The
I Hate
George W. Bush
R·E·A·D·E·R

The
I Hate
George W. Bush
R·E·A·D·E·R

WHY HE'S WRONG ABOUT
ABSOLUTELY EVERYTHING

EDITED BY CLINT WILLIS

THUNDER'S MOUTH PRESS
NEW YORK

THE I HATE GEORGE W. BUSH READER:
WHY HE'S WRONG ABOUT ABSOLUTELY EVERYTHING

Compilation copyright © 2004 by Clint Willis
Introductions copyright © 2004 by Clint Willis

Published by
Thunder's Mouth Press
An Imprint of Avalon Publishing Group Incorporated
245 West 17th St., 11th floor
New York, NY 10011

Library of Congress Cataloging-in-Publication Data is available.

ISBN 1-56025-589-7

Interior design by Paul Paddock

Printed in the United States of America

Distributed by Publishers Group West

For his victims

CONTENTS

INTRODUCTION

I have a confession to make: I don't hate anyone. That said, I sometimes find it difficult to love George W. Bush—although I do feel sorry for the miserable son of a bitch.

I pity the guy in part because he seems to lack any such empathic skills: Our current president doesn't feel sorry for anybody but himself. At times, he seems hardly aware that other people actually exist, let alone suffer. In that sense, George W. Bush is a sociopath.

Some sociopaths grow up to be serial killers; others grow up to be president, which is worse. George W. Bush presided over more than 150 executions as governor of Texas, and seemed to enjoy the role (see page 102). He has exploited the events of September 11, 2001 to launch an apparently endless crusade in pursuit of a new American empire (see page 285). That crusade already has claimed thousands of victims and inspired a new generation of terrorists. Meanwhile, George W. Bush has done almost nothing to protect us from the current generation of terrorists who are the supposed object of his endless war (see page 334).

The catalogue of GWB's crimes against America and the planet is virtually endless. His disingenuously named No Child Left Behind Act has poisoned our public school system (see page 227). His regressive tax cuts and other economic policies have created huge deficits (see page 117) and cost the nation more than two million jobs. His environmental record is the worst in history—he has done more to harm the environment than any human being in the history of the world (see page 237).

Why is he doing this? The answer is simple: George W. Bush is a willing slave to corporations and the rich people who own them. Those people launched his business career and made him a wealthy man—even though he bungled his business dealings (see page 256). The same wealthy and corrupt supporters financed his political career, and continue to do so.

Bush has used his presidency to repay these supporters. He has dismantled our government, our labor unions, our schools—any institution that unites us as a free and mutually supportive community (see page 139). Why? Because that community of compassionate, freedom-loving Americans represents a threat to corporate and personal greed—the headlong pursuit of short-term profit by people and organizations who are already rich.

What do Bush and his leading supporters want? Here's just a sampling from their wish list:

- They want free rein to pollute, to kill off species and plunder what little is left of our wilderness.
- They want to avoid the taxes that finance programs such as Medicare and Social Security, which offer us security in our old age—and which in doing so bind us to future and past generations.
- They want to turn our public schools into joyless trade schools so that our children learn skills that will make them good corporate drones rather than learning values that will make them better citizens and happier people.
- They want to destroy workers' unions and cut pensions and medical benefits to the bone. They want to reduce most foreign and many domestic workers to conditions of near-slavery so that companies like

Wal-Mart (an evil empire if there ever was one) can earn a higher profit margin.

• They want us to raise our children to be killers, and they want civilians to act more like soldiers.

• They want to monitor our activities so that they can hurt us when we step out of line—and they want to strip us of the right to defend ourselves from even the most arbitrary punishment.

The bottom line: George W. Bush and his cronies want us to stop looking out for ourselves and each other and get back to work—so that they can continue to accumulate ever-greater power and wealth.

Sadly—tragically—they have made great progress toward these goals during the past several years. They have done so through a variety of means. They lie. They intimidate. They cheat. They obfuscate. They kill.

How are we to respond to these outrages? For starters, we need to take action to rebuild and nurture the community that Bush is trying to destroy.

• We need to take good care of our children, and make sure they understand the values of a true community: values such as respect and love and generosity.

• We need to support and help each other—taking care of the old and the sick and the weak; finding ways to rehabilitate criminals; forcing corporations to take responsibility for actions that hurt workers and consumers.

• We need to build strong institutions, volunteering to help at our schools, building strong labor unions and coming together to support each other's spiritual, emotional and intellectual growth in churches, workshops, book clubs and elsewhere.

• We need to stand up for our beliefs in the workplace and in the voting booth, fighting oppression and choosing leaders and policies who will support our community and its deepest values.

• We need to complain when our freedoms are threatened, and we need to take a risk now and then to stand up for what we know is right.

• We need to get to know each other as human beings—so that we can appreciate each other's common values and needs.

• We need to be less greedy and more generous—knowing that our generosity will make the world better for everyone, including ourselves.

• We need to throw the bum out.

Fact is, George W. Bush's policies are inimical to America's most cherished ideals of community and compassion—his policies are hateful. But hating GWB and his policies won't solve our problems or improve our lives. True, we must do what's necessary (and legal) to remove him from office as soon as possible: That is the task of the moment. Meanwhile, however, we face another, greater task: We must learn to work together as Americans and as citizens of this increasingly small planet. If we can do that, we can build a community, a country and a world worthy of our better natures—a community, a country and a world ruled by love.

—Clint Willis

HE'S
A LIAR

with quotes by George W. Bush;
cartoons by Ruben Bolling and Garry Trudeau;
quizzes by Paul Slansky;
and anagrams

George W. Bush lies to America, to the world and to himself. Like all habitual liars, he sometimes forgets he is lying—which makes his lies harder to recognize. He lies because he can't afford to acknowledge his true agenda: to serve the likes of Wal-Mart and Halliburton. We all suffer the consequences of his lies, which range from environmental destruction to unnecessary wars to lost jobs to huge budget deficits.

Bush Lies, Media Swallows

from *The Nation* (11/25/02)

Eric Alterman

The more things change . . . Roughly ten years ago, I celebrated the criminal indictment of Elliott Abrams for lying to Congress by writing an Op-Ed in the *New York Times* on the increasing acceptance of official deception. (I was just starting my dissertation on the topic back then.) The piece got bogged down, however, when an editor refused to allow me even to imply that then-President Bush was also lying to the country. I noted that such reticence made the entire exercise feel a bit absurd. He did not dispute this point but explained that *Times* policy simply would not allow it. I asked for a compromise. I was offered the following: "Either take it out and a million people will read you tomorrow, or leave it in and send it around to your friends." (It was a better line before e-mail.) Anyway, I took it out, but I think it was the last time I've appeared on that page.

President Bush is a liar. There, I said it, but most of the mainstream media won't. Liberal pundits Michael Kinsley, Paul Krugman and Richard Cohen have addressed the issue on the Op-Ed pages, but almost all news pages and network broadcasts pretend not to notice. In the one significant effort by a national daily to deal with Bush's consistent pattern of mendacity, the *Washington Post*'s Dana Milbank could not bring himself (or was not allowed) to utter the crucial words. Instead, readers were treated to such complicated linguistic circumlocutions as: Bush's statements represented "embroidering key assertions" and were clearly "dubious, if not wrong." The President's "rhetoric has taken some flights of fancy," he has "taken some liberties," "omitted qualifiers" and "simply out-pace[d] the facts." But "Bush lied"? Never.

Ben Bradlee explains, "Even the very best newspapers have never learned how to handle public figures who lie with a straight face. No editor would dare print this ver-sion of Nixon's first comments on Watergate for instance. 'The Watergate break-in involved matters of national secu-rity, President Nixon told a national TV audience last night, and for that reason he would be unable to com-ment on the bizarre burglary. That is a lie.'"

Part of the reason is deference to the office and the belief that the American public will not accept a mere reporter calling the President a liar. Part of the reason is the culture of Washington—where it is somehow worse to call a person a liar in public than to be one. A final reason is political. Some reporters are just political activists with columns who prefer useful lies to the truth. For instance, Robert Novak once told me that he "admired" Elliott Abrams for lying to him in a television interview about illegal US acts of war against Nicaragua because he agreed with the cause.

Let us note, moreover, that Bradlee's observation, offered in 1997, did not apply to President Clinton. Reporters were positively eager to call Clinton a liar, although his lies were about private matters about which many of us, including many reporters, lie all the time. "I'd like to be able to tell my children, 'You should tell the truth,'" Stuart Taylor Jr. of the *National Journal* said on *Meet the Press*. "I'd like to be able to tell them, 'You should respect the President.' And I'd like to be able to tell them both things at the same time." David Gergen, who had worked for both Ronald Reagan and Richard Nixon as well as Clinton and therefore could not claim to be a stranger to official dishonesty, decried what he termed "the deep and searing violation [that] took place when he not only lied to the country, but co-opted his friends and lied to them." Chris Matthews kvetched, "Clinton lies knowing that you know he's lying. It's brutal and it subjugates the person who's being lied to. I resent deeply being constantly lied to." George Will, a frequent apologist for the lies of Reagan and now Bush, went so far as to insist that Clinton's "calculated, sustained lying has involved an extraordinarily corrupting assault on language, which is the uniquely human capacity that makes persuasion, and hence popular government, possible."

George W. Bush does not lie about sex, I suppose—merely about war and peace. Most particularly he has consistently lied about Iraq's nuclear capabilities as well as its missile-delivery capabilities. Take a look at Milbank's gingerly worded page-one October 22 *Post* story if you doubt me. To cite just two particularly egregious examples, Bush tried to frighten Americans by claiming that Iraq possesses a fleet of unmanned aircraft that could be used "for missions targeting the United States." Previously he insisted that a report by the International Atomic Energy Agency revealed the Iraqis to be "six months away from developing a weapon." Both of these statements were false, but they worked. Nearly three-quarters of Americans surveyed thought that Saddam was helping Al Qaeda; 71 percent thought it likely that he was personally involved in the 9/11 attacks.

What I want to know is why this kind of lying is apparently OK. Isn't it worse to refer "repeatedly to intelligence . . . that remains largely unverified"—as the *Wall Street Journal* puts it—in order to trick the nation into war, as Bush and other top US officials have done, than to lie about a blowjob? Isn't it worse to put "pressure . . . on the intelligence agencies to deliberately slant estimates," as *USA Today* worded its report? Isn't it more damaging to offer "cooked information," in the words of the CIA's former chief of counterterrorism, when you are asking young men and women to die for your lies? Don't we revile Lyndon Johnson for having done just that with his dishonest Gulf of Tonkin resolution?

Here's Bradlee again: "Just think for a minute how history might have changed if Americans had known then that their leaders felt the war was going to hell in a handbasket. In the next seven years, thousands of American lives and more thousands of Asian lives would have been saved. The country might never have lost faith in its leaders."

Reporters and editors who "protect" their readers and viewers from the truth about Bush's lies are doing the nation—and ultimately George W. Bush—no favors. Take a look at the names at that long black wall on the Mall. Consider the tragic legacy of LBJ's failed presidency. Ask yourself just who is being served when the media allow Bush to lie, repeatedly, with impunity, in order to take the nation into war.

He Said It . . .

"The reason I believe in a large tax cut because it's what I believe."
—Washington, DC, 12/18/00

"My pan plays down an unprecedented amount of our national debt."
—budget address to Congress, 2/27/01

Quiz
Paul Slansky

According to Dick Cheney, why was the wildly ballooning deficit not a cause for concern?

(a) Because the government could "turn it around overnight if we play our cards right" in John Poindexter's terrorism-futures market.

(b) Because, "if we need to, we can always borrow a few trillion from Halliburton."

(c) Because he is "a deficit hawk," and, even more reassuring, "so is the President."

(d) Because "the world could blow up tomorrow, and then all debts would be forgiven and we'd look pretty damn smart."

Answer: (c)

A Nation of Victims

from *The Nation* (6/30/03)

Renana Brooks

George W. Bush is generally regarded as a mangler of the English language. What is overlooked is his mastery of emotional language—especially negatively charged emotional language—as a political tool. Take a closer look at his speeches and public utterances, and his political success turns out to be no surprise. It is the predictable result of the intentional use of language to dominate others.

President Bush, like many dominant personality types, uses dependency-creating language. He employs language of contempt and intimidation to shame others into submission and desperate admiration. While we tend to think of the dominator as using physical force, in fact most dominators use verbal abuse to control others. Abusive language has been a major theme of psychological researchers on marital problems, such as John Gottman, and of philosophers and theologians, such as Josef Pieper. But little has been said about the key role it has come to play in political discourse, and in such "hot media" as talk radio and television.

Bush uses several dominating linguistic techniques to induce surrender to his will. The first is *empty language*. This term refers to broad statements that are so abstract and mean so little that they are virtually impossible to oppose. Empty language is the emotional equivalent of empty calories. Just as we seldom question the content of potato chips while enjoying their pleasurable taste, recipients of empty language are usually distracted from examining the content of what they are hearing. Dominators use empty language to conceal faulty generalizations; to ridicule viable alternatives; to attribute negative motivations to others, thus making them appear contemptible; and to rename and "reframe" opposing viewpoints.

Bush's 2003 State of the Union speech contained thirty-nine examples of empty language. He used it to reduce complex problems to images that left the listener relieved that George W. Bush was in charge. Rather than explaining the relationship between malpractice insurance and sky-rocketing healthcare costs, Bush summed up: "No one has ever been healed by a frivolous lawsuit." The multiple fiscal and monetary policy tools that can be used to stimulate an economy were downsized to: "The best and fairest way to make sure Americans have that money is not to tax it away in the first place." The controversial plan to wage another war on Iraq was simplified to: "We will answer every danger and every enemy that threatens the American people." In an earlier study, I found that in the 2000 presidential debates Bush used at least four times as many phrases containing empty language as Carter, Reagan, Clinton, Bush Senior or Gore had used in their debates.

Another of Bush's dominant-language techniques is *personalization*. By personalization I mean localizing the attention of the listener on the speaker's personality. Bush projects himself as the only person capable of producing results. In his post-9/11 speech to Congress he said, "I will not forget this wound to our country or those who inflicted it. I will not yield; I will not rest; I will not relent in waging this struggle for freedom and security for the

American people." He substitutes his determination for that of the nation's. In the 2003 State of the Union speech he vowed, "I will defend the freedom and security of the American people." Contrast Bush's "I will not yield" etc. with John F. Kennedy's "Ask not what your country can do for you, ask what you can do for your country."

The word "you" rarely appears in Bush's speeches. Instead, there are numerous statements referring to himself or his personal characteristics—folksiness, confidence, righteous anger or determination—as the answer to the problems of the country. Even when Bush uses "we," as he did many times in the State of the Union speech, he does it in a way that focuses attention on himself. For example, he stated: "Once again, we are called to defend the safety of our people, and the hopes of all mankind. And we accept this responsibility."

In an article in the January 16 *New York Review of Books*, Joan Didion highlighted Bush's high degree of personalization and contempt for argumentation in presenting his case for going to war in Iraq. As Didion writes: " 'I made up my mind,' he had said in April, 'that Saddam needs to go.' This was one of many curious, almost petulant statements offered in lieu of actually presenting a case. *I've made up my mind, I've said in speech after speech, I've made myself clear.* The repeated statements became their own reason."

Poll after poll demonstrates that Bush's political agenda is out of step with most Americans' core beliefs. Yet the public, their electoral resistance broken down by empty language and persuaded by personalization, is susceptible to Bush's most frequently used linguistic technique: *negative framework*. A negative framework is a pessimistic image of the world. Bush creates and maintains negative frameworks in his listeners' minds with a number of linguistic techniques borrowed from advertising and hypnosis to instill the image of a dark and evil world around us. Catastrophic words and phrases are repeatedly drilled into the listener's head until the opposition feels such a high level of anxiety that it appears pointless to do anything other than cower.

Psychologist Martin Seligman, in his extensive studies of "learned helplessness," showed that people's motivation to respond to outside threats and problems is undermined by a belief that they have no control over their environment. Learned helplessness is exacerbated by beliefs that problems caused by negative events are permanent; and when the underlying causes are perceived to apply to many other events, the condition becomes pervasive and paralyzing.

Bush is a master at inducing learned helplessness in the electorate. He uses pessimistic language that creates fear and disables people from feeling they can solve their problems. In his September 20, 2001, speech to Congress on the 9/11 attacks, he chose to increase people's sense of vulnerability: "Americans should not expect one battle, but a lengthy campaign, unlike any other we have ever seen. . . . I ask you to live your lives, and hug your children. I know many citizens have fears tonight. . . . Be calm and resolute, even in the face of a continuing threat." (Subsequent terror alerts by the FBI, CIA and Department of Homeland Security have maintained and expanded this fear of unknown, sinister enemies.)

Contrast this rhetoric with Franklin Roosevelt's speech

delivered the day after the Japanese attack on Pearl Harbor. He said: "No matter how long it may take us to overcome this premeditated invasion, the American people in their righteous might will win through to absolute victory. . . . There is no blinking at the fact that our people, our territory and our interests are in grave danger. With confidence in our armed forces—with the unbounding determination of our people—we will gain the inevitable triumph—so help us God." Roosevelt focuses on an optimistic future rather than an ongoing threat to Americans' personal survival.

All political leaders must define the present threats and problems faced by the country before describing their approach to a solution, but the ratio of negative to optimistic statements in Bush's speeches and policy declarations is much higher, more pervasive and more long-lasting than that of any other President. Let's compare "crisis" speeches by Bush and Ronald Reagan, the President with whom he most identifies himself. In Reagan's October 27, 1983, televised address to the nation on the bombing of the US Marine barracks in Beirut, he used nineteen images of crisis and twenty-one images of optimism, evenly balancing optimistic and negative depictions. He limited his evaluation of the problems to the past and present tense, saying only that "with patience and firmness we can bring peace to that strife-torn region—and make our own lives more secure." George W. Bush's October 7, 2002, major policy speech on Iraq, on the other hand, began with forty-four consecutive statements referring to the crisis and citing a multitude of possible catastrophic repercussions. The vast majority of these statements (for example: "Some ask how urgent this danger is to America and the world. The danger is already significant, and it only grows worse with time"; "Iraq could decide on any given day to provide a biological or chemical weapon to a terrorist group or individual terrorists") imply that the crisis will last into the indeterminate future. There is also no specific plan of action. The absence of plans is typical of a negative framework, and leaves the listener without hope that the crisis will ever end. Contrast this with Reagan, who, a third of the way into his explanation of the crisis in Lebanon, asked the following: "Where do we go from here? What can we do now to help Lebanon gain greater stability so that our Marines can come home? Well, I believe we can take three steps now that will make a difference."

To create a dependency dynamic between him and the electorate, Bush describes the nation as being in a perpetual state of crisis and then attempts to convince the electorate that it is powerless and that he is the only one with the strength to deal with it. He attempts to persuade people they must transfer power to him, thus crushing the power of the citizen, the Congress, the Democratic Party, even constitutional liberties, to concentrate all power in the imperial presidency and the Republican Party.

Bush's political opponents are caught in a fantasy that they can win against him simply by proving the superiority of their ideas. However, people do not support Bush for the power of his ideas, but out of the despair and desperation in their hearts. Whenever people are in the grip of a desperate dependency, they won't respond to rational criticisms of the people they are dependent on. They will respond to plausible and forceful statements and alternatives that put the American electorate back in touch with their core optimism. Bush's opponents must combat his dark imagery with hope and restore American vigor and optimism in the coming years. They should heed the example of Reagan, who used optimism against Carter and the "national malaise"; Franklin Roosevelt, who used it against Hoover and the pessimism induced by the Depression ("the only thing we have to fear is fear itself"); and Clinton (the "Man from Hope"), who used positive language against the senior Bush's lack of vision. This is the linguistic prescription for those who wish to retire Bush in 2004.

DIST. BY UNIVERSAL PRESS SYNDICATE ©2003 R. BOLLING 6-4- www.tom.thedancingbug.com

YOU KNOW WHY YOU'VE BEEN CALLED IN! AN **ASTEROID** 50 MILES WIDE HAS BEEN DISCOVERED TO BE LESS THAN A MONTH FROM **COLLIDING WITH EARTH!**

WE HAVE TO ACT **FAST** -- AND EACH OF YOU IS A **SPECIALIST**, HAND-PICKED TO RESPOND TO THIS DIRE SITUATION !

JIM HALER -- OIL DRILLING EXPERT !

YESSIR, PRESIDENT BUSH! I'M READY FOR ANYTHING !

GET UP TO THE ARCTIC NATIONAL WILDLIFE REFUGE IN **ALASKA** AND START **DRILLING**! WE'RE GONNA NEED **LOTS** OF **ENERGY** TO DEAL WITH THIS!

UH... OKAY.

DANIEL TIBMAN -- CONSTITUTION EXPERT! DRAFT A BILL GIVING THE GOVERNMENT UNFETTERED SURVEILLANCE POWERS !

I WANNA KNOW WHO COULD TRY TO SABOTAGE OUR EFFORTS!

ROGER KENT -- TAX EXPERT ! GET ME NEW LEGISLATION SLASHING **TAXES** ON THE **RICH!** WE DON'T NEED OUR MOST CREATIVE AMERICANS HAMPERED IN THIS DARK HOUR!

UM -- RIGHT!

AND, YES, GENERAL! **INVADE IRAN**! WE CAN'T BE BLINDSIDED BY AN EXTREMIST NATION AT THIS CRITICAL JUNCTURE!

THERE -- WE'VE DONE ALL WE CAN. LET US PRAY WE'RE NOT TOO LATE

NEXT: KILLER BEES!

DEREGULATE EVERYTHING NOW!

Science Friction

from *Washington Monthly* (July/August 2003)

Nicholas Thompson

THE GROWING—AND DANGEROUS—DIVIDE BETWEEN SCIENTISTS AND THE GOP.

Not long ago, President Bush asked a federal agency for evidence to support a course of action that many believe he had already chosen to take on a matter of grave national importance that had divided the country. When the government experts didn't provide the information the president was looking for, the White House sent them back to hunt for more. The agency returned with additional raw and highly qualified information, which the president ran with, announcing his historic decision on national television. Yet the evidence soon turned out to be illusory, and the entire policy was called into question.

Weapons of mass destruction in Iraq, you say? Actually, the above scenario describes Bush's decision-making process on the issue of stem-cell research. In August 2001, Bush was trying to resolve an issue he called "one of the most profound of our time." Biologists had discovered the potential of human embryonic stem cells—unspecialized cells that researchers can, in theory, induce to develop into virtually any type of human tissue. Medical researchers marveled at the possibility of producing treatments for medical conditions such as Parkinson's, Alzheimer's, and spinal cord injuries; religious conservatives quivered at the fact that these cells are derived from human embryos, either created in a laboratory or discarded from fertility clinics. Weighing those concerns, Bush announced that he would allow federal funding for research on 60-plus stem cell lines already taken from embryos, but that he would prohibit federal funding for research on new lines.

Within days, basic inquiries from reporters revealed that there were far fewer than 60 viable lines. The National Institutes of Health (NIH) has so far confirmed only 11 available lines. What's more, most of the existing stem cell lines had been nurtured in a growth fluid containing mouse tumor cells, making the stem cells prone to carrying infections that could highly complicate human trials. Research was already underway in the summer of 2001 to find an alternative to the mouse feeder cells—research that has since proven successful. But because these newer clean lines were developed after Bush's decision, researchers using them are ineligible for federal funding.

At the time of Bush's announcement, most scientists working in the field knew that although 60 lines might exist in some form somewhere, the number of robust and usable lines was much lower. Indeed, the NIH had published a report in July 2001 that explained the potential problems caused by the mouse feeder cells and estimated the total number of available lines at 30. Because that initial figure wasn't enough for the administration, according to *Time* magazine, Health and Human Services Secretary Tommy Thompson asked the NIH to see if more lines "might conceivably exist." When NIH representatives met with Bush a week before his speech with an estimate of 60 lines scattered around the world in unknown condition, the White House thought it had what it wanted. In his announcement, Bush proclaimed, without qualification, that there were "more than 60 genetically diverse stem cell lines."

After his speech, then–White House Counselor Karen Hughes said, "This is an issue that I think almost everyone who works at the White House, the president asked them their opinion at some point or another." However, Bush didn't seek the advice of Rosina Bierbaum, then-director of the White House's Office of Science and Technology Policy (OSTP). Hughes claimed that Bush had consulted other top federal scientists, including former NIH director Harold Varmus. That was partly true, but the conversation with Varmus, for example, took place during a few informal minutes at a Yale graduation ceremony. Later press reports made much of Bush's conversations with bioethicists Leon Kass and Daniel Callahan. Yet neither is a practicing scientist, and both were widely known to oppose stem-cell research. Evan Snyder, director of the stem-cell program at the Burnham Institute in La Jolla, Calif., says, "I don't think science entered into Bush's decision at all."

The administration's stem-cell stand is just one of many examples in which the White House has made policies that defy widely accepted scientific opinion. In mid-June, the Bush administration edited out passages in an E.P.A. report that described scientific concerns about the potential risks of global warming, according to *The New York Times*. That same week, the American Medical Association came out in opposition to the Bush adminstration's restrictions on stem-cell research. Why this administration feels unbound by the consensus of academic scientists can be gleaned, in part, from a telling anecdote in Nicholas Lemann's recent *New Yorker* profile of Karl Rove. When asked by Lemann to define a Democrat, Bush's chief political strategist replied, "Somebody with a doctorate."

Lemann noted, "This he said with perhaps the suggestion of a smirk." Fundamentally, much of today's GOP, like Rove, seems to smirkingly equate academics, including scientists, with liberals.

In this regard, the White House is not necessarily wrong. Most scientists today do lean Democratic, just as most of the uniformed military votes Republican—much to the annoyance of Democrats. And like the latter cultural divide, the former can cause the country real problems. The mutual incomprehension and distrust between the Pentagon and the Clinton White House, especially in its early years, led to such debacles as Somalia and the clash over allowing gays to serve openly in the military. The Bush administration's dismissiveness toward scientists could also have serious consequences, from delaying vital new medical therapies to eroding America's general lead in science. The Clinton administration quickly felt the sting of the military's hostility and worked to repair the relationship. It's not clear, however, that the Bush administration cares to reach out to scientists—or even knows it has a problem.

MAD SCIENTISTS

The GOP has not always been the anti-science party. Republican Abraham Lincoln created the National Academy of Sciences in 1863. William McKinley, a president much admired by Karl Rove, won two presidential victories over the creationist Democrat William Jennings Bryan, and supported the creation of the Bureau of Standards, forerunner of today's National Institutes of Science and Technology. Perhaps the most pro-science president of the last century was Republican Dwight D. Eisenhower, a former West Point mathematics and engineering student, and later president of Columbia University. Eisenhower established the post of White House science adviser, allowed top researchers to wander in and out of the West Wing, and oversaw such critical scientific advances as the development of the U2 spy plane and federally funded programs to put more science teachers in public schools. At one point, he even said that he wanted to foster an attitude in America toward science that paralleled the country's embrace of competitive sports. Scientists returned the affection, leaning slightly in favor of the GOP in the 1960 election.

The split between the GOP and the scientific community began during the administration of Richard Nixon. In the late 1960s and early 1970s, protests against the Vietnam War captured the sympathy of the liberal academic community, including many scientists, whose opposition to the war turned them against Nixon. The president characteristically lashed back and, in 1973, abolished the entire White House science advisory team by executive order, fuming that they were all Democrats. Later, he was caught ranting on one of his tapes about a push, led by his science adviser, to spend more money on scientific research in the crucial electoral state of California. Nixon complained, "Their only argument is that we're going to lose the support of the scientific community. We will never have their support." The GOP further alienated scientists with its "Southern strategy," an effort to broaden the party's appeal to white conservative Southerners. Many scientists were turned off by the increasing evangelical slant of Republicans and what many saw as coded appeals to white racists.

Scientists also tended to agree with Democrats' increasingly pro-environmental and consumer-protection stances, movements which both originated in academia. Gradually, as John Judis and Ruy Teixeira show in their recent book *The Emerging Democratic Majority*, professionals, the group of highly skilled workers that includes scientists, moved from the Republican camp to the Democratic. Yet that transition took a while, in large part because most professionals were still fiscally conservative, few sided with pro-union Democrats, and the Republican Party had not yet been overtaken by its more socially conservative factions. In the mid 1970s, for example, Republican President Gerald Ford showed a moderate streak while in the White House and reinstated the Office of Science and Technology Policy.

Ronald Reagan oversaw a widening gulf between the Republican Party and academic scientists. During the 1980 campaign, he refused to endorse evolution, a touchstone issue among scientists, saying, "Well, [evolution] is a theory—it is a scientific theory only, and it has in recent years been challenged in the world of science and is not yet believed in the scientific community to be as infallible as it was once believed." Though he aggressively funded research for military development, he alienated many in academia with his rush to build a missile defense system that most scientists thought unworkable.

George H. W. Bush tried to walk the tightrope. He pushed the Human Genome Project forward and elevated the position of chief science adviser from a special assistant to assistant. Yet he served during an acrimonious public debate about global warming, an issue that drove a wedge between academic scientists and the interests of the oil and gas industry—an increasingly powerful ally of the GOP. He generally sided with the oil industry and dismissed environmentalists' appeals for the most costly reforms. Yet he also tried to appease moderates by signing the landmark Framework Convention on Climate Change in Rio de Janeiro and helping pass the Clean Air Act, which aimed to reduce smog and acid rain. In the end, his compromising did him little good; environmentalists attacked him, and his rapprochement with liberal academic elites won him few friends with social conservatives. Bush faced a surprisingly tough primary challenge from Pat Buchanan in the 1992 election campaign, saw his support among evangelicals in the general election decline compared with 1988, and lost to the Democratic underdog Bill Clinton.

Newt Gingrich didn't make the same mistakes. When he became the House Speaker in 1995, Gingrich worked vigorously to cut budgets in areas with Democratic constituents—and he knew that by the time he came to office most scientists were supporting Democrats. The speaker took aim at research organizations such as the U.S. Geological Survey and National Biological Survey and dismissed action on global warming. He even abolished the Congressional Office of Technology Assessment, which served as the main scientific research arm of Capitol Hill. Gingrich claimed that OTA was too slow to keep up with congressional debates; agency defenders argued that the cut was fueled by partisan dislike of an agency perceived as a Democratic stronghold. Indeed, several years prior, OTA had published a report harshly critical of the predominantly GOP-backed missile defense project, the Strategic Defense Initiative.

By the mid 1990s, the GOP had firmly adopted a new paradigm for dismissing scientists as liberals. Gingrich believed, as Nixon did, that most scientists weren't going to support him politically. "Scientists tend to have an agenda, and it tends to be a liberal political agenda," explains Gingrich's close associate former Rep. Robert Walker (R-Pa.), the former chairman of the House Science Committee. In 1995, Rep. Dana Rohrabacher (R-Calif.), then-chairman of the House committee dealing with global warming, called climate change a "liberal claptrap." In interviews with *The Washington Post* in 2001, Texas Republican Tom DeLay dismissed evolution as unproven, said that we shouldn't need an EPA because "God charges us to be good stewards of the Earth," and denigrated scientific Nobel Prize winners as "liberal and extremist."

PH.D. PHOBIA

George W. Bush embodies the modern GOP's attitude toward science. He hails from a segment of the energy industry that, when it comes to global warming, considers science an obstacle to growth. He is strongly partisan, deeply religious, and also tied to evangelical supporters. And, like Reagan, he has refused to endorse the scientific principle of evolution. During the 2000 campaign, a *New York Times* reporter asked whether he believed in evolution. Bush equivocated, leading the *Times* to write that he "believes the jury is still out."

Bush has also learned from his father's experience that siding with scientists gains him little politically, and often alienates conservatives. Bush and Rove have tried to woo portions of other groups that traditionally trend Democratic—steel tariffs for unions, faith-based grants for African-American ministers—but scientists are different. They aren't a big voting bloc. They are generally affluent, but not enough so to be major donors. They are capable of organizing under the auspices of a university to lobby for specific grants, but they aren't organized politically in a general way. In short, scientists aren't likely to cause the GOP problems if they are completely alienated. Scientists have almost never turned themselves into anything like a political force. Even Al Gore, the apotheosis of many scientists' political hopes, received little formal support from them during the 2000 campaign.

Consequently, the White House seems to have pushed scientific concerns down toward the bottom of its list of priorities. Bush, for instance, has half as many Ph.D.s in his cabinet as Clinton had two years into his term. Among the White House inner circle, Condoleezza Rice's doctorate distinguishes her as much as her race and more than her sex. Consider also the length of time the administration left top scientific positions vacant. It took 20 months to choose an FDA director, 14 months to choose an NIH director, and seven months to choose a white House science adviser for the Office of Science and Technology Policy. Once Bush had appointed a head of OSTP, he demoted the rank of the position, moved the office out of the White House, and cut the number of associate directors from four to two. An OSTP spokeswoman argues that the administration's decision to move OSTP was inconsequential and that reducing the number of associate directors was just a way of "reducing the stovepipes." But geography and staff equal clout in Washington, and unarguably signal how much the people in power care about what you do.

Moreover, Bush appointed to one of the two associate director positions Richard Russell, a Hill aide credentialed with only a bachelor's degree in biology, and let him interview candidates for the job of director. "It bothers me deeply [that he was given that spot], because I don't think that he is entirely qualified," says Allen Bromley, George H. W. Bush's science adviser, who worked for some of his tenure out of prime real estate in the West Wing of the White House. "To my astonishment, he ended up interviewing some of the very senior candidates, and he did not do well. The people he interviewed were not impressed."

CYNICAL TRIALS

When required to seek input from scientists, the administration tends to actively recruit those few who will bolster the positions it already knows it wants to support, even if that means defying scientific consensus. As with Bush's inquiry into stem-cell research, when preparing important policy decisions, the White House wants scientists to give them validation, not grief. The administration has stacked hitherto apolitical scientific advisory committees, and even an ergonomics study section, which is just a research group and has no policy making role.

Ergonomics became a politicized issue early in Bush's term when he overturned a Clinton-era rule requiring companies to do more to protect workers from carpal tunnel syndrome and other similar injuries. Late last year, the Department of Health and Human Services rejected, without explanation, three nominees for the Safety and Occupational Health Study Section who had already been approved by Dana Loomis, the group's chair, but who also weren't clearly aligned with the administration's position on ergonomics. Loomis then wrote a letter saying that "The Secretary's office declined to give reasons for its decision, but they seem ominously clear in at least one case: one of the rejected nominees is an expert in ergonomics who has publicly supported a workplace ergonomics standard." Another nominee, who was accepted, said that she had been called by an HHS official who wanted to know her views on ergonomics before allowing her on the panel.

The administration has further used these committees as places for religious conservatives whose political credentials are stronger than their research ones. For example, on Christmas Eve 2002, Bush appointed David Hager—a highly controversial doctor who has written that women should use prayer to reduce the symptoms of PMS—to the FDA's Reproductive Health Drugs Advisory Commission.

Bush has also taken to unprecedented levels the political vetting of nominees for advisory committees. When William Miller, a professor of psychology at the University of New Mexico, was considered as a candidate for a panel on the National Institute of Drug Abuse, he was asked his views on abortion, the death penalty, and whether he had voted for Bush. He said no to the last question and never received a call back. "Not only does the Bush administration scorn science; it is subjecting appointments to scientific advisory committees and even study sections to political tests," says Donald Kennedy, editor in chief of *Science*, the community's flagship publication.

CONTROL GROUP POLITICS

Any administration will be tempted to trumpet the conclusions of science when they justify actions that are advantageous politically, and to ignore them when they don't. Democrats, for instance, are more than happy to tout the scientific consensus that human activity contributes to climate change, but play down evidence that drilling in the Arctic National Wildlife Refuge (which they oppose) probably will have little impact on the caribou there. But Democrats will only go so far down the path of ignoring scientific evidence because they don't want to alienate their scientific supporters. Increasingly, the Republicans feel little such restraint. Hence the Bush administration's propensity to tout scientific evidence only when it suits them politically. For instance, though numerous studies have shown the educational benefits of after-school programs, the Bush administration cited just one recent report casting doubt on those benefits to justify cutting federal after-school funding. Meanwhile, the White House has greatly increased the federal budget for abstinence-only sex education programs despite a notable lack of evidence that they work to reduce teen pregnancy. The administration vigorously applies cost-benefit analysis—some of it rigorous and reasonable—to reduce federal regulations on industry. But when the National Academy of Sciences concluded that humans are contributing to a planetary warming and that we face substantial future risks, the White House initially misled the public about the report and then dramatically downplayed it. Even now, curious reporters asking the White House about climate change are sent to a small, and quickly diminishing, group of scientists who still doubt the causes of global warming. Many scientists were shocked that the administration had even ordered the report, a follow-up to a major report from the 2,500-scientist Intergovernmental Panel on Climate Change, the world's leading climate research committee. Doing that was like asking a district court to review a Supreme Court decision.

EXPERTS IN EXILE

This White House's disinclination to engage the scientific community in important policy decisions may have serious consequences for the country. One crucial issue that Congress and the Bush administration will likely have to confront before Bush leaves office is human cloning. Researchers distinguish between "reproductive cloning," which most scientists abhor, and "therapeutic cloning," which may someday allow researchers to use stem cells from a patient's cloned embryo to grow replacement bone marrow, liver cells, or other organs, and which most scientists favor. When the President's Council on Bioethics voted on recommendations for the president, every single practicing scientist voted for moving therapeutic cloning forward. Bush, however, decided differently, supporting instead a bill sponsored by Sen. Sam Brownback (R-Kan.) to ban all forms of embryonic cloning.

John Marburger, the president's current scientific adviser—a longtime Democrat who says that he has good relations with Bush and is proud of the administration's science record—wrote in an email statement which barely conceals his own opinion: "As for my views on cloning, let me put it this way. The president's position—which is to ban all cloning—was made for a number of ethical reasons, and I do know that he had the best, most up-to-date science before him when he made that decision." Jack Gibbons, a former head of the Congressional Office of Technology Assessment, calls Bush's proposed ban "an attempt to throttle science, not to govern technology." Harold Varmus, the former NIH director, believes that "this is the first time that the [federal] government has ever tried to criminalize science."

Another potentially costly decision is the Bush administration's post–September 11 restrictions on the ability of foreign scientists to immigrate to the United States— restrictions which many scientists argue go far beyond reasonable precautions to keep out terrorists. In December 2002, the National Academy of Science, the National Academy of Engineering, and the Institute of Medicine issued a statement complaining that "recent efforts by our government to constrain the flow of international visitors in the name of national security are having serious unintended consequences for American science, engineering and medicine." Indeed, MIT recently abandoned a major artificial-intelligence research project because the school couldn't find enough graduate students who weren't foreigners and who could thus clear new security regulations.

UNSCIENTIFIC METHOD

Like Gingrich, Bush favors investments in scientific research for the military, health care, and other areas that garner strong public and industry support. Indeed, the White House quickly points to such funding increases whenever its attitude toward science is questioned. But for an administration that has boosted spending in a great number of areas, more money for science is less telling than how the Bush administration acts when specific items on its agenda collide with scientific evidence or research needs. In almost all of those cases, the scientists get tuned out.

Ignoring expert opinion on matters of science may never cause the administration the kind of political grief it is now suffering over its WMD Iraq policy. But neither is it some benign bit of anti-elitist bias. American government has a history of investing in the capabilities and trusting the judgments of its scientific community—a legacy that has brought us sustained economic progress and unquestioned scientific leadership within the global intellectual community. For the short-term political profits that come with looking like an elite-dismissing friend of the everyman, the Bush administration has put that proud, dynamic history at real risk.

He Said It . . .

"For a century and a half now, America and Japan have formed one of the great and enduring alliances of modern times."
—Tokyo, 2/18/02

"Neither in French nor in English nor in Mexican."
—declining to answer reporters' questions at the Summit of the Americas, 4/21/01

ANAGRAM

Bush Administration:
Must do Arabs in hit

Ten Appalling Lies We Were Told About Iraq

from *AlterNet* (6/27/03)

Christopher Scheer

"The Iraqi dictator must not be permitted to threaten America and the world with horrible poisons and diseases and gases and atomic weapons."
—*George Bush, Oct. 7, 2002, in a speech in Cincinnati.*

There is a small somber box that appears in the *New York Times* every day. Titled simply "Killed in Iraq," it lists the names and military affiliations of those who most recently died on tour of duty. Wednesday's edition listed just one name: Orenthal J. Smith, age 21, of Allendale, South Carolina.

The young, late O.J. Smith was almost certainly named after the legendary running back, Orenthal J. Simpson, before that dashing American hero was charged for a double-murder. Now his namesake has died in far-off Mesopotamia in a noble mission to, as our president put it on March 19, "disarm Iraq, to free its people and to defend the world from grave danger."

Today, more than three months after Bush's stirring declaration of war and nearly two months since he declared victory, no chemical, biological or nuclear weapons have been found, nor any documentation of their existence, nor any sign they were deployed in the field.

The mainstream press, after an astonishing two years of cowardice, is belatedly drawing attention to the unconscionable level of administrative deception. They seem surprised to find that when it comes to Iraq, the Bush administration isn't prone to the occasional lie of expediency but, in fact, *almost never told the truth.*

What follows are just the most outrageous and significant of the dozens of outright lies uttered by Bush and his top officials over the past year in what amounts to a systematic campaign to scare the bejeezus out of everybody:

Lie #1:"The evidence indicates that Iraq is reconstituting its nuclear weapons program . . . Iraq has attempted to purchase high-strength aluminum tubes and other equipment needed for gas centrifuges, which are used to enrich uranium for nuclear weapons." —*President Bush, Oct. 7, 2002, in Cincinnati.*

Fact: This story, leaked to and breathlessly reported by Judith Miller in the *New York Times,* has turned out to be complete baloney. Department of Energy officials, who monitor nuclear plants, say the tubes could not be used for enriching uranium. One intelligence analyst, who was part of the tubes investigation, angrily told the *New Republic*: "You had senior American officials like Condoleezza Rice saying the only use of this aluminum really is uranium centrifuges. She said that on television. And that's just a lie."

Lie #2: "The British government has learned that Saddam Hussein recently sought significant quantities of uranium from Africa."—*President Bush, Jan. 28, 2003, in the State of the Union address.*

Fact: This whopper was based on a document that the White House already knew to be a forgery thanks to the CIA. Sold to Italian intelligence by some hustler, the document carried the signature of an official who had been out of office for 10 years and referenced a constitution that was no longer in effect. The ex-ambassador who the CIA sent to check out the story is pissed: "They knew the Niger story was a flat-out lie," he told the *New Republic*, anonymously. "They [the White House] were unpersuasive about aluminum tubes and added this to make their case more strongly."

Lie #3: "We believe [Saddam] has, in fact, reconstituted nuclear weapons." —*Vice President Cheney on March 16, 2003 on "Meet the Press."*

Fact: There was and is absolutely zero basis for this statement. CIA reports up through 2002 showed no evidence of an Iraqi nuclear weapons program.

Lie #4: "[The CIA possesses] solid reporting of senior-level contacts between Iraq and al-Qaeda going back a decade." —*CIA Director George Tenet in a written statement released Oct. 7, 2002 and echoed in that evening's speech by President Bush.*

Fact: Intelligence agencies knew of tentative contacts between Saddam and al-Qaeda in the early '90s, but found no proof of a continuing relationship. In other words, by tweaking language, Tenet and Bush spun the intelligence 180 degrees to say exactly the opposite of what it suggested.

Lie #5: "We've learned that Iraq has trained al-Qaeda members in bomb-making and poisons and deadly gases . . . Alliance with terrorists could allow the Iraqi regime to attack America without leaving any fingerprints."—*President Bush, Oct. 7.*

Fact: No evidence of this has ever been leaked or produced. Colin Powell told the U.N. this alleged training took place in a camp in northern Iraq. To his great embarrassment, the area he indicated was later revealed to be outside Iraq's control and patrolled by Allied war planes.

Lie #6: "We have also discovered through intelligence that Iraq has a growing fleet of manned and unmanned aerial vehicles that could be used to disperse chemical or biological weapons across broad areas. We are concerned that Iraq is exploring ways of using these UAVs [unmanned aerial vehicles] for missions targeting the United States."—*President Bush, Oct. 7.*

Fact: Said drones can't fly more than 300 miles, and Iraq is 6,000 miles from the U.S. coastline. Furthermore, Iraq's drone-building program wasn't much more advanced than your average model plane enthusiast. And isn't a "manned aerial vehicle" just a scary way to say "plane"?

Lie #7: "We have seen intelligence over many months that they have chemical and biological weapons, and that they have dispersed them and that they're weaponized and that, in one case at least, the command and control arrangements have been established."—*President Bush, Feb. 8, 2003, in a national radio address.*

Fact: Despite a massive nationwide search by U.S. and British forces, there are no signs, traces or examples of chemical weapons being deployed in the field, or anywhere else during the war.

Lie #8: "Our conservative estimate is that Iraq today has a stockpile of between 100 and 500 tons of chemical weapons agent. That is enough to fill 16,000 battlefield rockets." —*Secretary of State Colin Powell, Feb. 5, 2003, in remarks to the U.N. Security Council.*

Fact: Putting aside the glaring fact that not one drop of this massive stockpile has been found, as previously reported on AlterNet the United States' own intelligence reports show that these stocks—if they existed—were well past their use-by date and therefore useless as weapon fodder.

Lie #9: "We know where [Iraq's WMD] are. They're in the area around Tikrit and Baghdad and east, west, south, and north somewhat." —*Secretary of Defense Donald Rumsfeld, March 30, 2003, in statements to the press.*

Fact: Needless to say, no such weapons were found, not to the east, west, south *or* north, somewhat or otherwise.

Lie #10: "Yes, we found a biological laboratory in Iraq which the U.N. prohibited."—*President Bush in remarks in Poland, published internationally June 1, 2003.*

Fact: This was reference to the discovery of two modified truck trailers that the CIA claimed were potential mobile biological weapons labs. But British and American experts—including the State Department's intelligence wing in a report released this week—have since declared this to be untrue. According to the British, and much to Prime Minister Tony Blair's embarrassment, the trailers are actually exactly what Iraq said they were: facilities to fill weather balloons, sold to them by the British themselves.

So, months after the war, we are once again where we started—with plenty of rhetoric and absolutely no proof of this "grave danger" for which O.J. Smith died. The Bush administration is now scrambling to place the blame for its lies on faulty intelligence, when in fact the intelligence was fine; it was their abuse of it that was "faulty."

Rather than apologize for leading us to a preemptive war based on impossibly faulty or shamelessly distorted "intelligence" or offering his resignation, our sly madman in the White House is starting to sound more like that other O.J. Like the man who cheerfully played golf while promising to pursue "the real killers," Bush is now vowing to search for "the true extent of Saddam Hussein's weapons programs, no matter how long it takes."

On the terrible day of the 9/11 attacks, five hours after a hijacked plane slammed into the Pentagon, retired Gen. Wesley Clark received a strange call from someone (he didn't name names) representing the White House position: "I was on CNN, and I got a call at my home saying, 'You got to say this is connected. This is state-sponsored terrorism. This has to be connected to Saddam Hussein,'" Clark told "Meet the Press" anchor Tim Russert. "I said, 'But—I'm willing to say it, but what's your evidence?' And I never got any evidence."

And neither did we.

The Revision Thing: A history of the Iraq war, told entirely in lies

from Harpers.org
Sam Smith

All text is verbatim from senior Bush Administration officials and advisers. In places, tenses have been changed for clarity.

Once again, we were defending both ourselves and the safety and survival of civilization itself. September 11 signaled the arrival of an entirely different era. We faced perils we had never thought about, perils we had never seen before. For decades, terrorists had waged war against this country. Now, under the leadership of President Bush, America would wage war against them. It was a struggle between good and it was a struggle between evil.

It was absolutely clear that the number-one threat facing America was from Saddam Hussein. We know that Iraq and Al Qaeda had high-level contacts that went back a decade. We learned that Iraq had trained Al Qaeda members in bomb making and deadly gases. The regime had long-standing and continuing ties to terrorist organizations. Iraq and Al Qaeda had discussed safe-haven opportunities in Iraq. Iraqi officials denied accusations of ties with Al Qaeda. These denials simply were not credible. You couldn't distinguish between Al Qaeda and Saddam when you talked about the war on terror.

The fundamental question was, did Saddam Hussein have a weapons program? And the answer was, absolutely. His regime had large, unaccounted-for stockpiles of chemical and biological weapons—including VX, sarin, cyclosarin, and mustard gas, anthrax, botulism, and possibly smallpox. Our conservative estimate was that Iraq then had a stockpile of between 100 and 500 tons of chemical-weapons agent. That was enough agent to fill 16,000 battlefield rockets. We had sources that told us that Saddam Hussein recently authorized Iraqi field commanders to use chemical weapons—the very weapons the dictator told the world he did not have. And according to the British government, the Iraqi regime could launch a biological or chemical attack in as little as forty-five minutes after the orders were given. There could be no doubt that Saddam Hussein had biological weapons and the capability to rapidly produce more, many more.

Iraq possessed ballistic missiles with a likely range of hundreds of miles—far enough to strike Saudi Arabia, Israel, Turkey, and other nations. We also discovered through intelligence that Iraq had a growing fleet of manned and unmanned aerial vehicles that could be used to disperse chemical or biological weapons across broad areas. We were concerned that Iraq was exploring ways of using UAVs for missions targeting the United States.

Saddam Hussein was determined to get his hands on a nuclear bomb. We knew he'd been absolutely devoted to trying to acquire nuclear weapons, and we believed he had, in fact, reconstituted nuclear weapons. The British government learned that Saddam Hussein had recently sought significant quantities of uranium from Africa. Our intelligence sources told us that he had attempted to purchase high-strength aluminum tubes suitable for nuclear-weapons production. When the inspectors first went into Iraq and were denied, finally denied access, a report came out of the [International Atomic Energy Agency] that they were six months away from developing a weapon. I didn't know what more evidence we needed.

Facing clear evidence of peril, we could not wait for the final proof that could come in the form of a mushroom cloud. The Iraqi dictator could not be permitted to threaten America and the world with horrible poisons and diseases and gases and atomic weapons. Inspections would not work. We gave him a chance to allow the inspectors in, and he wouldn't let them in. The burden was on those people who thought he didn't have weapons of mass destruction to tell the world where they were.

We waged a war to save civilization itself. We did not seek it, but we fought it, and we prevailed. We fought them and imposed our will on them and we captured or, if necessary, killed them until we had imposed law and order. The Iraqi people were well on their way to freedom. The scenes of free Iraqis celebrating in the streets, riding American tanks, tearing down the statues of Saddam Hussein in the center of Baghdad were breathtaking. Watching them, one could not help but think of the fall of the Berlin Wall and the collapse of the Iron Curtain.

It was entirely possible that in Iraq you had the most pro-American population that could be found anywhere in the Arab world. If you were looking for a historical analogy, it was probably closer to post-liberation France. We had the overwhelming support of the Iraqi people. Once we won, we got great support from everywhere.

The people of Iraq knew that every effort was made to spare innocent life, and to help Iraq recover from three decades of totalitarian rule. And plans were in place to provide Iraqis with massive amounts of food, as well as medicine and other essential supplies. The U.S. devoted unprecedented attention to humanitarian relief and the prevention of excessive damage to infrastructure and to unnecessary casualties.

The United States approached its postwar work with a two-part resolve: a commitment to stay and a commitment to leave. The United States had no intention of determining the precise form of Iraq's new government. That choice belonged to the Iraqi people. We have never been a colonial power. We do not leave behind occupying armies. We leave behind constitutions and parliaments. We don't take our force and go around the world and try to take other people's real estate or other people's resources, their oil. We never have and we never will.

The United States was not interested in the oil in that region. We were intent on ensuring that Iraq's oil resources remained under national Iraqi control, with the proceeds made available to support Iraqis in all parts of the country. The oil fields belonged to the people of Iraq, the government of Iraq, all of Iraq. We estimated that the potential income to the Iraqi people as a result of their oil could be somewhere in the $20 [billion] to $30 billion a year [range], and obviously, that would be money that would be used for their well-being. In other words, all of Iraq's oil belonged to all the people of Iraq.

We found the weapons of mass destruction. We found biological laboratories. And we found more weapons as time went on. I never believed that we'd just tumble over weapons of mass destruction in that country. But for those who said we hadn't found the banned manufacturing devices or banned weapons, they were wrong, we found them. We knew where they were.

We changed the regime of Iraq for the good of the Iraqi

people. We didn't want to occupy Iraq. War is a terrible thing. We've tried every other means to achieve objectives without a war because we understood what the price of a war can be and what it is. We sought peace. We strove for peace. Nobody, but nobody, was more reluctant to go to war than President Bush.

It is not right to assume that any current problems in Iraq can be attributed to poor planning. The number of U.S. forces in the Persian Gulf region dropped as a result of Operation Iraqi Freedom. This nation acted to a threat from the dictator of Iraq. There is a lot of revisionist history now going on, but one thing is certain—he is no longer a threat to the free world, and the people of Iraq are free. There's no doubt in my mind when it's all said and done, the facts will show the world the truth. There is absolutely no doubt in my mind.

He Said It . . .

"The British government has learned that Saddam Hussein recently sought significant quantities of uranium from Africa."
—State of the Union speech, January 28, 2003

"What's the difference?"
—12/16/03, claiming that it didn't matter
whether Saddam actually possessed WMDs or
merely wanted them

**"The Kay report identified dozens of
weapons of mass destruction–related program activities."**
—1/20/04, coining a cumbersome and silly
new term in yet another attempt to confuse
and mislead Americans

*George W. Bush's claim that Saddam Hussein had tried to acquire
uranium was based on faulty intelligence—which his administration knew was faulty. The president's lie convinced many listeners
that Iraq posed a nuclear threat to the United States.*

Taking Responsibility

A version of this article appeared on AlterNet.org
(8/15/03)

Sheldon Rampton and John Stauber

"I take personal responsibility for everything I say, of
course. Absolutely," responded President Bush on July
28, 2003, to a question posed at a rare news conference.

Weeks of media debate and discussion went into parsing a mere sixteen words from Bush's State of the Union speech in which he falsely claimed to have knowledge that Iraq had attempted to purchase uranium in Niger.

Rather than taking responsibility for his words, Bush and his advisors did everything to *avoid* taking responsibility. They first attempted to justify the inclusion of the Niger claim, which they knew was dubious, by attributing it to Tony Blair's government. CIA director George Tenet stepped forward to accept the blame for Bush's words and was rewarded by Bush declaring his confidence in Tenet.

The purpose behind this game of musical chairs, of course, was to muddy the waters so that no one had to take responsibility for the president's false remarks. Harry Truman had a plaque on his desk that read, "The buck stops here." If Bush had a plaque on his desk, it would say, "The buck stops with Blair, or Tenet, or Condoleezza Rice—but I forgive them all." In addition to treating responsibility for the president's words like a hot potato, his public relations advisors tried to pretend that expecting him to tell the truth about Iraq's alleged weapons of mass destruction constituted petty quibbling over details. The subtle spin behind all this talk about a mere 16 words was the insinuation that everyone was making a mountain out of a molehill. Why make such a big deal, they implied, over a single sentence in which the president may have misspoken.

The reality is that the Bush administration's phony claims about Iraq went well beyond those mere 16 words in the State of the Union address. With respect to weapons of mass destruction alone, those falsehoods included the following:

• On Sept. 7, 2002, Bush cited a report by the International Atomic Energy Agency, which he said proved that the Iraqis were on the brink of developing nuclear weapons. "I would remind you that when the inspectors first went into Iraq and were denied, finally denied access, a report came out of the Atomic—the IAEA—that they were six months away from developing a weapon," he said. "I don't know what more evidence we need." Actually, no such report existed. The IAEA did issue a report in 1998, around the time weapons inspectors were denied access to Iraq, but what it said was, "Based on all credible information to date, the IAEA has found no indication of Iraq having achieved its program goal of producing nuclear weapons or of Iraq having retained a physical capability for the production of weapon-useable nuclear material or having clandestinely obtained such material." Responding to the Bush speech, IAEA chief spokesman Mark Gwozdecky said, "There's never been a report like that issued from this agency."

• In his Sept. 12, 2002, address to the United Nations, Bush spoke ominously of Iraq's "continued appetite" for nuclear bombs, pointing to the regime's purchase of thousands of high-strength aluminum tubes, which he said were "used to enrich uranium for nuclear weapons." In fact, the IAEA said in a January 2003 assessment, the size of the tubes made them ill-suited for uranium enrichment, but they were identical to tubes that Iraq had used previously to make conventional artillery rockets. Nevertheless, Colin Powell repeated the aluminum-tubes charge in his speech to the UN on Feb. 5, 2003.

• In an Oct. 7, 2002, speech to the nation, Bush warned that Iraq has a growing fleet of unmanned aircraft that could be used "for missions targeting the United States." Actually, the puny aircraft lacked the range to reach the United States.

• In the same speech, Bush also stated that in 1998, "information from a high-ranking Iraqi nuclear engineer who had defected revealed that despite his public promises, Saddam Hussein had ordered his nuclear program to continue." Bush's statement implied that this information was current as of 1998. In fact, the nuclear defector to whom he referred was Khidhir Hamza, who had actually retired from Iraq's nuclear program in 1991 and fled the country in 1995. Bush also neglected to note that Hussein Kamal, whose earlier defection and debriefing by UNSCOM investigators served as the basis for part of the Bush administration's claims about Iraqi weapons, told investigators that he regarded Hamza as a "professional liar."

• Hussein Kamal—Saddam Hussein's son-in-law who was later murdered by the Iraqi regime as punishment for his defection from Iraq—was also cited repeatedly by the Bush administration to bolster its case that inspections were not working and that Iraq's weapons programs were continuing. Actually,

Kamal had told UNSCOM interrogators during his debriefing that "after the Gulf War, Iraq destroyed all its chemical and biological weapons stocks and the missiles to deliver them. . . . Nothing remained. . . . All weapons—biological, chemical, missile, nuclear were destroyed." Kamal also told his debriefers that UN inspection teams were "very effective in Iraq."

This list shows only a few of the lies and distortions related to the Bush administration's claims about Iraqi weapons. In our book *Weapons of Mass Deception*, we provide a long list of other falsehoods with which the Bush administration made the rest of its case for war, such as its attempt to insinuate that Iraq was in cahoots with Al Qaeda, or its promises that the Iraqi people would welcome American troops as liberators.

There was no follow-up question from reporters to Bush's hollow claim to "take responsibility." One obvious follow-up could have been, "Did you know this story was a lie when you told it in your state of the union address, if not why not, and if so why did you lie anyway?" Instead the news conference came to a close, and the mainstream U.S. news media all but dropped the subject of the 16 words, failing to press further with investigations into the many other instances of phony claims for war that we document in our book. Despite being a best seller in both the U.S. and the UK, our book was itself ignored by most major American media and reviewed by only one major U.S. newspaper, the *San Francisco Chronicle*.

The complacent pseudo-journalists who acted as state propagandists in helping sell the U.S. war on Iraq have shown no interest in examining the way it was sold. To look closely would risk exposing their own complicity. If the public wants a real investigation into the lies that led us into war, it will have to look outside the narrow window of the corporate media and seek alternative sources of information.

Bush claimed to "take responsibility" for his words, but taking responsibility means facing the consequences, and thus far the Bush administration has suffered no consequences whatsoever. The people who have experienced the consequences of Bush's many deceptions are the U.S. soldiers who remain targets of daily attack inside Iraq, the Iraqi people themselves, and of course the American taxpayers who are footing the massive bill for it all. Everyone, it seems, is expected to shoulder some of the burden of responsibility for the President's words, except for Bush himself.

Quiz
Paul Slansky

What do engineering experts believe was the likely purpose of the two trailers whose discovery inspired George W. Bush to announce that portable biological-weapons labs—"weapons of mass destruction"—had been found in Iraq?

(a) They were used to transport dozens of Saddam Hussein look-alikes around the country.

(b) They were used as "dubbing dens" for bootleg CDs.

(c) They were used to produce hydrogen for weather balloons.

(d) They were used by Uday and Qusay Hussein to store pornography.

Answer: (c)

Quiz
Paul Slansky

Three of these statements were uttered by George W. Bush. Which was spoken by Defense Secretary Donald Rumsfeld?

(a) "The war on terror involves Saddam Hussein because of the nature of Saddam Hussein, the history of Saddam Hussein, and his willingness to terrorize himself."

(b) "For those who urge more diplomacy, I would simply say that diplomacy hasn't worked."

(c) "There are known knowns. These are things we know that we know. There are known unknowns. That is to say, there are things that we know we don't know. But there also are unknown unknowns. There are things we don't know we don't know."

(d) "Republicans and Democrats stood with me in the Rose Garden to announce their support of a clear statement of purpose [to Saddam]: You disarm or we will."

Answer: (c)

ANAGRAM

George W. Bush:
He grew bogus

A silver lining view of George Bush's not attending military funerals, lest he become associated with bad news

from *The Nation* (12/1/03)

Calvin Trillin

At least there's no Bush eulogy
On why they had to die
It's better that they're laid to rest
Without another lie

HE'S MEAN

with quotes by George W. Bush;
cartoons by Jeffrey Stahler, Ruben Bolling, and Gary Trudeau;
quizzes from Paul Slansky;
and anagrams

George W. Bush is petty, ungenerous and down-right cruel. In short, he's mean.

Where's the Compassion?

from *The Nation* (8/28/03)

Joe Conason

I am a fiscal conservative and a family conservative. And
I am a compassionate conservative, because I know my
philosophy is optimistic and full of hope for every American." So George W. Bush described himself and his beliefs
on the eve of his first campaign for President. With that
speech, the Texas governor hoped to finesse a paradox of
national politics. To win the nomination of the Republican Party, he had to be acceptable to every kind of conservative, from the libertarian to the fundamentalist; to
win the presidency itself, he also had to embody an alternative to the angry conservatism that Americans had
found increasingly repellent during the Clinton years.

Moderate, suburban voters were alienated by the parti-
sanship, self-righteous hypocrisy and antigovernment
extremism of Newt Gingrich's Republican "revolution-
aries." By 1999 the House Speaker's colleagues had immo-
lated him, but his brief tenure and the impeachment
fiasco he sponsored left behind a cloud of acrid smoke.

Bush and his political adviser Karl Rove knew that he
could ill afford his father's mistake of alienating the far
right. At the same time, they knew he had to avoid being
isolated politically on the right. "Compassionate conservatism" was their answer. So deft was this gambit that it
left journalists gawking and scratching their heads, as if
they had witnessed the candidate literally running in two
directions at once.

During the election year to come, Bush and Rove will

renew the "compassionate conservatism" theme to draw independent, female and minority voters, balancing the appeal of a "wartime presidency" that is already beginning to lose its luster. The President recently returned to emphasizing buzzwords like "inclusive, positive and hopeful" in a June speech to the Urban League.

Indeed, "compassion" is a featured topic on the new website put up by Bush-Cheney '04 (www.georgew bush.com), where "news" about the President's agenda of compassion includes highlights like "President stresses importance of health and fitness." The need for such filler reflects how thin the Administration's portfolio for the poor remains. The site's most noticeable feature is a "compassion photo album" consisting almost entirely of photos of the smiling Bush with smiling black children. This is almost identical to the public-relations material Bush and his advisers rolled out during the 2000 campaign (and the minstrel-show GOP convention in Philadelphia), repackaged to remind voters that he is, or purports to be, a "different kind of Republican."

Distinguishing son from father was a process that began during George W.'s second gubernatorial campaign in 1998, with a massive wave of television advertising created by Mark McKinnon, formerly a top Democratic consultant in Austin. McKinnon honestly believed that George W. Bush was a "different kind of Republican," a bipartisan leader who cared about the poor, and that belief showed in his advertising. Later, McKinnon, Rove and other advisers developed the same themes into a more sophisticated strategy that drew from the two most successful politicians of the postwar era, Bill Clinton and Ronald Reagan.

From Reagan, the Bush advisers borrowed the friendly

optimism, the down-home cowboy boots and the lavishly produced Morning in America style of advertising, which they retitled "Fresh Start." (If that sounded like a breakfast cereal or deodorant, it was entirely appropriate.) From Clinton, they adopted the supple tactics of repositioning their rhetoric toward the center and rephrasing issues to neutralize any partisan disadvantage.

This wasn't the first time, of course, that attractive branding had sold the nation a phony product. After two years of skewed tax cuts, destructive deregulation and social regression, nobody doubts Bush's conservatism. But where's the compassion?

To paraphrase a famous man, it depends on what the meaning of that word is.

Americans normally understand compassion to mean caring for the ill, homeless, hungry, unemployed, destitute and defenseless. "Compassionate" softens "conservative," a word that tends to be associated with smug stinginess rather than benevolence or mercy. "Compassionate conservative" acknowledges that unfortunate stereotype, indicating a person of right-wing inclination who nevertheless feels an obligation to lift up the downtrodden. In the modern context, the term also suggests acceptance of government responsibility—since private charity has never been sufficient to relieve social distress.

But the ideological authors of Bush's "philosophy" have devised their own definition of compassionate conservatism. The phrase itself usually refers to the policy prescriptions of Marvin Olasky, a professor of journalism at the University of Texas who also publishes World, an ultra-conservative, fundamentalist-Christian newsweekly. With the assistance of the Heritage Foundation and other think tanks on the right, Olasky has written three books extolling religious charity as a moral alternative to the sinful welfare state.

In early 1996, Newt Gingrich wrote a gushing introduction to Olasky's book *Renewing American Compassion.* Four years later, Bush contributed the foreword to Olasky's next volume, *Compassionate Conservatism: What It Is, What It Does, and How It Can Transform America. Christian Century*'s reviewer called it "less a book than an advertisement for Bush's presidential campaign." Although Bush used rhetoric about compassion to distance himself publicly from Gingrich, their overlapping relationships with Olasky showed how little ideological space really existed between them. Both had endorsed the rebranding of conservatism with a human face. Both had done favors for this idea's "godfather" and accepted favors from him. Both were determined to dismantle the programs of the New Deal and the Great Society, from Social Security to Medicare.

But Gingrich couldn't redecorate his threatening image in comforting pastels. He wasn't sufficiently nimble to move in two directions at once. Bush, having entered the national consciousness as an unknown figure marked only by his father's famous name, had no need to remake a damaged image. He rolled himself out as the "conservative with a heart," and profited by contrasting himself with the disgraced former Speaker. And if Bush's differences with Gingrich were a pretense—as they surely were—that easy deception only reflected the more profound dishonesty of the "compassion" strategy.

Now, after observing Bush's first few years in the Oval

Office, we have a clearer understanding of what his words meant on that auspicious day in New Hampshire. Being a "fiscal conservative" meant passing lopsided tax cuts for the wealthy few and leaving the federal budget in deficit for the foreseeable future. Being a "family conservative" meant looking after certain families, particularly if their annual incomes are higher than $200,000 and their estates are valued at more than $2 million. And so far, being a "compassionate conservative" appears to mean nothing very different from being a hardhearted, stingy, old-fashioned conservative.

Bush's budgets prove that he still emphatically prefers cutting the taxes of wealthy individuals and corporations to maintaining living standards for poor and working-class families. States and localities, their economies soured and their budgets overstrained, are unable to maintain services for their neediest citizens. Food deliveries to many of the helpless elderly will end. Nearly a million Americans are losing their Medicaid benefits in what the National Governors Association describes as "the worst fiscal crisis since World War II." For the first time in a decade, the rate of poverty is rising again, with 1.3 million Americans falling below the poverty line in 2001.

The most vigorous response of the Bush White House to these grim prospects is to propose abolishing "double taxation" of stock dividends. "That is very much pro-poor," according to R. Glenn Hubbard, the former chairman of Bush's Council of Economic Advisers, even though the poor won't get any of the benefits.

While he is fighting to allow the highest income class to pay nothing on investment earnings, he is tightening the requirements for those who seek the earned-income tax credit—meaning the working poor. Essentially a refund of a portion of regressive payroll taxes paid by low-income workers, the EITC is one of the most successful government initiatives directed toward Americans who work full-time but cannot earn enough to keep their families above the poverty line. In 1999, at the zenith of his compassionate phase, Bush stood up as a defender of the EITC against Congressional Republicans who were trying to reduce it. He quite rightly denounced the scheme pushed by his fellow Texan Tom DeLay, a professing Christian, as an attempt to balance the federal budget "on the backs of the poor." But having since legislated mammoth tax cuts for the wealthy and run up a record deficit, Bush won't defend EITC from conservatives in the White House and Congress who are seeking to cut it, eliminate the funds that help workers apply for it, impose harsher audits on families that claim it—or even eliminate it.

Originally, the twin centerpieces of Bush's compassionate conservatism were his education plan, "No Child Left Behind," and his "faith-based initiative" to direct federal funds toward private charities, including religious institutions. Owing to the deficits caused by the recession and his tax cuts, however, the education bill he negotiated with Senator Edward Kennedy fell far short of the funding he had originally promised. Although his budget proposal increased education spending, the proposed rise was the lowest in several years. He cut a billion dollars from programs specified in his own bill. One statistic summed up Bush's priorities: His tax cuts for the rich amounted to more than fifty times the total amount he requested for new education spending.

Bush's vaunted "faith-based initiative" met an even more disgraceful fate. In the winter of 2002, Bush got a lump of coal in his Christmas stocking from John DiIulio, the former director of the White House Office of Faith-Based and Community Initiatives. The University of Pennsylvania professor is probably the leading neoconservative exponent of compassionate conservatism. As a devout Catholic and lifelong Democrat, he didn't share Marvin Olasky's religious or social views, but he joined the Republican Administration because he hoped to create innovative programs to assist the poor.

In a devastating, emotional seven-page letter quoted by journalist Ron Suskind in *Esquire* magazine, DiIulio depicted a White House dominated by partisan cynicism and devoid of competent policy-makers. Karl Rove and his aides dominated every discussion of domestic issues, always emphasizing media and political strategy at the expense of substance and analysis. DiIulio told Suskind that when he objected to a proposal to kill the earned-income tax credit, he suddenly realized that he was arguing with libertarians who understood little about the workings of government and had no interest in learning.

"There is no precedent in any modern White House for what is going on in this one: a complete lack of a policy apparatus," he said. "What you've got is everything—and I mean everything—being run by the political arm. It's the reign of the Mayberry Machiavellis." That was DiIulio's nickname for Karl Rove and his aides, "who consistently talked and acted as if the height of political sophistication consisted in reducing every issue to its simplest black-and-white terms for public consumption, then steering legislative initiatives or policy proposals as far right as possible."

The result is that the President's "faith-based initiative" has been transformed into a patronage operation. During the 2002 midterm-election campaign, Administration officials suddenly showed up at inner-city churches, seeking to entice African-American ministers with federal funding. A half-million-dollar grant was quickly slated for Pat Robertson's quasi-charitable Operation Blessing International Relief and Development Corporation, which the Christian Coalition founder has in the past used to advance his diamond-mining ventures in the Congo region.

The White House staff, he said, "winked at the most far-right House Republicans, who, in turn, drafted a so-called faith bill that . . . satisfied certain fundamentalist leaders and Beltway libertarians but bore few marks of compassionate conservatism. . . . Not only that, but it reflected neither the president's own previous rhetoric on the idea nor any of the actual empirical evidence." He declared, "There is a virtual absence as yet of any policy accomplishments that might, to a fair-minded nonpartisan, count as the flesh on the bones of so-called compassionate conservatism."

"So-called compassionate conservatism." That phrase, written by a man who said he still loved and admired George W. Bush, resounded with disillusion. Still, DiIulio held out hope that someday in the years to come, his ideal of a spirited movement to uplift the poor might be realized. There was no domestic policy, but in two years, or six years, something might happen.

The saddened professor couldn't quite admit that this President is unlikely ever to fulfill the expectations he raised—because in a White House ruled so thoroughly and ruthlessly by pious conservatives, there is so little room for compassion.

ANAGRAM

G. Dubya:
Bad Guy

He Said It . . .

"I know what I believe. I will continue to articulate what I believe and what I believe—I believe what I believe is right."
—Rome, Italy, 7/22/01

Quiz
Paul Slansky

True or False:

When critics of George W. Bush's tax cuts pointed out that the wealthiest 1 percent of tax-payers would divvy up 28 percent of the windfall, while the poorest 60 percent would split 8 percent of the benefits, Bush accused them of engaging in "class warfare."

Answer: True

ANAGRAM

President George Walker Bush:
Ruthless Breed. Wanker. Ego pig.

*Language is a sacred trust as is the presidency. Bush's proposed
budget for 2004 manipulated both our language and exploited
his office in an attempt to hijack the federal government from
its rightful owners and beneficiaries—the rest of us.*

Get Rich or Get Out

from *Harper's* (June 2003)

Thomas Frank

ATTEMPTED ROBBERY WITH A LOADED FEDERAL BUDGET

The Bush Administration's proposed budget for 2004 fills
five phone book–size volumes; it is 2,866 pages long. The
list of authors alone runs to hundreds of names, arranged
alphabetically, occupying four pages of four columns
each. The UPS man who delivered my copy had to carry it
on his shoulder, puffing as he climbed three flights of
stairs. When he plunked it down on the floor of my apartment, the dishes rattled in the cupboard.

The five-volume budget set includes a book of precise
details in microscopic type, a book of tables showing how
much was spent on the various programs over the years, a
book of hints for unlucky staffers who have been assigned
to think about matters budgetary, and a main volume—a
reader-friendly book featuring a continuous prose narrative, full-color pictures of your government in action,
items of interest set off in attractively typeset boxes, and a
reassuring abundance of the familiar phrases of bureau-
cracy: "homeland," "stewardship," "caregiver." "Transition"
gets used a lot as a verb.

I don't have too much of a problem with the budget's
desk-crushing backup volumes. I find it kind of interesting

to read seven pages of tables detailing highway expenditures from 1940 to the present. It's the part of the budget I'm supposed to like that I really can't stand.

Let me upgrade that remark: The 2004 budget is toxic. It is an epic of distortion and evasion and contradiction and misleading rhetorical ploys. The object of this malodorous epic is to outline the Bush Administration's plan for plunging the nation from surplus into deficit and to cast the blame for the ensuing disaster on the very people—the retired, the sick, the poor—who will feel the brunt of its effects. Whether Congress alters this budget, reduces its tax cuts, or rejects it altogether is beside the point. This document we will have always with us, an indelible reminder of what the Bush team would do if they possibly could.

There is nothing inherently wrong with deficits, even massive ones, as a tool of state policy. In wars and recessions it is right and even proper for the federal government to spend more than it takes in, so as to ensure that resources continue to flow to consumers and to those hardest hit, and thus stimulate the economy. The 2004 budget is not concerned with any of that. Here war and recession are merely pretexts for getting the crudest social trends of the last twenty years moving again. This deficit is designed to enrich those at the very top of the social pyramid while cutting services for those lower down. This is not cyclical Keynesianism. This is not a helpful or even a merely benign program of deficit spending. It is a blueprint for sabotage. It is an instruction manual for how to power up a complicated machine and dash it headlong into a stone wall.

After which the president will turn to us and say, "See? I told you big government doesn't work."

We know he will say this, because his budget pretty much says it now. In the early days of his administration, George Bush was hailed as the "CEO president," an M.B.A.-bearing true believer who would put management theory into practice. This was thought to mean that he was a practical man who would make things work smoothly, just like they supposedly do in a corporation. What such interpretations overlooked was that management theory holds government to be a uniquely depraved social actor.

M.B.A.-speak is intertwined with contempt for government throughout the 2004 budget. A preliminary chapter called "Governing with Accountability," for example, simply heaps blame on federal shoulders. When corporate scoundrels are accused of wrongdoing, of course, they try to defend themselves, or at least take the Fifth; here the White House can be seen confessing, on behalf of previous administrations and, indeed, the entire federal workforce, to just about anything you care to think of. "Federal agencies," for example, are said to be so out of touch that they have "not managed themselves well enough to know whether they had the right people with the right skills to do their work." Among federal workers "pay and performance are generally unrelated," which is apparently not a problem in the private sector. Another chapter spreads the blame to federal efforts generally, lamenting that "in most cases, we do not know what we are getting for our money." This in turn is said to be a failing of "the Washington mentality," which "has wasted untold billions of dollars . . ." The books tell of gaping loopholes in the Social Security system, credit-card abuse by federal employees, and preposterous agricultural price supports, all of these problems flowing together to give the overall impression that government is simply a gigantic boondoggle.

When government is relieved of its duties by the private sector, though, the narrative turns chirpy and upbeat. Indeed, the highlight of the budget is meant to be the administration's proposal that every single federal operation embrace a little M.B.A. magic: outsourcing, merit pay, the setting up of websites. Congratulation is due whenever a department manages to toss a bone to the private sector, such as the construction of housing on Army bases or even the taking of bids on the printing of the budget itself, which is such a big deal that it receives its own brag box on page 39. It is surely not a coincidence that the Department of Defense, one of the only departments Dubya likes enough to increase its funding, is flattered on the very first page of its chapter by being compared to a "large corporation." Call it Regime Change, Inc.

That there might also be waste and inefficiency and even fraud in the private sector is a topic the budget chooses to ignore, just as the National Energy Policy, developed by Vice President Dick Cheney in consultation with a cabal of energy executives, refused to acknowledge that electricity problems in California were caused by corporations gaming the system. In the case of the Department of Defense, that organization so like a "large corporation," the problem of private pork is known to be particularly severe. But although the budget tells proudly of a Navy base that has found a way to save on heating bills, the epidemic of mismanagement at defense contractors and the enormous divide between pay and performance all across the private sector are neither described nor criticized. Nor is market manipulation by electricity traders, though it cost the government immense sums. Nor is cherry-picking by the HMOs, into which this budget wants to push even more Medicare recipients. Nor are the disastrous conflicts of interest on Wall Street, even though one of the supplementary budget volumes suggests that Wall Street is a good place for our Social Security savings. Nor are the practices of the oil companies that the budget proposes to turn loose on the Arctic National Wildlife Refuge and, soon enough, on Iraq. That waste and inefficiency is just not up for debate.

Much of the press commentary on this budget has focused on the deficits into which it proposes to plunge us. The budget's authors have, of course, anticipated this reaction. That surplus for which everyone pines was, we are helpfully informed, nothing more than a "revenue bubble" propelled by a bull market that was "already in the process of popping" when the businessman president took office. Although it is obviously true that the booming stock market pumped up tax receipts, and although it was foolish for anyone to count on those inflated tax receipts continuing into the future, to call the surplus a "bubble" is to confuse the issue. In ordinary usage, a "bubble" is a pitfall of the private sector, a situation in which prices are driven to unsustainable heights by collective fantasies of stupendous future profits. A bubble is a swindle—you know, like the NASDAQ. Here the term is simply used to imply that the surplus was doomed all along and that the current administration, unlike its predecessor, is in no way to blame for its disappearance. Those tax cuts enacted two years ago? They did not cause the deficit. The budget would have been in deficit anyway because of falling revenues after the stock-market crash. Tax cuts, therefore, aren't important. Slam door, walk away.

What this fails to consider is that the deficit is worse, is more bad, than it otherwise would have been had those tax cuts not been enacted.[*] What this further fails to consider are the deficits going forward, which the budget expects to get bigger as we begin to feel the effects of the mammoth new tax cuts that are proposed only four pages earlier in this selfsame document.

But no. "The Real Fiscal Danger," the budget tells us in a chapter of that title, is Social Security and Medicare. When you cut rich people's taxes, no harm can possibly come. When you offer insurance for the average person's health care and retirement, however, you're playing with fire. The Bush Administration has already distinguished itself by the lengths to which it will go to libel Social Security—its handpicked commission on privatizing the program actually implied that it was somehow *racist*— but here the administration outdoes itself in cynical innuendo. The budget implies that these programs are in such staggering ill repair that they may in fact be responsible for the overall deficit. Here is a sentence that actually occurs on page 31 of the main volume of the 2004 federal budget:

> But in 2002 the combined shortfall in Social Security and Medicare of nearly $18 trillion was

[*] A study by the Center on Budget and Policy Priorities shows that the 2001 and 2002 tax cuts caused roughly 30 percent of the decline into deficit and that if they had not been enacted the budget would soon be back in surplus.

about five times as large as today's publicly held national debt.

An eighteen trillion dollar shortfall! Frightening, is it not? Until you read further and realize that, in fact, both programs are today in surplus, that Social Security will remain in surplus for fourteen years to come (it will be able to function on the money in its Trust Fund until 2042),* and that the $18 trillion figure is a cumulative seventy-five-year estimate based on extreme long-term projections that will probably turn out to bear as much resemblance to reality then as the Futurama exhibit at the 1939 World's Fair does to our reality today. None of this is admitted, however, until the chapter is nearly over, even though the mind-bending $18 trillion number has already been unleashed to do its terrifying work on the very first page. The chapter also includes a boxed heart attack headed "What Does $18 Trillion Mean To You?" which invites the reader to believe that in order to pay for Social Security and Medicare "the federal government

---

* The Social Security Trust Fund is not mentioned in the main budget document. This date is given in the 2003 report of the Social Security trustees. It is a revealing number in and of itself. We have been hearing catastrophic predictions about Social Security for almost ten years now, and yet during this time the date when economists expect the Social Security Trust Fund to run dry keeps getting pushed further and further into the future. The Social Security Trustees' report for 2000 gave the expiration date for the Trust Fund as 2037; this year's report gives it as 2042, yielding a gain of five future years per every three actual years. If that rate holds, by 2017, the year the budget names as the beginning of the end, economists will be gravely warning us that the Trust Fund will expire in 2064.

would have to confiscate almost half of all household wealth . . . "

This is irresponsible even on the budget's own terms. In the preceding chapter, the one about deficits, the authors had insisted that federal budgets need only look ahead five years (rather than ten, which had been the previous standard), on the grounds that longer-term forecasts vary so much they are largely worthless. But not if those forecasts might help to impugn Social Security and Medicare! When that is the object, it seems, no technique, however inconsistent or speculative or fanciful or simply wrong, is out of bounds.

By the terms of normal human interaction, this stuff is so dishonest it's well-nigh Enronian. According to one economist I talked to, the $18 trillion number is so groundless that it can have been introduced here only in order to panic and deceive. It is a transparent effort to redirect the blame for the massive cuts in government spending that Bush's tax cut will necessitate. And, one might add, to come up with some figure that might rival the actual, present-day, real-world destruction of more than $7 trillion of household wealth by the collapse of the stock market—the very place, as it happens, that this administration would rather we put our Social Security money.

Medicare's share of the imaginary $18 trillion is $13 trillion. No one denies that the system is in trouble; health-care costs in America have been out of control for years, soaring above what they are in every other industrialized country, even those that are healthier than we are, even those with socialized medicine. To arrive at its frightening number, the administration projects that this situation will continue and even worsen, with health-care costs ascending at such a rate that they will eventually wreck the entire economy, private sector and all. For normal readers, this prediction is as shattering an indictment of the free-market way as anything ever dreamed up by Eugene Debs. But in keeping with their general belief in the infallibility of markets, the authors of the budget offer no plan for restraining health-care costs, as is done in so many other countries. They take it for granted that all we will care about as the world goes to managed-care hell is this one shocking number, the tab the taxpayer might have to pay, fished up from who knows where and manipulated to imply that the basic idea of social insurance is somehow to blame.

For Social Security that one shocking number is given as $4.6 trillion. The budget asks the reader to imagine this A-bomb of a number, piled up over the next seventy-five years, as though some cosmic collection agency were phoning us night and day demanding we cough it up right now. This is like those pro-abstinence posters that tried to convince us that since the total amount a parent spends on a child over the course of the child's life is something like $100,000, we shouldn't even contemplate having a kid until we'd saved the hundred grand. Consider also that seventy-five years from now the United States will be a much richer country than it currently is; asking us to pay off a debt today from that bigger, wealthier nation of 2078 is sort of like asking Haiti to pay off France's debt.

In truth the only way to understand projected future public debt is as a percentage of projected future economic output. Economist Dean Baker of the Center for Economic Policy Research points out that over the same seventy-five-year horizon gross domestic product is also expected to grow, keeping the Social Security shortfall at less than one percent of future GDP. Measured this way, Baker continues, the $75 billion that President Bush requested from Congress in April to pay for the war in Iraq is "bigger, relative to GDP, than the amount of money needed to make Social Security fully solvent for the next seventy-five years."

Even if you accept the administration's wildly pessimistic view of Social Security's future, the problem is dwarfed by the size of the administration's tax cuts. The Center for Budget and Policy Priorities estimates that this budget's proposed tax cuts, added to those of 2001, will, over the course of seventy-five years, outweigh Social Security's estimated long-term shortfall by a factor of three. Take into consideration who will benefit from each policy choice—fund Social Security, help out the average American; go ahead with the tax cuts, help out the very wealthiest stratum of society—and it is clear that what is being proposed here is an historic reconfiguration of the machinery of government to serve the rich rather than the poor or even the middle class.

The real problem with Social Security, of course, is that it is a popular and successful program. Its existence confirms that there are economic functions better served by government than by business, and as such it provides a foundation for the activist government that pro-business conservatives like the current president have dedicated their lives to destroying.

The title that the budget's authors chose to put on the chapter introducing the administration's proposed tax cuts is "For Everyone Willing to Work, a Job." Willingness to work has nothing to do with it, though. To receive the stock dividends that the chapter proposes to make tax-free you don't even have to get out of bed in the morning. Dividends merely require that you have excess money lying around. This budget is the administration's way of showing its support for a population of unproductive freeloaders, as long as they're rich freeloaders.

The rest of us have to work, of course. And as recent headlines confirm, work is becoming scarcer by the day. Hence, I suppose, the chapter's oddly socialist-sounding title. But there is, of course, no full-employment program offered here. In fact, jobs also have nothing to do with what the chapter proposes, except as a hoped-for by-product of the torrential economic activity meant to flow from the dividend windfall for the idle rich. A more accurate title would have been "For Everyone Who Has a Million Dollars, Some More."

For all the media attention that has been paid to the administration's tax package, the budget itself gives the subject surprisingly short shrift. The tax-cut chapter is only four pages long, the figures that it presents are apparently unrelated to those being used by the media, and the breakdown of who will benefit from the tax cuts is as predictably misleading as everything else in this feculent document, proceeding by age group and marital status rather than by the more obvious and useful category of income.

This is unfortunate, at least from a literary standpoint. The tax cut is by far the most daring and controversial and hence interesting aspect of the 2004 budget; if passed by Congress, it would surely be the golden cross on which federal budgets for years to come were crucified. And yet these five volumes and countless words of text give us almost no idea of what the tax cut actually looks like.

So let's put a face on it. The genius of the administration's new tax-cut plan is that it balloons over time as different tax cuts kick in. Passing it now would take only $40 billion or so out of the federal revenues, but by the year 2013 it will have rolled up a total cost, according to the Citizens for Tax Justice, of nearly $2 trillion, including interest. Add to that the $1.6 trillion in lost revenue that will eventually result from the 2001 tax cut, and you can see the vague outlines of the vise in which legislators ten years from now will find themselves squeezed.

Who will benefit from this? According to the administration, we all will; people in the highest income brackets are only the immediate beneficiaries. In fact, 77 percent of this year's tax cuts will go to society's richest 20 percent. Fully 32 percent of the total tax cuts this year will go to society's richest 1 percent. While the average person will get a tax cut of $289 in 2003, people who take in more than a million dollars a year will get tax cuts of more than $30,000 each. Ironically, these are the same people who benefited from the great bull market of the 1990s, as well as from the great bull market of the 1980s. The bull may have exhausted himself now, but with George W. Bush taking up the slack these same folks are going to get their third up-decade in a row.

Just imagine how the president's writers might have illustrated this aspect of the budget. Rather than photos of impoverished children getting school lunches and handicapped people working in a garden, the documents might have included pictures of high-income Americans posing proudly on their new sailboat, or pointing to the gleaming copper gutters they've had installed on their suburban manse, or sharing a laugh with the eager young staff of the rule-breaking libertarian magazine they've endowed. We could gawk at their titanium tree house designed by Frank

Gehry, their Turnbull & Asser ties, their friend the congressman, their trip through Indochina on a sedan chair.

Think also of the drama lurking on the other side of the ledger. One of the reasons the Bush people love tax cuts is that tax cuts defund government—but gradually and indirectly, allowing plenty of time for blame evasion later. Although it may not look like much now, this tax cut is a time bomb planted in the heart of activist government: as it grows, the whopping giveaway to the rich will compel massive cuts in government spending somewhere down the road. Imagine as all the deficit-reduction battles of the early nineties are fought all over again, only with much greater stakes. Imagine the look of dawning desperation on those politicians' faces as they begin to understand Bush's masterful fait accompli. Like the U.N. delegates Bush has similarly outmaneuvered, they will vote and speechify in vain. The public will laugh at their impotence. And then will come the moment of hard truth. On whom will death set his fateful hand? Who will be defunded? Maybe it will be Head Start. Or Medicaid. Or Food Stamps. Or perhaps the windbags in D.C. will accede at long last to the administration's desires and do the only thing that will rescue them from this elegant trap—gut Social Security.

Cutting the taxes of the wealthy while heaping calumny on Social Security and Medicare for not having enough money in the bank might seem to many readers like a perverse way of doing things, but through the prism of management thought it makes perfect sense. After all, the Bush plan certainly does "build shareholder value," doesn't it? And it rewards top management in the manner to which they are most decidedly accustomed. Everyone knows that to attract and retain top talent you have to offer top compensation packages.

Consider also how the 2004 budget deals with labor, the chronic buzz-kill of the M.B.A. world. In the spirit of such classic market-model solutions as medical savings accounts and school vouchers, it unveils what it calls "Personal Re-employment Accounts" (PRAs), a bold new program that may someday supplant traditional unemployment insurance altogether. The budget describes our existing unemployment system as "an unwieldy relic," mainly because it relies on taxes levied on the worker's former employer, and because "employers complain that their federal unemployment taxes are too high." Awww. PRAs, on the other hand, will provide the unemployed worker with a fixed sum of money (up to $3,000, apparently regardless of the worker's expenses or previous state of employment), doled out to her in installments while she remains unemployed, the balance deliverable as soon as she finds work. The PRA is thus supposed to give the worker—get this—an incentive to find a job. Evidently that's what's lacking in these recessionary times: the will of workers to get off their ass and stop being poor.

Imagine how an observer who is utterly innocent of American ways might respond to this. "Won't this incentive business simply be negated by the above-described dividend business?" they might ask. "Won't those unemployed workers simply fall back on their newly tax-free dividends and continue their lazy ways?" Imagine how the room would fall silent and everyone would blush at the stranger's naïveté, how some thoughtful Bushite would take him aside and explain to him that we have, in America, something called social class. The policies aren't contradictory, since the people who receive unemployment and the people who receive dividends come from very, very different groups. Handouts are okay for the rich, who own most of the stock, but workers—well, workers need to learn discipline.

The groups that claim to represent workers need to be taught a lesson, too. Just as Secretary of Labor Elaine Chao recently took the opportunity of addressing the AFL-CIO's annual meeting to read aloud from a list of union-related crimes, the budget for the Department of Labor proposes, under the heading "Standing Up for the Rights of Union Members," to increase the budget for investigating and prosecuting unions. "Cracking Down on Labor Racketeering," as the budget puts it, might be of some benefit, but it is by no means a burning requirement of the moment. (Did unions destroy the NASDAQ?) The notion's prominent place in the budget is yet another blame-dispersal device, this one lifted from the playbook of the auto industry: whatever goes wrong, blame the unions. In the meantime, the initiative will impose costs on innocent unions as well as villainous ones, and is thus a clear signal of where the administration's sympathies lie. The Labor Department budget is getting smaller, remember, not bigger, and while the dollars flow for down-cracking, other programs from the days when unions had a say in how the country was run are simply being defunded.

Every kid growing up in Kansas in the seventies knew, as I did, that the Republicans were the party of sound government. Whereas Democrats practiced a degraded politics of tax and tax, spend and spend, elect and elect, Republicans were upright men who stood for balanced budgets and deplored the dalliance with deficits in which the country had engaged since the 1930s. Republicans were insiders, responsible businessmen, people with a personal stake in the fiscal probity of our public institutions.

Now all that stuff sounds like the quaint idealism of youth, something akin to my Boy Scout faith that the United States would never strike first in a war. To believe either today you'd have to have spent a long time on another planet.

There still are honorable, balanced-budget Republicans, of course. But the dominant, conservative strain of the party's thought and rhetoric has gone way beyond probity. Today the GOP is not the responsible government party; it is the antigovernment party.

"Government is not the solution to our problem," Ronald Reagan famously said in his first inaugural address. "Government is the problem." Today the phrase reverberates across the years, echoed by a mighty chorus: Limbaugh, Coulter, Liddy, North, O'Reilly, Hannity; Fox News, Conrad Black, FreeRepublic.com; Gingrich, Barr, DeLay; Hayworth, Gramm, Santorum. Yesterday's far right is today's mainstream, and the belief that government is merely misguided has given way to the belief that government is unredeemable; that the liberals who staff it are elitist, un-American, treasonable. Talk to the average Kansan about politics today and you will find that he despises the federal government the way one would despise a colonial tyrant. He believes it has nothing to offer him, despite the fact that it paid for his college education and has subsidized his way of life with agricultural price supports. He imagines that by writing government-hating emails on some listserv, he is participating in a noble brotherhood of revolutionary patriots not unlike the Founding Fathers.

Much of the GOP's most spectacular initiatives over the last ten years seem to have been designed less to accomplish some overt object than to throw a wrench into the works of this despised institution. Conservatives turn a budget debate into a crusade to shut the government down. They paralyze the executive branch with harassing investigations and impeachment proceedings. They joke about assassinating a Democratic president. They fantasize about abolishing entire departments. They cut the wages of federal workers. They dream up ways to make the tax code bear more heavily on the poor, in order to turn the poor against government and "get [their] blood boiling with tax rage," as the *Wall Street Journal* recently put it.[*] They suggest that they might default on government bonds. They "strengthen" Social Security by making it appear weaker. Even Republican blunders such as Watergate wind up reinforcing their message: You just can't trust government!

Reckless, massive deficits have become, since Reagan, the signature gesture of Republican administrations. The goal is not so much to prime the economic pump, as in the liberals' beloved Keynesian theory, but to break it. And along the way, to do unto the despised liberals as the conservatives believe the liberals have done unto

---

[*] In my home state of Kansas, which is currently caught in a budget crisis of its own thanks to rabid tax cutting in the 1990s, the Republican-dominated state legislature proposed to deal with the problem by delaying state tax refunds. This will, of course, infuriate voters, but, as Mike Hendricks of the *Kansas City Star* recently pointed out, their fury will likely fall not on the stridently anti-tax Republicans who did this to them but on the usual targets—the state revenue department and the machinery of state government, which happens to have a Democratic governor at its head.

them for decades. Traditional deficit spending, according to conservative dogma, redistributes the hard-earned wealth of real Americans down into the pockets of liberalism's contemptible constituents. Republican deficit spending, by contrast, reverses this flow and redistributes wealth upward, into the bank accounts of their people.

That's the goal if you believe this has all been thought through. It seems equally likely that this budget document, in both its juvenile rhetorical tricks and its idiotic plans for the nation, is merely supposed to teach us a lesson in how badly government can misbehave. Conservatives know that what will be discredited as we slide toward the inevitable reckoning is not the Republican Party but deficit spending, the whole hated concept of an interventionist government.

Historians often describe the New Deal of the 1930s as an effort to save capitalism from itself. Maybe that's what the policies of the Bush Administration are, too, coming as they do after a systemic crisis that in many ways resembles that of 1929–33. The technique, however, is different. The Bush team seems bent on so battering and stigmatizing the only institution capable of policing capitalism that we will be left with no practical alternative. They will fritter away the surplus. They will squander the goodwill of the world. They will jam the locomotive into reverse, toss something heavy on the throttle, and jump for it.

In 1981 the conservative thinker George Gilder published *Wealth and Poverty*, a fire-breathing damnation of government's interference with capitalism that inspired the Reagan Administration's own strategy of deficit-inducing tax cuts. Twenty-two years later, Gilder is still hammering away at the villainy of government, though the particulars of the indictment have changed a little. Today it's all about "trust," a property the private sector is said to possess in great abundance but that government lacks. In a free market, Gilder asserts in the December issue of *Forbes* magazine, "the truth will out in a relatively short time," and the laws of nature will see to it that those who have abused our trust will face the consequences. Weasely, unaccountable government, however, screws up everything that it touches—naturally, Gilder finds malevolent significance in the term "antitrust"—and the moral gulf between government and the pursuit of private profit strikes Gilder as so vast that he "trust[s] Kenneth Lay of Enron and Bernard Ebbers of WorldCom" even more than he trusts Justices Rehnquist and Scalia.

Gilder apparently has much to teach us about the ways in which trust and accountability work in America circa 2003. After writing speeches for Reagan, he became a freelance prophet of Silicon Valley, discovering that the microchip agreed with Reagan in many important respects. He was a one-man *Wired* magazine, with heavy religious overtones: constructing a virtual theology of what he called the "telecosm," worshiping at the shrine of the entrepreneur, becoming a superstar stock picker. And he bore as much responsibility for puffing the "New Economy" bubble as anyone in America.

Today the telecoms have imploded, and Gilder's portfolio of tech-stock picks, the subject of journalistic awe three years ago, has lost more than 90 percent of its peak value. If you trusted Gilder, you would be sorry now. Yet here he is, like those CEOs who walk away with millions while their companies die, still at it, inveighing against government in the pages of *Forbes*, proclaiming that the only way to react to the economic downturn he insists capitalism didn't cause is by doing absolutely nothing, by letting the market enforce its trust laws in its own mysterious way. Were one not struck speechless by the self-serving audacity of Gilder's arguments, one might respond that his own continuing prominence rather neatly disproves the whole accountability myth.

Gilder is able to soldier on because the fantasy world he imagines in such vivid colors—that perfect libertarian universe in which markets work flawlessly and the blame for anything that goes wrong can be neatly outsourced to government—is one in which the very, very wealthy dearly like to believe. In March, I attended one of Gilder's high-tech business conferences, this one having to do with what he calls "Storewidth." The high point of the gathering was not the technical presentations, even with their projections of amazing entrepreneurship to come; it was a political stem-winder delivered by Gilder's friend and patron Steve Forbes, the publisher and onetime presidential candidate.

Naturally the Bush tax plan was prominent in Forbes's thoughts. In fact, he was ecstatic about the prospects, calling the elimination of the dividends tax a "step forward to the flat tax," his own pet idea for enriching the rich. With those who complain about the return of deficits Forbes had no patience at all, since obviously the federal shortfalls would quickly be made good by the economic growth that the tax cuts would surely unleash. The doubters, he went on, were motivated by a congenital hatred of the very idea of tax cuts; besides, Washington used accounting that would "make Enron look honest." And this was an odd thing to say: Wasn't Forbes's own magazine one of the many business publications that literally did make Enron look honest? And not just Enron, but electricity deregulation itself, the billions to be made in bandwidth, the whole New Economy swindle?

Maybe so, but Forbes was showing no contrition. The business class had led us into disaster, but now they thought they deserved some help from Uncle Sam. They wanted what Forbes called "the dead weight of Washington" off their backs. They wanted the entire world to embrace their deregulatory agenda. They wanted a tax cut.

Walking around the luxurious hotel in which the conference was being held, it wasn't hard to see why. The St. Regis Monarch Beach Resort & Spa was built two years ago, at the tail end of the bull market, in the southern California city of Dana Point, just a little inland from the even posher Ritz-Carlton. It's the kind of place that sifts people like me out even before we get inside: arriving by car, you either pay the valet and come sweeping in the grand, chandeliered main entrance or you park it yourself and enter via an unmarked door tucked away behind the registration counter. The hotel has its own high-end antiques store; it has its own bakery/coffee shop with old-style wood trimmings; it has a fine restaurant with the requisite jeroboams of champagne posted by the door; it has a Versailles-size fountain and a golf course overlooking the Pacific; hanging over the bar it has an enormous reproduction of Maxfield Parrish's *Garden of Allah*, one of those idyllic dream-scenes in which everything shimmers in a golden haze. And aside from the conference attendees, the hotel was almost deserted.

I sat by myself on the hotel's vast, sweeping veranda and looked out past the empty balconies of the hotel rooms, the empty deck chairs by the empty swimming pool, the empty terrace with the oversize planters, out to the brand new empty suburb erupting from a nearby hillside, all the

ocher-colored homes ready to be occupied. The instant civilization of upper-class America was all here, antiques to
zabaglione, but no one had come to consume it.

They call this "excess capacity." Just like in Gilder's
beloved telecom industry, which so overbuilt during the
bubble years that only 5 percent of all fiber-optic lines
worldwide are currently in use, someone had made a huge
miscalculation here. They had plunked down an enormous
bet on good times for the rich carrying on forever, just when
the free money from Silicon Valley was starting to dry up.

But now comes George W. Bush, savior of his class, to get
the good times rolling again, to give us a tax cut of such
magnitude that it may well replace the NASDAQ and keep
the people of southern California relaxing in style. Social
Security will be steered deliberately into the ground, but
excess capacity in the luxury industry is one problem that
the federal budget for 2004 will undoubtedly solve. Their
coffers swelled with tax-free dividends and inheritances,
the Republicans will soon be back in Monarch Beach. Tan
men dressed in business casual will pull up to the grand
entrance in Boxsters and Ferraris. Cosmopolitans will clink
under the Maxfield Parrish. Hungover heiresses will chew
biscotti in the European-style coffee shop. And the venture
capitalists will return at last, toasting their clients out on the
veranda, opening that jeroboam, celebrating as though
none of it had ever happened.

He Said It . . .

"I want everybody to hear loud and clear that I'm going to be the president of everybody."
—Washington, DC, 1/18/01

George W. Bush has enormous power to provide help to citizens who need it most—but that is one power he doesn't care to use.

Warm in the White House
from *Bushwhacked* (2003)
Molly Ivins and Lou Dubose

First and first and foremost, we've got to make sure we fully fund LIHEAP, which is a way to help low-income folks, particularly here in the East, pay their high fuel bills.
—*George W. Bush, Presidential Debate, Boston, October 2000*

Let's begin by demonstrating our grasp of the obvious: George W. Bush has never faced the choices Luz Cruz wakes up to every day. He doesn't know much about cold houses. Maybe that's why he refused to release the $300 million in federal funds that would have helped Cruz keep her house warm in the winter of 2003. This remarkable example of compassionate conservatism is enough to make you wonder if the country has completely lost its gag reflex. While the president was cutting the heating subsidy for people in Luz Cruz' desperate circumstances, he was also pushing a $337 billion cut in dividend taxes that benefits only the very rich. Bloomberg News Service applied Bush's proposed tax cuts to Bush's own 2002 tax returns and to those of Vice President Cheney. The resulting savings would be $44,500 for Bush and $326,555 for Cheney.

If you think Bush later changed his mind and released $200 million in the Low Income Home Energy Assistance Program (LIHEAP) funds in January 2003, you have been misinformed. The story was just complex enough so that it was reported wrong.

More on that later.

On a Saturday morning in late January 2003 Luz Cruz sat at the kitchen table in her North Philadelphia home. Her three children sprawled on the floor watching cartoons. Piles of bills were scattered across the kitchen table waiting for Cruz to puzzle her way through them. It was 15 degrees F. outside and the house was almost warm, but the bills had Cruz sweating. The eastern seaboard was in the grip of a cold spell that brought snow to the Carolinas' Outer Banks and single-digit temperatures to Philadelphia. Cruz owed the gas company $992.45 and had no idea how she was going to pay it. In a rich Puerto-Rican-flavored Spanish sprinkled with English, she told the story of how she got into this fix.

"*Mi mamá era mi* backup," she said. Unfortunately, *mamá* the backup died a year ago. Luz' husband divorced her and went back to Puerto Rico. She has yet to see her first child-support check. Her eleven-year-old daughter, Jennifer, a child with large, expressive eyes who is timid in two languages, has chronic asthma. At times Jennifer requires treatment every four hours with a nebulizer, a portable appliance that allows her to breathe a medicated mist. When she goes into respiratory distress, she checks into a nearby hospital. After her mother's death, Cruz left her job as a hairdresser in order to take care of Jennifer. The family lives on the $248.50 the Pennsylvania Department of Public Welfare provides every two weeks. Like taxation, welfare is redistribution of wealth. Based on her current income, it would take Cruz fifty-four years to get the $326,555 redistributed to Dick Cheney under Bush's 2003 tax plan.

Cruz' North Philly neighborhood doesn't have a lot of curb appeal. Some of the row houses are tagged with condemned signs. Some have already been demolished, and the lots between the standing homes give the effect of missing teeth. Some are occupied by squatters. But the Cruz house is well kept and painted a tropical blue and yellow that looks like better times in Puerto Rico. The mortgage payment is $341.

Cruz said she is lucky the gas company didn't cut her off in the fall when she was trying to negotiate a payment plan. The city doesn't allow cutoffs in winter. She was trying to cut costs and deal with her bills so she wouldn't get cut off in spring or summer and face the following winter with no heat. That had already happened to ten thousand Philadelphia households.

In order to save $10 a week, her son rides the *"wawa"* to school in the morning but walks home when it's warmer in the afternoon. (When Cruz talks about the *wawa*, you realize you can take the girl out of Puerto Rico, but you can't take the Puerto Rico out of the girl. A *wawa* in Puerto Rico is an *autobus* in most Latin American countries.) Joshua's walk home from the local high school is only a couple of miles. No big deal, he said. He's a tall, healthy kid who wants to be a chef. The $40 he saves each month will help pay the gas bill down enough so maybe the gas won't be shut off in the spring.

Cruz washes clothes at the Laundromat because it's cheaper than using her own water and electricity. She keeps the thermostat as low as she can without risking the children's health. She has no car so there are no car expenses. She tries to cut costs at the grocery store, *"pero es muy difícil,"* she said. She would like to go back to work but doesn't see a way out.

The last thing Luz Cruz needs is for George Bush to make her life harder. When Bush cut $300 million from the annual budget of LIHEAP—the heating-oil and gas subsidy program designed to help people in Luz Cruz' situation—her assistance was put on hold. She has gotten LIHEAP assistance in the past but is having a hard time in 2003. Even if she does get it, the $250 annual stipend from the federally funded program will not cover her delinquent bill. In fact, it won't even cover the current bills, which run about a hundred dollars a month. "It would help," she said. "Sometimes I think I'll let them have the house and go back to Puerto Rico. I can find work in a beauty salon there, and it's never cold."

It was probably not a bad time for Cruz to leave. The Delaware hadn't seen this much ice since George Washington crossed it. There were ice-skaters on the Schuylkill. Household energy prices this winter were up 19 percent for natural gas, 45 percent for heating oil, and 22 percent for propane. Two rounds of Bush tax cuts for the wealthy made the federal budget harder to balance. By moving just 500,000 low-income families off LIHEAP—in the direction of energy independence—the president saved $300 million, *one thousandth of his dividend tax cut*. Too easy for him to pass up.

The Low Income Home Energy Assistance Program has been in place since 1974. By 2001 it was helping 4.6 million low-income families, half with children under eighteen, keep their homes warm in winter. Bush didn't intend to wipe out the subsidy for all of them, just for half a million. His numbers-crunchers even came up with a plan to get two bangs for their buck. A warm winter in 2001 had left LIHEAP $500 million in surplus funds, which could be rolled back into general revenue if not spent. The president's 2003 budget provided $1.4 billion instead of the $1.7 appropriated the previous year. Add the $500 million surplus from 2002 to the $300 million cut from the budget in 2003, and you have practically a billion dollars to apply to tax cuts. All you have to do is cut off heat for people who rarely turn out to vote and never make political contributions.

If there are cold hearts in the White House, at least there are heroes in one of the country's most durable community organizations. In her quirky mix of Spanish and English, Cruz said she was hanging her hopes on a grassroots group known by its odd arboreal acronym. "ACORN *tuve* an action," Cruz said. The leaders and members of the Association of Community Organizations for Reform Now are perennial trench fighters for economic justice in the nation's cities. The "action" Cruz referred to was a protest in Philadelphia. But ACORN's work extended beyond Philadelphia. During the big freeze of 2003, ACORN members and organizers seemed to be everywhere, or at least everywhere the poor were caught between the harsh realities of an arctic cold spell and George Bush's budget. Among its more creative efforts were takeovers of Republican Party headquarters.

In Chicago, for example, fifty ACORN families moved into the party offices, over the objection of the party's employees. They found their way to the databases and faxed and phoned Washington. They advised the White House switchboard that ACORN had taken over the Republican Party of Illinois and would give it back when President Bush released the emergency LIHEAP funds. Their timing was driven by more than cold weather. They moved into the offices the night before the president was to arrive in Chicago to lay out his budget: the budget that cut $300 million in LIHEAP funding. And to make the case for eliminating the taxes investors pay on stock dividends.

As Dubya Bush's advance team checked into their hotel, ACORN squatters were checking into the Republican Party office. "This place is warmer than most people's homes," said a man sitting on the floor. WGN-TV put the claim to the test, dispatching reporter Juan Carlos Fanjul to the living room of eighty-one-year-old Doris Rodgers, one of the people occupying Republican Party headquarters. The temperature on Fanjul's digital thermometer read 32 degrees F. The cops decided to arrest two elderly women. Eighty-one-year-old Mahaley Somerville and sixty-nine-year-old Gwendolyn Stewart were "cuffed and stuffed" into a patrol car in front of the party offices. "It's warm in jail," said Somerville as they hauled her away. "It's cold in my house."

TV news is done by formula. Every newscast began with a variation on "When President Bush arrives in Chicago tomorrow, he'll find that for some people it's just as cold inside their homes as it is on the city's streets . . ." Most stories went on to describe conditions facing fourteen thousand households without heat. WGN even sent a reporter into the Cook County Jail to ask Somerville what she would like to say to the president.

ACORN was equally imaginative in Rhode Island, where forty-five poor, urban protestors confronted Republican state party chair Bradford Gorham in the law offices of Gorham & Gorham. (Why do these folks always have names that sound like the *Mayflower* passenger manifest?) "I still don't know why they were here," Gorham told a reporter from *The Providence Journal*. "I kept asking the chief fellow, and he kept saying, 'I'm cold, it's warm in here.'

"It disrupted the place. . . . I mean people were shouting at the top of their lungs. They filled the whole downstairs of the office building. They were leaning against the fax machine, leaning against the printers and the computers. After that, one guy got very insulting. I said, 'Would you please leave,' and he just stood there looking stupid."

Gorham said the demonstrators had "sleeping bags and things like that. They were ready to camp out there on the floor. I said, 'Oh, Lord, I've got a sit-in demonstration.' And after the police came, they left."

When a reporter asked Gorham if the protesters had a point about Bush's budget cuts, Gorham said he wasn't sure. Then he wavered: "Nobody wants to see people cold or hungry or anything. I don't want to see that happen."

There were also a few heroes in Congress. Even before ACORN raided the Rhode Island Republican chairman's office, the state's Democratic senator had drafted an amendment to the appropriations bill. Jack Reed's amendment took all discretionary LIHEAP funding away from the president and restored it to mandatory "formula" funding that Bush cannot control. The amendment increased LIHEAP funding from the $1.4 billion proposed by Bush to $2 billion. The amendment won on an 88–4 vote.

Then Reed and Maine Republican Susan Collins fired off a letter to the president, urging him to immediately release the emergency contingency money, since it was no longer under his discretion. They demanded he use the power of the executive branch to get the money to the people who needed it. The senators' language was diplomatic, but one of Reed's staffers said the amendment intentionally took all discretionary funds from the president. Bush could either wait to see the money spent in the following fiscal year or release it immediately. He could no longer deny it to people who couldn't afford heating oil and gas.

Fort Worth writer Sam Hudson tells young reporters that "trousers are the most manly ass-covering, though some men try to cover their asses with paper." In a response to the 88–4 Senate vote and the letter from the two senators, George Bush covered his with paper. Two sheets, to be precise. One was an executive order releasing $200 million from the discretionary funds over which he was losing his discretion. The other was a press release in which the president announced the release of funds. This adroit move allowed him to save his face and cover his ass at the same time. By releasing $200 million of the $300 million in the fund, he maintained the illusion that he had a choice. The $100 million he didn't order spent will be included in the mandatory funding for LIHEAP in the year to come.

The president's press release provided the angle for most news reporters writing about LIHEAP. Some news stories went so far as to describe the Senate vote and make it clear that the president had no choice, but most people concluded that President Bush had done right by millions of Americans in need of help with their heating.

It was too late for many. The money, released in late January, could not ensure that the ten thousand households without heat in Philadelphia would have their heat turned on. Or the fourteen thousand freezing homes in Chicago. But it did help tens of thousands of people across the country, where states responded to increased fuel costs and increased demands for help by reducing the size of LIHEAP grants, cutting staff, and reducing the number of months covered.

If you don't believe the help is desperately needed, get into your car. In any city in the country you are a short drive from the people Michael Harrington described fifty years ago in *The Other America*.

In Philadelphia there are entire neighborhoods where a reporter can find "heat-or-eat" horror stories by knocking on doors and asking a few questions. If you're aiming for diversity, within four miles of Philly's Center City hotels, where dinner for two means a $200 tab, there's a heap of multicultural LIHEAP stories. Luz Cruz lives four miles north of Center City, in the shadow of Temple University. Four miles west, near the University of Pennsylvania, Frances Hassell lives in an eighty-year-old row house that seems to be collapsing from the front porch inward. "Look for the torn blue tarp on my roof," Hassell said. "That's how I tell people to find my house." She is a tall, fair-skinned woman with red hair, struggling to make it on a $570 monthly SSI check. Her husband, a World War II veteran who was almost twenty years her senior, died a few years ago. She's disabled and on her own. Last year her $250 LIHEAP grant helped. "It hasn't come through yet this year," she said. She has been unable to complete the application process because when she calls all she gets is a recording. Her gas bill is averaged over twelve months. "I'm supposed to pay sixty-four dollars and some change. This month they sent me a bill for one hundred sixty-four dollars. How am I going to pay one hundred sixty-four dollars?"

Four miles northwest of City Hall Alma Brown keeps her thermostat set well below seventy. Brown, a seventy-year-old African-American woman living on Social Security, is also disabled. "I get only Social Security, but I been managing pretty good," she said. For years she sewed uniforms at the Army Quartermaster Building in South Philadelphia. LIHEAP has helped in the past, but with temperatures in the low teens in January, she was still waiting for a response to her 2003 application. "I'll get it," she said. "But it's not going to be as much as last year. They cut everybody back." Brown was just starting to do the numbers. She had been managing pretty good, but a lower LIHEAP grant, fuel bills up by 45 percent, and a fixed income make it much harder.

Funds get cut and people "fall through the cracks." *The Philadelphia Inquirer* reported in late January that Delia Brown, seventy, Betty Clark, sixty-six, and Bobby Rivers, seventy-seven, had fallen through the cracks. Big-time. On the weekend most Americans were watching the Super Bowl, they died in their homes. Their heat had been cut off. The cause of their deaths was a combination of heart disease and hypothermia. They froze to death. The County Assistance Office would not say whether they had applied for LIHEAP assistance. The Philadelphia Gas Works does not discuss customer accounts.

Quizzes
Paul Slansky

Who commented on Bush's "almost giddy readiness to kill"?

(a) Senator Chuck Hagel (R-Nebraska)
(b) MSNBC's Chris Matthews
(c) CBS's Dan Rather
(d) General Tommy Franks

Answer: (b)

Three of these statements were made by George W. Bush. Which one was made by Donald Rumsfeld?

(a) "I think war is a dangerous place."
(b) "First, let me make it very clear: poor people aren't necessarily killers. Just because you happen to be not rich doesn't mean you're willing to kill."
(c) "The true strength of America happens when a neighbor loves a neighbor just like they'd like to be loved themselves."
(d) "Stuff happens."

Answer: (d)

He Said It . . .

"[I] understand how unfair the death penalty is . . . er . . . the death tax."
—Omaha, NE, 2/28/01

George W. Bush was a creepily enthusiastic enforcer of the death penalty in Texas, which performed more than 150 executions during his time as the state's governor.

Encyclopedia Brown and the Case of Death Row Dubya

from *The Modern Humorist* (5/15/00)

John Warner

Encyclopedia Brown and his partner Sally were about to close up shop at the detective agency for the day when a large bus with "Bush 2000" painted in three-foot-high letters on the side pulled into the driveway. A man wearing cowboy boots, a dark suit and a smirk got out of the bus and strode toward Encyclopedia and Sally. He was followed closely by a group of well-dressed men and women who are called handlers. A handler is someone who tells a political candidate what to say, think and feel.

As the group approached, Encyclopedia and Sally

both shivered as though they were in the presence of something without soul or conscience.

The smirking man spoke. "My name is George W. Bush, governor of the great state of Texas, and the next president of your United States. Encyclopedia Brown, I need your help as an American in the case of Rudy Roy Clifford." A handler placed a quarter on Encyclopedia's table and gave him a case file stamped DEATH ROW. The handler held a cattle prod loosely in his left hand. A cattle prod is a small device that delivers an electric charge and is used for the purposes of training and conditioning certain species of animals.

"Who's Rudy Roy Clifford?" Encyclopedia asked warily while looking at crime-scene photos.

"Look at me, I'm Rudy Roy Clifford," George W. Bush whimpered, his lips pursed in mock desperation. "Please don't kill me."

With a zap from the cattle prod, the handler dropped George W. Bush to his knees.

"Unnnnnuhhhaaahhhg," George W. Bush said. As he raised himself from the ground, he spoke again to Encyclopedia and Sally.

"What I meant to say is that Rudy Roy Clifford is the perpetrator of a heinous convenience store triple murder and is scheduled to be executed in precisely one hour. Of course, no innocent person has ever been executed in Texas, and I'm confident that justice is being done in this case, but because the final determination of innocence or guilt is among the most profound and serious decisions a person can make, I am exhausting all possible avenues of inquiry." George W. Bush winked at Sally.

Encyclopedia and Sally turned their attention to the file

for only a few moments when Sally shouted, "Wait, you can't execute Rudy Roy Clifford, and I know why!"

WHAT WAS SO OBVIOUS TO SALLY THAT THEY DIDN'T EVEN NEED ENCYCLOPEDIA?

Sally noticed in the case file that Rudy Roy Clifford had a documented IQ of 35. That means that he had the mental capacity of a four-year-old and could not understand the consequences of his actions and thus could not be judged competent to stand trial and punishment. Therefore, according to the law, as well as the principles of simple human decency, he should not be executed.

However, as Encyclopedia patted Sally on the back and suggested they go out for ice cream to celebrate her solving the case, George W. Bush said, "I understand those concerns, but I'm afraid that that particular issue has already been ruled upon many times by various levels of our judiciary who at every step have found Rudy Roy Clifford fit for punishment, and I cannot consider this factor as I make my final decision on clemency. But above all, we wish for justice, both for the accused and the victim, to be served."

Encyclopedia looked at one of the crime scene photos and noted that the splatter pattern on the wall angled downward where the victims had been killed. The splatter pattern is the manner in which human blood and viscera are dispersed by a gunshot.

George W. Bush described the crime to Encyclopedia and Sally. "On the afternoon of January 1st, Rudy Roy Clifford entered a Shop N' Go outside of Dallas, ordered the two store employees and one patron up against a wall and killed each of them with a single gunshot to the head. What did he kill them for?"

The handler with the cattle prod frowned as George W. Bush continued the story. "Thirty-seven dollars, which he probably took back to the slum and spent it on crack like they all do. How much crack—"

The handler zapped George W. Bush again. George W. Bush rolled under the table and curled into a defensive, fetal position. The fetal position is a resting position in which the body is curved, the legs and arms are bent and drawn toward the chest, and the head is bowed forward, which is used in some forms of psychic regression. "Mommy?" George W. Bush asked.

"I'm scared, Encyclopedia," Sally said. "What are we going to do?"

"Don't worry, Sally," Encyclopedia said. "I have one question that I think will solve this once and for all. How tall is Rudy Roy Clifford?"

"Five foot one," answered George W. Bush, coming briefly out of his daze.

Encyclopedia bolted from his chair, "Rudy Roy Clifford did not commit these murders and I can prove it!" he shouted triumphantly.

WHAT DID ENCYCLOPEDIA SEE IN THE CRIME PHOTOS?
Encyclopedia observed that the splatter pattern on the wall angled downward, suggesting that the fatal shots came from an angle *above* the victims, which would be impossible for the five foot one inch Rudy Roy Clifford unless he were standing on a stepstool, which wasn't found at the crime scene.

Furthermore, Encyclopedia noted that, according to the

police report, when asked by the police to merely hold a gun, the developmentally disabled Rudy Roy Clifford held it backwards, with the barrel pointed at himself.

Encyclopedia and Sally turned to go inside for dinner, but the handler, while nudging at George W. Bush with his foot, spoke quickly. "What Governor Bush would like to say is that he understands the limitations of forensic science, and the occasionally contradictory nature of some of the evidence. However, a jury of Mr. Clifford's peers, upon hearing all of the evidence and testimony have found him guilty . . ."

"That's right!" George W. Bush shouted from under the table, smiling up at the handler.

"But—" began Encyclopedia.

The handler ignored him. "And fortunately, in this case there is an eyewitness identification of Rudy Roy Clifford as the shooter. So, in the absence of other, more compelling evidence, in order to insure that justice is to be done, Governor Bush must rely on the uncontroverted account of Mr. Meany."

"Bugs Meany! I knew it!" Sally and Encyclopedia cried simultaneously.

"I'm cold," George W. Bush said from the floor, still rocking in the fetal position.

Entering the Tigers' clubhouse, Encyclopedia, Sally, George W. Bush and his handlers were confronted with a media frenzy. In a corner, Geraldo Rivera interviewed himself, while next to him, ABC's Cokie Roberts checked her reflection in Sam Donaldson's shiny forehead and nearby, CNBC's Chris Matthews and NBC's Tim Russert sat painting each other's toes with glitter as they engaged in empty rhetoric. Empty rhetoric sounds like this: blah blah blah di blah blah.

Encyclopedia and Sally dodged through the crowd. They found Bugs Meany in the center of it all, stroking the inner thigh of Republican strategist Ann Coulter as he recounted witnessing the murders to CNN's Bernard Shaw. Bernard Shaw is a television reporter and commentator with a perfectly rectangular head.

"It was New Year's Day, and I was on my way to watch the Sugar Bowl game with my uncle, Buck Meany, when he said he needed some Corn Nuts." Corn Nuts are a type of snack food made out of road pebbles that are painted yellow, then kiln-fired to a fine glaze. "So we pulled into the store, and as I went inside to get the corn-nuts, plain as day, I saw Rudy Roy Clifford off those people," Bugs continued, dabbing at his eye with a hanky. "It was terrible," Bugs said, turning and finding solace in Ann Coulter's cleavage.

Finally, completely exasperated, Encyclopedia shouted, "Stop this madness!" and all the talking heads turned to face the boy sleuth. "Once and for all, Rudy Roy Clifford is innocent and I can, absolutely, beyond a shadow of a doubt, prove it!"

Encyclopedia heard Bugs say that he was on the way to the Sugar Bowl with his uncle, Buck Meany, but as any sports fan knows, the Sugar Bowl is played in New Orleans, not Dallas, which is the home of the Cotton Bowl. Tripped up by his mistake, Bugs admitted that he'd made the whole story up to collect the $1,500 dollars in reward money for the case.

Sent into a flurry of activity, one of the handlers said,

"He's got to show the proper sensitivity," while another said, "The important thing is that he remains consistent." Finally, after consulting the latest poll figures and throwing the twenty-sided die, the handlers huddled, then whispered into George W. Bush's ear as they straightened his tie.

In a solemn voice that contradicted his often lighthearted nature, George W. Bush faced the multitude of assembled cameras and said, "I recognize that there are good people who oppose the death penalty. I have heard their message and I respect their heartfelt point of view, but after considering all the facts, I'm confident that justice is being done and I will not intervene in the case of Rudy Roy Clifford."

At 8:11 p.m., Rudy Roy Clifford was put to death by lethal injection.

Afterwards, Encyclopedia and Sally tried to cheer themselves up by going out for ice cream with Vice President Al Gore. As they waited in line, Al Gore said, "I'm in favor of the death penalty, but I do think we need to take a good hard look at the system to make sure that no one is being wrongly executed," before hastening to add, "But I do not know the record in Texas."

Al Gore smiled and ordered a pineapple sundae. Suddenly, Encyclopedia and Sally weren't hungry at all, couldn't imagine eating, actually, and went home early.

THE BUSH ADMINISTRATION WILL NOT ALLOW THOSE PROMOTING A "GAY AGENDA" TO SUBVERT THE INSTITUTION OF MARRIAGE-- TO CHANGE ITS **TRADITIONAL** DEFINITION:

AN EXCHANGE OF PROPERTY ARRANGED BY THE PARENTS OF STRANGERS!

THAT'S WHY WE INTRODUCED the DEFENSE OF TRADITIONAL MARRIAGE ACT

THIS IS HOW MARRIAGE STARTED CENTURIES AGO-- AND **THIS** IS HOW WE'RE KEEPIN' IT!

§2.01. The Parents shall arrange for the Bride, no younger than 12 years of age, to become the possession of the Groom, with a Dowry of no less than three livestock animals.

HI. I'M MICHELLE. PLEASED TO MARRY YOU.

§2.02. Marriage by abduction is legally proscribed, although if the Groom later pays a Bride-Price, it will be recognized.

DO YOU ACCEPT PAYPAL?

§2.03. Among Nobility, Marriages may be arranged between Reigning Families for the purpose of reinforcing geo-political alliances.

HERE YA GO, PRINCE! SHE'S A KEEPER!

THANK YOU, VICE PRESIDENT CHENEY!

UH, DAD.

He Said It . . .

"For every fatal shooting, there were roughly three non-fatal shootings. And, folks, this is unacceptable in America. It's just unacceptable. And we're going to do something about it."
—Philadelphia, 5/14/01

"And so, in my State of the—my State of the Union—or state—my speech to the nation, whatever you want to call it, speech to the nation—I asked Americans to give 4,000 years—4,000 hours over the next— the rest of your life—of service to America. That's what I asked—4,000 hours."
—Bridgeport, CT, 4/9/02

LOOK, WITH ALL DUE RE-
SPECT TO THE MILLION
MOMS, THIS GUN THING
IS WAY OVER-
BLOWN!

TO BEGIN WITH, A LOT
OF GUN DEATHS ARE
SUICIDES, AND NOT
MURDERS, OKAY?

5-17

IN JAPAN, WHERE GUNS ARE
ILLEGAL, PEOPLE KILL THEM-
SELVES WITH KNIVES! WHICH
WOULD YOU RATHER HAVE —
A SLOW, PAINFUL DEATH
THROUGH DISEMBOWELMENT,
OR A QUICK LIGHTS-OUT?

SO ONCE
AGAIN,
IT'S ABOUT
COMPAS-
SION?

GUILTY AS
CHARGED!

Quizzes
Paul Slansky

Match the Bush judicial nominee with his or her decision or statement.

1. James Leon Holmes
2. William Pryor
3. Carolyn Kuhl
4. Priscilla Owen

(a) Ruled against a woman who claimed that her privacy had been violated by a doctor who allowed a drug salesman to hang out in the room with them—and laugh at her—while the doctor examined her breasts.

(b) Argued that the Violence Against Women Act was unconstitutional.

(c) Consistently ruled to restrict access to abortion without parental consent.

(d) "The wife is to subordinate herself unto her husband . . . to place herself under the authority of the man."

Answers: 1(d), 2(b), 3(a), 4(c)

Who did what?

1. Comedian Mort Sahl
2. Senator Rick Santorum (R-PA)
3. Nobel Prize–winning economist George A. Akerlof
4. MSNBC's Chris Matthews

(a) Defended George W. Bush's economic priorities—refusing to roll back any of his hundred-billion-dollar tax cuts for the rich, while keeping down spending on child care for mothers trying to get off welfare—by pointing out that "making people struggle a little bit is not necessarily the worst thing."

(b) Declared that "the Bush fiscal policy is the worst policy in the last two hundred years."

(c) Participated in a phone conversation with Karl Rove in which Rove called Valerie Plame, the C.I.A. agent who is married to the Bush critic Joseph Wilson, "fair game."

(d) Said that George W. Bush is "the first President who likes to hang out with his father's friends."

Answers: 1(d), 2(a), 3(b), 4(c)

HE'S
ANTI-AMERICAN

*with quotes by George W. Bush;
a cartoon by Garry Trudeau;
a quiz from Paul Slansky;
and an anagram*

George W. Bush isn't a real American: He hates real Americans. Real Americans are a mutually supportive community of fair-minded, generous, freedom-loving people. George W. Bush—judgmental, stingy and power-mad—despises that community. He seeks to destroy the ties that bind and protect us, so that corporations and the rich people who control them can rule our lives.

> *"Well, it's an unimaginable honor to be the president during the Fourth of July of this country. It means what these words say, for starters. The great inalienable rights of our country. We're blessed with such values in America. And I—it's—I'm a proud man to be the nation based upon such wonderful values."*
> —at the Jefferson Memorial, 7/2/01

Rolling Back the 20th Century
from *The Nation* (5/12/03)
William Greider

I. BACK TO THE FUTURE

George W. Bush, properly understood, represents the third and most powerful wave in the right's long-running assault on the governing order created by twentieth-century liberalism. The first wave was Ronald Reagan, whose election in 1980 allowed movement conservatives finally to attain governing power (their flame was first lit by Barry Goldwater back in 1964). Reagan unfurled many bold ideological banners for right-wing reform and established the political viability of enacting regressive tax cuts, but he accomplished very little reordering of government, much less shrinking of it. The second wave was Newt Gingrich, whose capture of the House majority in 1994 gave Republicans control of Congress for the first time in two generations. Despite some landmark victories like welfare reform, Gingrich flamed out quickly, a zealous revolutionary ineffective as legislative leader.

George Bush II may be as shallow as he appears, but his presidency represents a far more formidable challenge than either Reagan or Gingrich. His potential does not emanate from an amiable personality (Al Gore, remember, outpolled him in 2000) or even the sky-high ratings generated by 9/11 and war. Bush's governing strength is anchored in the long, hard-driving movement of the right that now owns all three branches of the federal government. Its unified ranks allow him to govern aggressively, despite slender GOP majorities in the House and Senate and the public's general indifference to the right's domestic program.

The movement's grand ambition—one can no longer say grandiose—is to roll back the twentieth century, quite literally. That is, defenestrate the federal government and reduce its scale and powers to a level well below what it was before the New Deal's centralization. With that accomplished, movement conservatives envision a restored society in which the prevailing values and power relationships resemble the America that existed around 1900, when William McKinley was President. Governing authority and resources are dispersed from Washington, returned to local levels and also to individuals and private institutions, most notably corporations and religious organizations. The primacy of private property rights is re-established over the shared public priorities expressed in government regulation. Above all, private wealth—both enterprises and individuals with higher incomes—are permanently insulated from the progressive claims of the graduated income tax.

These broad objectives may sound reactionary and destructive (in historical terms they are), but hard-right conservatives see themselves as liberating reformers, not destroyers, who are rescuing old American virtues of self-reliance and individual autonomy from the clutches of collective action and "statist" left-wingers. They do not expect any of these far-reaching goals to be fulfilled during Bush's tenure, but they do assume that history is on their side and that the next wave will come along soon (not an unreasonable expectation, given their great gains during the past thirty years). Right-wingers—who once seemed frothy and fratricidal—now understand that three steps forward, two steps back still adds up to forward progress. It's a long march, they say. Stick together, because we are winning.

Many opponents and critics (myself included) have found the right's historic vision so improbable that we tend to guffaw and misjudge the political potency of what it has put together. We might ask ourselves: If these ideas are so self-evidently cockeyed and reactionary, why do they keep advancing? The right's unifying idea—get the government out of our lives—has broad popular appeal, at least on a sentimental level, because it represents an authentic core value in the American experience ("Don't tread on me" was a slogan in the Revolution). But the true source of its strength is the movement's fluid architecture and durability over time, not the passing personalities of Reagan-Gingrich-Bush or even the big money from business. The movement has a substantial base that believes in its ideological vision—people alarmed by cultural change or injured in some way by government intrusions, coupled with economic interests that have very strong reasons to get government off their backs—and the right has created the political mechanics that allow these disparate elements to pull together. Cosmopolitan corporate executives hold their noses and go along with Christian activists trying to stamp out "decadent" liberal culture. Fed-up working-class conservatives support business's assaults on their common enemy, liberal government, even though they may be personally injured when business objectives triumph.

The right's power also feeds off the general decay in the political system—the widely shared and often justifiable resentments felt toward big government, which no longer seems to address the common concerns of ordinary citizens.

I am not predicting that the right will win the governing majority that could enact the whole program, in a kind of right-wing New Deal—and I will get to some reasons why I expect their cause to fail eventually. The farther they advance, however, the less inevitable is their failure.

II. The McKinley Blueprint

In the months after last November's elections, the Bush Administration rattled progressive sensibilities with shock and awe on the home front—a barrage of audacious policy initiatives: Allow churches to include sanctuaries of worship in buildings financed by federal housing grants. Slash hundreds of billions in domestic programs, especially spending for the poor, even as the Bush tax cuts kick in for the well-to-do. At the behest of Big Pharma, begin prosecuting those who help the elderly buy cheaper prescription drugs in Canada. Compel the District of Columbia to conduct federally financed school voucher experiments (even though DC residents are overwhelmingly opposed). Reform Medicaid by handing it over to state governments, which will be free to make their own rules, much like welfare reform. Do the same for housing aid, food stamps and other long-established programs. Redefine "wetlands" and "wilderness" so that millions of protected acres are opened for development.

Liberal activists gasped at the variety and dangerous implications (the public might have been upset too but was preoccupied with war), while conservatives understood that Bush was laying the foundations, step by step, toward their grand transformation of American life. These are the concrete elements of their vision:

- Eliminate federal taxation of private capital, as the essential predicate for dismantling the progressive income tax. This will require a series of reform measures (one of them, repeal of the estate tax, already accomplished). Bush has proposed several others: elimination of the tax on stock dividends and establishment of new tax-sheltered personal savings accounts for the growing "investor class." Congress appears unwilling to swallow these, at least this year, but their introduction advances the education-agitation process. Future revenue would be harvested from a single-rate flat tax on wages or, better still, a stiff sales tax on consumption. Either way, labor gets taxed, but not capital. The 2003 Economic Report of the President, prepared by the Council of Economic Advisers, offers a primer on the advantages of a consumption tax and how it might work. Narrowing the tax base naturally encourages smaller government.

• Gradually phase out the pension-fund retirement system as we know it, starting with Social Security privatization but moving eventually to breaking up the other large pools of retirement savings, even huge public-employee funds, and converting them into individualized accounts. Individuals will be rewarded for taking personal responsibility for their retirement with proposed "lifetime savings" accounts where capital is stored, forever tax-exempt. Unlike IRAs, which provide a tax deduction for contributions, wages are taxed upfront but permanently tax-sheltered when deposited as "lifetime" capital savings, including when the money is withdrawn and spent. Thus this new format inevitably threatens the present system, in which employers get a tax deduction for financing pension funds for their workers. The new alternative should eventually lead to repeal of the corporate tax deduction and thus relieve business enterprise of any incentive to finance pensions for employees. Everyone takes care of himself.

• Withdraw the federal government from a direct

role in housing, healthcare, assistance to the poor and many other long-established social priorities, first by dispersing program management to local and state governments or private operators, then by steadily paring down the federal government's financial commitment. If states choose to kill an aid program rather than pay for it themselves, that confirms that the program will not be missed. Any slack can be taken up by the private sector, philanthropy and especially religious institutions that teach social values grounded in faith.

• Restore churches, families and private education to a more influential role in the nation's cultural life by giving them a significant new base of income—public money. When "school choice" tuitions are fully available to families, all taxpayers will be compelled to help pay for private school systems, both secular and religious, including Catholic parochial schools. As a result, public schools will likely lose some of their financial support, but their enrollments are expected to shrink anyway, as some families opt out. Although the core of Bush's "faith-based initiative" stalled in Congress, he is advancing it through new administrative rules. The voucher strategy faces many political hurdles, but the Supreme Court is out ahead, clearing away the constitutional objections.

• Strengthen the hand of business enterprise against burdensome regulatory obligations, especially environmental protection, by introducing voluntary goals and "market-driven" solutions. These will locate the decision-making on how much progress is achievable within corporate managements rather than enforcement agencies (an approach also championed in this year's Economic Report). Down the road, when a more aggressive right-wing majority is secured for the Supreme Court, conservatives expect to throw a permanent collar around the regulatory state by enshrining a radical new constitutional doctrine. It would require government to compensate private property owners, including businesses, for new regulations that impose costs on them or injure their profitability, a formulation sure to guarantee far fewer regulations [see Greider, "The Right and US Trade Law," October 15, 2001].

• Smash organized labor. Though unions have lost considerable influence, they remain a major obstacle to achieving the right's vision. Public-employee unions are formidable opponents on issues like privatization and school vouchers. Even the declining industrial unions still have the resources to mobilize a meaningful counterforce in politics. Above all, the labor movement embodies the progressives' instrument of power: collective action. The mobilizations of citizens in behalf of broad social demands are inimical to the right's vision of autonomous individuals, in charge of their own affairs and acting alone. Unions may be taken down by a thousand small cuts, like stripping "homeland security" workers of union protection. They will be more gravely weakened if pension funds, an enduring locus of labor power, are privatized.

Looking back over this list, one sees many of the old peevish conservative resentments—Social Security, the income tax, regulation of business, labor unions, big government centralized in Washington—that represent the great battles that conservatives lost during early decades of the twentieth century. That is why the McKinley era represents a lost Eden the right has set out to restore. Grover Norquist, president of Americans for Tax Reform and a pivotal leader in the movement's inside-outside politics, confirms this observation. "Yes, the McKinley era, absent the protectionism," he agrees, is the goal. "You're looking at the history of the country for the first 120 years, up until Teddy Roosevelt, when the socialists took over. The income tax, the death tax, regulation, all that." (In foreign policy, at least, the Bush Administration could fairly be said to have already restored the spirit of that earlier age. Justifying the annexation of the Philippines, McKinley famously explained America's purpose in the world: "There was nothing left for us to do but to take them all, and to educate the Filipinos, and uplift and civilize and Christianize them, and by God's grace do the very best we could by them, as our fellow men for whom Christ also died.")

But the right employs a highly selective memory. McKinley Republicans, aligned with the newly emergent industrial titans, did indeed hold off the Progressive advocates of a federal income tax and other reforms, while their high tariffs were the equivalent of a stiff consumption tax. And their conservative Supreme Court blocked regulatory laws designed to protect society and workers as unconstitutional intrusions on private property rights.

But the truth is that McKinley's conservatism broke down not because of socialists but because a deeply troubled nation was awash in social and economic conflicts, inequities generated by industrialization and the awesome power consolidating in the behemoth industrial corporations (struggles not resolved until economic crisis spawned the New Deal). Reacting to popular demands, Teddy Roosevelt enacted landmark Progressive reforms like the first federal regulations protecting public health and safety and a ban on corporate campaign contributions. Both Roosevelt and his successor, Republican William Howard Taft, endorsed the concept of a progressive income tax and other un-Republican measures later enacted under Woodrow Wilson.

George W. Bush does not of course ever speak of the glories of the McKinley era or acknowledge his party's retrograde objectives (Ari Fleischer would bat down any suggestions to the contrary). Conservatives learned, especially from Gingrich's implosion, to avoid flamboyant ideological proclamations. Instead, the broader outlines are only hinted at in various official texts. But there's nothing really secretive about their intentions. Right-wing activists and think tanks have been openly articulating the goals for years. Some of their ideas that once sounded loopy are now law.

III. The Ecumenical Right

The movement "is moving with the speed of a glacier," explains Martin Anderson, a senior fellow at Stanford's Hoover Institution who served as Reagan's house intellectual, the keeper of the flame, and was among the early academics counseling George W. Bush. "It moves very slowly, stops sometimes, even retreats, but then it moves forward again. Sometimes, it comes up against a tree and seems stuck, then the tree snaps and people say, 'My gosh, it's a revolution.'" To continue the metaphor, Anderson thinks this glacier will run up against some big boulders that do not yield, that the right will eventually be stopped short of grand objectives like small government or elimination of the income tax. But they've made impressive progress so far.

For the first time since the 1920s, Congress, the White House and the Supreme Court are all singing from the same hymnal and generally reinforcing one another. The Court's right-wing majority acts to shrink federal authority, block citizen challenges of important institutions and hack away at the liberal precedents on civil rights, regulatory law and many other matters (it even decides an election for its side, when necessary).

Bush, meanwhile, has what Reagan lacked—a Reaganite majority in Congress. When the Gipper won in 1980, most Republicans in Congress were still traditional conservatives, not radical reformers. The majority of House Republicans tipped over to the Reaganite identity in 1984, a majority of GOP senators not until 1994. The ranks of the unconverted—Republicans who refuse to sign Norquist's pledge not to raise taxes—are now, by his count, down to 5 percent in the House caucus, 15 percent in the Senate.

This ideological solidarity is a central element in Bush's governing strength. So long as he can manage the flow of issues in accord with the big blueprint, the right doesn't shoot at him when he makes politically sensitive deviations (import quotas for steel or the lavish new farm-subsidy bill). It also helps that, especially in the House, the GOP leaders impose Stalinist discipline on their troops. Bush also reassures the far right by making it clear that he is one of them. Reagan used to stroke the Christian right with strong rhetoric on social issues but gave them very little else (the man was from Hollywood, after all). Bush is a true believer, a devout Christian and exceedingly public about it. Bush's principal innovation—a page taken from Bill Clinton's playbook—is to confuse the opposition's issues by offering his own compassion-lite alternatives, co-opting or smothering Democratic initiatives. Unlike Clinton, Bush does not mollify his political base with empty gestures. Their program is his program.

"Reagan talked a good game on the domestic side but he actually didn't push for much," says Paul Weyrich, leader of the Free Congress Foundation and a movement pioneer. "Likewise, the Gingrich era was a lot of rhetoric. This Administration is far more serious and disciplined. . . . they have better outreach than any with which I have dealt. These people have figured out how to communicate regularly with their base, make sure it understands what they're doing. When they have to go against their base, they know how to inoculate themselves against what might happen."

Norquist's ambition is that building on its current strength, the right can cut government by half over the next twenty-five years to "get it down to the size where we can drown it in the bathtub" [see Robert Dreyfuss, "Grover Norquist: 'Field Marshal' of the Bush Tax Plan," May 14, 2001]. The federal government would shrink from 20 percent of GDP to 10 percent, state and local government from 12 to 6 percent. When vouchers become universally available, he expects public schools to shrink from 6 to 3 percent of GDP. "And we'll have better schools," he assures. People like Norquist play the role of constantly pushing the boundaries of the possible. "I'm lining up support to abolish the alternative minimum tax," he says. "Has Bush spoken to this? No. I want to run ahead, put our guys on the record for it. So I will be out in front of the Bush Administration, not attacking the Bush Administration. Will he do everything we want? No, but you know what? I don't care."

Americans for Tax Reform serves as a kind of "action central" for a galaxy of conservative interests, with support from corporate names like Microsoft, Pfizer, AOL Time Warner, R.J. Reynolds and the liquor industry. "The issue that brings people to politics is what they want from government," Norquist explains. "All our people want to be left alone by government. To be in this coalition, you only need to have your foot in the circle on one issue. You don't need a *Weltanschauung,* you don't have to agree with every other issue, so long as the coalition is right on yours. That's why we don't have the expected war within the center-right coalition. That's why we can win."

One of the right's political accomplishments is bringing together diverse, once-hostile sectarians. "The Republican Party used to be based in the Protestant mainline and aggressively kept its distance from other religions," Norquist observes. "Now we've got observant Catholics, the people who go to mass every Sunday, evangelical Christians, Mormons, orthodox Jews, Muslims." How did it happen? "The secular left has created an ecumenical right," he says. This new tolerance, including on race, may represent meaningful social change, but of course the right also still feeds on intolerance too, demonizing those whose values or lifestyle or place of birth does not conform to their idea of "American."

This tendency, Norquist acknowledges, is a vulnerability. The swelling ranks of Latino and Asian immigrants could become a transforming force in American politics, once these millions of new citizens become confident enough to participate in election politics (just as European immigrants became a vital force for liberal reform in the early twentieth century). So Bush labors to change the party's anti-immigrant profile (and had some success with Mexican-Americans in Texas).

Norquist prefers to focus on other demographic trends that he believes insure the right's eventual triumph: As the children of the New Deal die off, he asserts, they will be replaced by young "leave me alone" conservatives. Anderson, the former Reagan adviser, is less certain. "Most of the people like what government is doing," he observes. "So long as it isn't overintrusive and so forth, they're happy with it."

IV. SHOW ME THE MONEY

Ideology may provide the unifying umbrella, but the real glue of this movement is its iron rule for practical politics: Every measure it enacts, every half-step it takes toward the grand vision, must deliver concrete rewards to one constituency or another, often several—and right now, not in the distant future. Usually the reward is money. There is nothing unusual or illegitimate about that, but it sounds like raw hypocrisy considering that the right devotes enormous energy to denouncing "special-interest politics" on the left (schoolteachers, labor unions, bureaucrats, Hollywood). The right's interest groups, issue by issue, bring their muscle to the cause. Bush's "lifetime savings" accounts constitute a vast new product line for the securities industry, which is naturally enthused about marketing and managing these accounts. The terms especially benefit the well-to-do, since a family of four will be able to shelter up to $45,000 annually (that's more than most families earn in a year). The White House has enlisted Fortune 500 companies to spread the good news to the investor class in their regular mailings to shareholders.

Bush's "market-friendly" reforms for healthcare would reward two business sectors that many consumers regard as the problem—drug companies and HMOs. Big Pharma would get the best of all worlds: a federal subsidy for prescription drug purchases by the elderly, but without any limits on the prices. The insurance industry is invited to set up a privatized version of Medicare that would compete with the government-run system (assuming there are enough senior citizens willing to take that risk).

Some rewards are not about money. Bush has already provided a victory for "pro-lifers" with the ban on late-term abortions. The antiabortionists are realists now and no longer badger the GOP for a constitutional amendment, but perhaps a future Supreme Court, top-heavy with right-wing appointees, will deliver for them. Republicans are spoiling for a fight over guns in 2004, when the federal ban on assault rifles is due to expire. Liberals, they hope, will try to renew the law so the GOP can deliver a visible election-year reward by blocking it. (Gun-control advocates are thinking of forcing Bush to choose between the gun lobby and public opinion.)

The biggest rewards, of course, are about taxation, and the internal self-discipline is impressive. When Reagan proposed his huge tax-rate cuts in 1981, the K Street corporate lobbyists piled on with their own list of goodies and the White House lost control; Reagan's tax cuts wound up much larger than he intended. This time around, business behaved itself when Bush proposed a tax package in 2001 in which its wish list was left out. "They supported the 2001 tax cuts because they knew there was going to be another tax cut every year and, if you don't support this year's, you go to the end of the line next time," Norquist says. Their patience has already been rewarded. The antitax movement follows a well-defined script for advancing step by step to the ultimate goal. Norquist has organized five caucuses to agitate and sign up Congressional supporters on five separate issues: estate-tax repeal (already enacted but still vulnerable to reversal); retirement-savings reforms; elimination of the alternative minimum tax; immediate business deductions for capital investment expenses (instead of a multiyear depreciation schedule); and zero taxation of capital gains. "If we do all of these things, there is no tax on capital and we are very close to a flat tax," Norquist exclaims.

The road ahead is far more difficult than he makes it sound, because along the way a lot of people will discover that they are to be the losers. In fact, the McKinley vision requires vast sectors of society to pay dearly, and from their own pockets. Martin Anderson has worked through the flat-tax arithmetic many times, and it always comes out a political loser. "The conservatives all want to revolutionize the tax system, frankly because they haven't thought it through," Anderson says. "It means people from zero to $35,000 income pay no tax and anyone over $150,000 is going to get a tax cut. The people in between get a tax increase, unless you cut federal spending. That's not going to happen."

Likewise, any substantial consumption tax does severe injury to another broad class of Americans—the elderly. They were already taxed when they were young and earning and saving their money, but a new consumption tax would now tax their money again as they spend it. Lawrence Lindsey, Bush's former economic adviser, has advocated a consumption-based flat tax that would probably require a rate of 21 percent on consumer purchases (like a draconian sales tax). He concedes, "It would be hitting the current generation of elderly twice. So it would be a hard sell."

"School choice" is also essentially a money issue, though this fact has been obscured by the years of Republican rhetoric demonizing the public schools and their teachers. Under tuition vouchers, the redistribution of income will flow from all taxpayers to the minority of American families who send their children to private schools, religious and secular. Those children are less than 10 percent of the 52 million children enrolled in K–12. You wouldn't know it from reading about the voucher debate, but the market share of private schools actually declined slightly during the past decade. The Catholic parochial system stands to gain the most from public financing, because its enrollment has declined by half since the 1960s (to 2.6 million). Though there was some growth during the 1990s, it was in the suburbs, not cities. Other private schools, especially religious schools in the South, grew more during the past decade (by about

400,000), but public schools expanded far faster, by 6 million. The point is, the right's constituency for "school choice" remains a small though fervent minority.

Conservatives have cleverly transformed the voucher question into an issue of racial equality—arguing that they are the best way to liberate impoverished black children from bad schools in slum surroundings. But educational quality notwithstanding, it is not self-evident that private schools, including the Catholic parochial system, are disposed to solve the problem of minority education, since they are highly segregated themselves. Catholic schools enroll only 2.5 percent of black students nationwide and, more telling, only 3.8 percent of Hispanic children, most of whom are Catholic. In the South hundreds of private schools originated to escape integration and were supported at first by state tuition grants (later ruled unconstitutional). "School choice," in short, might very well finance greater racial separation—the choice of whites to stick with their own kind—and at public expense.

The right's assault on environmental regulation has a similar profile. Taking the lead are small landowners or Western farmers who make appealing pleas to be left alone to enjoy their property and take care of it conscientiously. Riding alongside are developers and major industrial sectors (and polluters) eager to win the same rights, if not from Congress then the Supreme Court. But there's one problem: The overwhelming majority of Americans want stronger environmental standards and more vigorous enforcement.

V. ARE THEY RIGHT ABOUT AMERICA?

"Leave me alone" is an appealing slogan, but the right regularly violates its own guiding principle. The antiabortion folks intend to use government power to force their own moral values on the private lives of others. Free-market right-wingers fall silent when Bush and Congress intrude to bail out airlines, insurance companies, banks—whatever sector finds itself in desperate need. The hard-right conservatives are downright enthusiastic when the Supreme Court and Bush's Justice Department hack away at our civil liberties. The "school choice" movement seeks not smaller government but a vast expansion of taxpayer obligations. Maybe what the right is really seeking is not so much to be left alone by government but to use government to reorganize society in its own right-wing image. All in all, the right's agenda promises a reordering that will drive the country toward greater separation and segmentation of its many social elements—higher walls and more distance for those who wish to protect themselves from messy diversity. The trend of social disintegration, including the slow breakup of the broad middle class, has been under way for several decades—fissures generated by growing inequalities of status and well-being. The right proposes to legitimize and encourage these deep social changes in the name of greater autonomy. Dismantle the common assets of society, give people back their tax money and let everyone fend for himself.

Is this the country Americans want for their grandchildren or great-grandchildren? If one puts aside Republican nostalgia for McKinley's gaslight era, it was actually a dark and troubled time for many Americans and society as a whole, riven as it was by harsh economic conflict and social neglect of everyday brutalities.

Autonomy can be lonely and chilly, as millions of Americans have learned in recent years when the company canceled their pensions or the stock market swallowed their savings or industrial interests destroyed their surroundings. For most Americans, there is no redress without common action, collective efforts based on mutual trust and shared responsibilities. In other words, I do not believe that most Americans want what the right wants. But I also think many cannot see the choices clearly or grasp the long-term implications for the country.

This is a failure of left-liberal politics. Constructing an effective response requires a politics that goes right at the ideology, translates the meaning of Bush's governing agenda, lays out the implications for society and argues unabashedly for a more positive, inclusive, forward-looking vision. No need for scaremongering attacks; stick to the well-known facts. Pose some big questions: Do Americans want to get rid of the income tax altogether and its longstanding premise that the affluent should pay higher rates than the humble? For that matter, do Americans think capital incomes should be excused completely from taxation while labor incomes are taxed more heavily, perhaps through a stiff national sales tax? Do people want to give up on the concept of the "common school"—one of America's distinctive achievements? Should property rights be given precedence over human rights or society's need to protect nature? The recent battles over Social Security privatization are instructive: When the labor-left mounted a serious ideological rebuttal, well documented in fact and reason, Republicans scurried away from the issue (though they will doubtless try again).

To make this case convincing, however, the opposition must first have a coherent vision of its own. The Democratic Party, alas, is accustomed to playing defense and has become wary of "the vision thing," as Dubya's father called it. Most elected Democrats, I think, now see their role as managerial rather than big reform, and fear that even talking about ideology will stick them with the right's demon label: "liberal." If a new understanding of progressive purpose does get formed, one that connects to social reality and describes a more promising future, the vision will not originate in Washington but among those who see realities up close and are struggling now to change things on the ground. We are a very wealthy (and brutally powerful) nation, so why do people experience so much stress and confinement in their lives, a sense of loss and failure? The answers, I suggest, will lead to a new formulation of what progressives want.

The first place to inquire is not the failures of government but the malformed power relationships of American capitalism—the terms of employment that reduce many workers to powerless digits, the closely held decisions of finance capital that shape our society, the waste and destruction embedded in our system of mass consumption and production. The goal is, like the right's, to create greater self-fulfillment but as broadly as possible. Self-reliance and individualism can be made meaningful for all only by first reviving the power of collective action.

My own conviction is that a lot of Americans are ready to take up these questions and many others. Some are actually old questions—issues of power that were not resolved in the great reform eras of the past. They await a new generation bold enough to ask if our prosperous society is really as free and satisfied as it claims to be. When conscientious people find ideas and remedies that resonate with the real experiences of Americans, then they will have their vision, and perhaps the true answer to the right wing.

Quiz
Paul Slansky

Which headline did *not* appear in a daily or weekly U.S. newspaper?

(a) "ADMINISTRATION ESTABLISHES NEW WET-LANDS GUIDELINES; TWENTY MILLION ACRES COULD LOSE PROTECTED STATUS, GROUPS SAY"

(b) "ASHCROFT ORDERS U.S. ATTORNEYS TO SEEK DEATH IN MORE CASES"

(c) "BUSH SEEKS STIFFER PROOF FOR POOR TO OBTAIN AID"

(d) "BUSH PLANS TO LET RELIGIOUS GROUPS GET BUILDING AID; WORSHIP SITES INVOLVED"

(e) "BUSH ORDERS A THREE-YEAR DELAY IN OPENING SECRET DOCUMENTS"

(f) "BUSH PUSHES PLAN TO CURB APPEALS IN MEDICARE CASES; BENEFIT DENIALS AT ISSUE"

(g) "BUSH DECLARES WAR; WARNS NATION MANY SACRIFICES WILL BE NECESSARY"

(h) "PENTAGON SEEKING TO DEPLOY MISSILES BEFORE FULL TESTING"

(i) "EPA TO ALLOW POLLUTERS TO BUY CLEAN WATER CREDITS"

Answer: (g)

ANAGRAM

President George W. Bush:
White person begrudges

He Said It . . .

"I appreciate that question because I, in the state of Texas, had heard a lot of discussion about a faith-based initiative eroding the important bridge between church and state."

—1/29/01

Bush to states (especially liberal ones): Drop dead.

Getting the Blues
from *The Nation* (8/4/03)

Peter Schrag

In the winter and early spring of 2001, when Dick Cheney was telling Californians that their sky-high electricity bills were their own tree-hugging fault, you might have thought the Administration was just covering for Enron CEO Ken Lay and George W. Bush's other Texas energy friends and, as an added bonus, sticking it to the lotus-eaters on the Left Coast who'd given Al Gore his million-vote California majority.

But that was just the paranoia of the innocent. In the past year, as the nation's deficit-ridden states were pleading for federal help, Washington was telling them all to drop dead, reserving harshest treatment for the "blues," meaning the liberal states that voted for Democrats. While California was not alone, it was certainly the biggest target, as the only large state with a Democratic governor, Democratic legislature and a Congressional delegation dominated (32-to-20) by Democrats. "They view California," said a Washington lobbyist, "as a foreign land." Some of that you can ascribe to the Administration's efforts to suck every possible dollar of the cost of Bush's tax cuts from the states. But behind the fiscal policies; the unfunded mandates (i.e., new federal requirements without funds to help states comply); the cost of NCLB, Bush's "No Child Left Behind" education law; the childcare expenses made necessary by the Administration's proposed new federal work rules for welfare recipients, there seemed to be an ideological thrust, bordering on vindictiveness, aimed at teaching the liberal states a lesson.

Late in April, as states like Oregon were preparing to close schools weeks before the end of the term, and others were dumping hundreds of thousands off the Medicaid rolls, laying off cops and raising college tuition to close a collective two-year deficit estimated by the nonpartisan National Conference of State Legislatures (NCSL) at upwards of $100 billion, Grover Norquist said he'd like to see a state or two go bankrupt.

Norquist, who runs the conservative Americans for Tax

Reform and heads what Bill Moyers has called a politburo of conservative strategy, is also joined at the hip with Karl Rove, the President's political brain and one of his chief policy advisers. "I hope a state has real trouble getting its act together," Norquist told the *New York Times*'s David Firestone. "We need a state to be a bad example, so that the others will start to make the serious decisions they need to get out of this mess." When Norquist speaks on such issues, you're never sure whether he's the ventriloquist or Rove's talking dog.

Brian Riedl, a fellow at the Heritage Foundation, put it more mildly, but it amounted to the same thing. "Deficits," he said, "provide states with a golden opportunity to examine their budgets and reduce wasteful and ineffective spending, which helps them keep taxes low and aid the economic recovery." Lay off those teachers, kick poor working mothers off the rolls of those who get help with childcare, close a few more parks. Norquist's and Riedl's remarks were generally directed at "states," but it didn't take much parsing to conclude that they weren't referring to Nebraska or Alabama. It was the liberal states—the Democratic states with the relatively generous social welfare programs and the more progressive tax rates—that they were talking about.

Forget that Washington, with Bush's multi-trillion-dollar tax cuts, is running deficits that are proportionally larger than those of the states; forget that at least part of the states' problems resulted not just from their unchecked boom-era spending and from a recession compounded by misbegotten federal economic policies but from their own tax cuts, which could have come straight out of Norquist's playbook. Both New York and California would have $13–$14 billion more in annual revenues had they not cut their own taxes during the mid- and late 1990s. Which is to say that the states' problems are also compounded by Norquist's White House friends and his allies in the Republican Congress.

Nor, of course, is it just the blue states that are being hit. Altogether, according to the NCSL, as of mid-April unfunded and underfunded mandates imposed on state and local governments totaled between $23.5 billion and $82.5 billion a year. When Democrats and Republican moderates like Maine's Olympia Snowe pressured Congress in May to add a $20 billion, two-year state fiscal-assistance package to Bush's $800 billion tax cut, therefore, it covered less than half of the lowest estimate of just the unfunded-mandate part of the gap, itself a fraction of a long list of other federal impositions. (And because the new federal tax cuts include cuts in dividend and capital gains tax rates, they also make equities more attractive and thus raise the cost to states and municipalities of the bonds they issue.)

The fiscal assistance package prompted NCSL to issue a handout praising Congress for the help. But privately, state officials said it was far too little: NCSL itself had wanted $40 billion. The Democratic Governors Association wanted $63 billion in aid and infrastructure investments. Among the most effective stimulus packages are strong state programs in public works, education and social services.

Lobbyists for state organizations in Washington will also tell you privately that the White House has "thoroughly intimidated" Republican governors—and some Democrats as well. "The Republicans are so disciplined," said a frustrated lobbyist for a Democratic governor. "The White House has imposed enormous pressure on the GOP governors, which is why you don't see the National Governors Association making much noise." Snowe, Pennsylvania Senator Arlen Specter and other Republican moderates, who've been savagely attacked by conservative organizations like the Club for Growth, know the price of even minor departures from the White House line.

You hear the same thing from people in the nonpartisan organizations, though none of them want to be identified either. This, said one, "is the most political administration I've seen in thirty years. If you're part of the team, you get access, but once you leave the reservation, that's it. Anyone who's not on board is done, and anything that shows blue is suspect." Norquist and fellow conservatives are using the long arms of the White House and Congress to discipline the states.

Even before Bush was elected, according to people like Tim Ransdell, who runs the California Institute, a nonpartisan research organization supplying data to that state's Congressional delegation, the structure of federal formulas made California and the Northeastern states the big "donor states"—those that paid more in federal taxes than they got back in federal programs and contracts. For every dollar California pays in taxes, it gets back 82 cents; for every dollar New Jersey pays, it gets back 67 cents; for every dollar Montana pays, it gets back $1.75.

Bush-era unfunded mandates and impositions, like expenses for homeland security, however, have been particularly hard on the so-called blue states. In part that's because they tend to be the states with the poorer people, the larger welfare and Medicaid loads, and, not coincidentally, the tougher environmental regulations, none of them beloved by this Administration.

But of course these are also the states that voted for Gore and thus, with the exception of the states that may be in play in 2004, find no particular hospitality in the Bush Administration. According to Representative Bob Matsui, a Democrat, and others in the California delegation, even staunch California Republicans, like Representative David Dreier, head of California's GOP caucus, have a hard time getting access to the White House. "Dreier's staff," said a staff member for another Californian, "feel like stepchildren. The White House pays attention to swing states like Pennsylvania and Illinois, but California"—where Bush was trounced in 2000 and where Gray Davis won re-election as governor in 2002 despite a major White House effort to beat him—"has been humiliating for Rove. He ended with egg on his face. . . . They're not going to do a damn thing for us."

In April 2001, after California's misbegotten energy deregulation scheme opened the state to big-time price gouging by Enron and other Texas energy marketers, Cheney met with Congress members from the Northwest, but according to Representative Jay Inslee of Washington, only on condition that Californians be kept out of the meeting. If California hadn't thought it could conserve its way out of its energy needs, Cheney said, it wouldn't have blocked the construction of new power plants. It could expect no regulatory help from Washington—and it got none until Senator James Jeffords quit the GOP and control of the Senate changed hands in June 2001.

Cheney's charge was a bum rap. It was the energy

producers' own caution about market prospects that kept
them from proposing new California plants; it was a
Republican governor who, in 1996, approved California's
wrongheaded deregulation scheme; and, as the country
later learned, it was market manipulation, abetted by the
failure of both the state and federal governments to act,
that helped drive energy prices through the roof. But the
list of particulars runs far beyond energy.

• House approval (still pending in the Senate) of
the Administration's tougher work rules under TANF,
Temporary Assistance for Needy Families. Those
requirements—to work forty hours a week rather
than the current thirty—would be virtually impossible to meet for workers in the low-wage restaurant
and hotel jobs in which many ex–welfare recipients
find themselves. That would create a need not only
for more state-funded public service jobs at a time
when states are laying off thousands of workers but
for billions in additional state childcare money. In
California alone, according to the state's nonpartisan
Legislative Analyst, those changes would cost $2.8
billion over the next five years. If the rules go into
effect, State Senator Raymond Meier of New York, a
Republican, told a House committee, "it will force
states to reallocate TANF funding away from creative
and innovative services [to get people off welfare] and
exacerbate the difficulties states face in providing
childcare to those on welfare and poor working
families."

• A gap of at least $6 billion annually between what

Bush promised and Congress authorized under NCLB to pay for the mandated education programs— "highly qualified" teachers in every classroom by 2005–06, intensive reading programs for at-risk children and the required yearly progress in test scores. One researcher in Vermont calculated that it would take more than $84 billion to comply with NCLB annual progress requirements. Bush has proposed $1 billion. Every state, from New Hampshire to Washington, is feeling that pinch; New Hampshire's school administrators say that for every dollar the state gets from the Feds, it has to kick in $7 to meet the NCLB requirements.

• Ongoing underfunding of the costs of homeland security. According to federal formulas, the $2 billion that Congress is now providing gives states like Wyoming and South Dakota—those magnets for terrorists—between eight and ten times as much per resident as California or New York. And even that money hardly compensates for cuts in other federal law-enforcement assistance. A new study conducted for the Council on Foreign Relations concluded that tight state and local budgets had sharply reduced police manpower in many places and that federal funding for state and local security over the next five years fell short by some $98 billion—a huge figure but, in the words of study adviser Richard Clarke, "decimal dust" compared with the Defense Department budget.

• The effects of the first round of Bush tax cuts,

which Representative John Spratt of South Carolina, the senior Democrat on the House Budget Committee, says has cost the states about $75 billion. The Bush Administration, he told the *Times*, is "just indifferent to the problem they're causing."

Those discrepancies are partly the result of formulas—and the clout of senators—that always give small states proportionally more money than populous states. But in this Administration and Congress, there's special relish in whacking the liberal states.

Maybe you can write off the Administration's double standard in agreeing to buy back oil leases off the Florida coast last year, but refusing to do the same in California. Since Governor Jeb Bush, the President's brother, was running for reelection, call that politics as usual. But what are we to make of the Justice Department's unprecedented decision to join auto makers (in this case General Motors) in their lawsuit attacking state emission control regulations, as the Feds did last year in California?

What of changed EPA rules on so-called new source review, which, to please energy industry contributors—who kicked in some $44 million to the Bush campaign—allow factories, refineries and power plants to expand and build without installing the most advanced emission controls? Those changes came in the face of vehement protests and lawsuits from the Northeastern states, where ecosystems are being damaged by acid rain created by pollution from Midwestern power plants.

What of the move to allow the Pentagon, in the name of national defense, to get around all federal toxic-dumping rules on its military installations, despite protests from agencies like the California EPA, and regardless of the fact that a lot of the toxics leach into neighboring wells and groundwater? According to a study for the Environmental Group conducted by Texas Tech University, perchlorate, a rocket fuel component that can depress thyroid function and impede development in fetuses and newborn babies, has already contaminated water in nineteen states and has been found in lettuce at four times the level the EPA regards as safe in drinking water.

And what of the intense, relentless campaign launched by Attorney General John Ashcroft and drug czar John Waiters to gut voter-enacted state medical marijuana laws? At a time when federal law-enforcement authorities are supposedly stretched thin by terrorism threats, what perverse passion would drive them to devote precious investigative and prosecutorial resources to that dubious purpose? Eight states, including Arizona, have approved such laws in the past seven years, all but one by voter initiative, but it's been California and Californians that have been virtually the sole target.

The same Justice Department vehemence has been directed toward eviscerating Oregon's doctor-assisted-suicide law, approved twice by voters in that state. That attempt, still blocked in the courts, has implications far beyond assisted suicide, since it could subject any physician using morphine or other drugs to relieve the pain of cancer or other diseases in terminally ill patients to prosecution or denial of the right to prescribe, which is tantamount to a denial of the right to practice.

Ashcroft says that federal Drug Enforcement Administration operatives can easily discern the "important medical, ethical and legal distinctions between intentionally causing a patient's death and providing sufficient dosages of pain medication necessary to eliminate or alleviate pain." But as any doctor can tell you, that's baloney. The very process of alleviating pain may hasten death.

What's particularly notable about Ashcroft's crusade is its intrusion into an area constitutionally reserved to the states by an Administration professing to honor states' rights headed by a former governor who has promised to be sensitive to the problems of the states.

In February, Ashcroft, a longtime friend of the gun lobby, threatened to criminally prosecute California officials for what he claims is illegal use of a federal data bank to track down illegal gun users. Ashcroft had also threatened to go after Georgia officials for denying gun permits to people that the federal data bank showed had been arrested for felonies but not convicted. Georgia complied, and according to the *Atlanta Journal-Constitution*, seventeen or eighteen people facing felony charges are now given Georgia gun permits daily.

You can get endless arguments about the motives. Is the White House's ugly treatment of the states simply the result of political expedience by an Administration that even opponents like Matsui say is highly astute politically, or is there an unbending ideological streak that, in ways never before attempted, seeks to use federal muscle to beat back liberalism in the states with nearly the same vehemence and determination it applies to federal policy?

Through the past two and a half years, the Administration, often flying the flag of the terrorism war, has altered federal policy in ways that couldn't have been imagined before the 2000 election—in its radical aggrandizement of the power to investigate, wiretap and detain suspects; in the concomitant rollback of civil liberties; in its tolerance for polluters and offshore tax dodges; in its multi-trillion-dollar tax breaks for the wealthiest Americans; in its roll-back of countless social programs.

But the attempt, often successful, to extend those efforts into the states, to use local cops to search out undocumented immigrants for detention, to go after liberal state laws—auto emission controls, medical marijuana, doctor-assisted suicide, welfare and childcare—is unprecedented. Without fanfare or discussion, the Administration appears to be putting the screws to liberal state programs with the same determination it is applying to things like tax cuts (which, of course, are the key to all other domestic policy).

Consistent with that effort, in March the White House decided no longer to publish a key document called Budget Information for States, which reported annually how much states receive under each federal program, and thus made it easy for local officials and advocacy groups to keep track of how their programs were treated. Eliminating the book, said a spokesman for the Office of Management and Budget, will eliminate the cost of the paper and production of the volume. How frugal. Who would have thought that it would be a Republican—and an ex-governor to boot—who'd bring federalism to its knees?

Republicans call liberals soft on crime—but Bush has abandoned the nation's crime-fighters. His betrayal of our nation's police is another example of the ways Bush works to destroy government and the community it should protect.

Bush's War on Cops

from *The Washington Monthly* (September 2003)

Benjamin Wallace-Wells

I am riding through Richmond, Va., with Sergeant David Wallis of the city police, and it is raining at a nearly biblical level—silver–dollar–sized fat splats of water slapping against every surface. It's one of those late afternoon summer thunderstorms that starts out looking like it's got to be over in half a minute, and somehow just lasts and lasts. The city's streets are deserted and, Sgt. Wallis says, it's a good bet anyone still outside is a threat to public safety. We find them, camped outside an impregnable-looking housing project called Whitcomb Court. A few teenagers are standing spaced sentry-like, every thousand feet or so, along the project's main road. They have umbrellas cocked over their shoulders, but are still getting drenched. They're street-level crack dealers, says Wallis, the advance guard for the municipal menace. Even in these conditions they stay outside, like hardy weeds, peering jumpily down the road, hoping for a sale. Wallis drives by slowly, but the scrawny, soaked dealers don't scamper away, they just shoot him pugnacious you-can't-touch-me smirks. This is usual, Wallis says: "They know we've got no backup, and so they're not even scared of us anymore."

It wasn't always like this. Ten years ago, Wallis and a

25-officer narcotics squad cleaned out Whitcomb Court. They set up surveillance teams in the elementary school that abuts the project and staged regular raids, cops piling out of a suddenly arrived line of six, eight, 10 cars to snatch all the dealers and guns they could. Within three months, the dealer pyramid in Whitcomb Court had been broken, its principals in jail and the project quiet.

Afterwards when Wallis and his squad would ride through Whitcomb Court, the older residents would sometimes cheer.

Richmond's police were praised from all points on the political spectrum—from the Clinton administration to the NRA—for halving the city's murder rate in the 1990s. One hundred and sixty people were killed in Richmond in 1994, and 70 in 2001. Richmond's method was simple: a concentrated program of aggressive beat policing and strict enforcement of gun laws.

But now, Wallis and many of his colleagues report, they simply can't mount such focused campaigns. Richmond is in the throes of a manpower shortage that has stripped cops off street beats and forced the city to change its neighborhood policing strategies. "All we're able to do right now is respond to calls which come in," the department's chief, Andre Parker, told me. "We don't have enough men to do any proactive policing. It's very worrying."

Aggressive programs like the ones Richmond used to bring down crime require extra officers, so that while some cops are responding to ongoing crimes, others can stalk crooks. Now, Richmond deploys 90 fewer active officers (the department has 670 total) than it did when crime was plummeting. It's no coincidence, police officials here and criminologists nationwide argue, that the city's murder rate, after seven consecutive years of decline, jumped by 20 percent in 2002 and by another 15 percent in the first six months of 2003. With fewer detectives, fewer of Richmond's murders can be solved—only 22 percent of murders were solved last year, compared to 35 percent in 2000. Other crimes, particularly robbery, are also increasingly common—trends, say community leaders, that are endangering inner-city Richmond's fragile revitalization.

Richmond is a dramatic example of a trend that is beginning to appear around the country. After eight straight years of decline in the 1990s, the murder rate has begun to increase: by 2.5 percent in 2001, and then another 0.8 percent in 2002. Those two slight increases have meant hundreds more violent deaths each year.

Dips and surges in the crime rate, locally and nationally, depend on many complicated factors, from the health of the economy to the number of criminals in prison to the abundance of guns and drugs on the street. Criminologists have said that the present surge in many cities' crime rates is due in part to the recession and in part from a simple law of averages—crime can't go down forever. But more police on the street is one of the most effective ways to keep crime down—it's also the one factor that lies immediately within the control of government.

Tellingly, those cities, like Richmond, that suffer from the worst cop shortages are also experiencing the most dramatic spikes in crime. Police in Portland, Ore., which is 64 officers short of its full 1,000-officer staffing, have noticed a rise in crime across the board in the first four months of 2003. Chief Mark Kroeker says he thinks the "scariest" jump in violent crime is yet to come. Minneapolis, normally a 900-officer department, is some 200 cops short, and crime is up 46 percent since Sept. 11, 2001. Los Angeles is more than 1,000 cops short of full staffing. Crime there jumped by 7 percent in the last half of 2001 and by another 1 percent in 2002, a year in which the murder rate jumped by 11 percent.

How can cities be so foolish as to cut their police forces and spark an inevitable rise in crime? Part of the problem is the state and local fiscal crisis that has hit communities across the nation. But faced with the need to trim budgets, most cities have first cut health, education, and transportation spending, and tried to preserve their police forces. The real cause of the police shortage is not in City Hall but in the White House. The Bush administration's first budget eliminated all direct funding for street cops. The war in Iraq, fought largely without allies, has required the call-up of huge numbers of reserves, many of whom are cops. And instead of using the men in blue as eyes and ears on the domestic war on terrorism, the administration has, in effect, used them as glorified security guards. The federal government's repeated directives to local police to beef up patrols at potential terrorist targets have taken officers away from their regular duties. And because the feds have not paid for many of these extra patrols, homeland security has stretched local budgets even further.

On his Sept. 14, 2001, visit to Ground Zero, the president famously addressed a group of cops and firemen through a bullhorn, from the top of a pile of mangled steel. When someone in the crowd called out that he couldn't hear the president, Bush said, spontaneously: "I can hear you. The rest of the world can hear you." But now many cops feel they're not being heard. During an interview in late July, Richmond's Chief Parker told me he's been "dismayed at the current administration's attitude towards local law enforcement." The administration, he said, has not "seemed to grasp what we face."

THE THINNING BLUE LINE

If the sudden disintegration of police forces and, in Richmond and so many other cities, the correlative return of crime have not yet caught the attention of most of the public, it may be at least in part because after eight straight years of declining crime in the 1990s, most of us have come to assume that the issue has been defanged. Much has been written about that dramatic drop. Criminologists, journalists, and criminal scientists ascribed crime's decline to the decade's sustained economic boom, the subduing of the crack epidemic, and a profound national shift in policing—a change often described as community policing. The new model, which emphasized a tangible police presence in the community, solving neighborhood problems, and talking with residents, became working doctrine in the nation's precinct houses.

In many ways, community policing was a return to the neighborhood-based model that developed after large, urban departments first began to be formed around the turn of the 20th century. For the next 30 years, policing was local: Officers walked beats on streets they frequently had grown up on. Complex criminal investigations were rare, so cops responded to calls about crime and community disorder—from vandalism to robbery to brawls. Urban police departments, which tended to be highly politicized and run by party bosses, were also frequently tools for dispensing social services and other forms of political patronage.

By the 1940s, this model was on the way out. As city bosses lost their firm control over police departments, cops moved towards a more professional, military model. They were more frequently armed, and more likely than not were riding in cruisers rather than walking the streets. Their focus became understanding the criminal mind and thwarting its ambitions. The archetype had shifted from the half-corrupt Irish beat cop, swiping a peddler's apple while driving loiterers off the sidewalk, to Joe Friday's just-the-facts-ma'am crime solver, who believed that the citizenry should be dealt with at an always-suspicious distance.

With the emptying out of the urban middle and working classes and a bulge in the populations of black and Hispanic young men—a tough set of demographic changes for the nation's police—crime began to balloon in the 1960s. An influx of Vietnam veterans into the policing ranks only strengthened the existent culture—hardened and Army-like. Jim Bueermann, who is now the chief of the Redlands, Calif., police department and is considered a pioneer of community policing, joined up with this generation, as did most of the officers now in what cops call "command positions." The dominant culture in the 1970s "was very purely law and order," Bueermann said. "There are bad guys out there who were disrupting the community, and our job was to catch them."

But as the Vietnam-veteran generation climbed through the ranks, in the 1970s and 1980s, the militaristic reputation of police officers preceded them into the neighborhoods, and more and more citizens began to view patrol officers as agents of fear, not trust. The 70s and 80s had seen corruption scandals, baton-wielding cop thugs standing at ready attention at protest marches, and finally,

in 1991, the Rodney King beating, and the riots that followed. Cops in movies and on television, even when they
were depicted heroically, were Dirty Harrys clearing out
ghettos with guns, and playing fast and loose with the
rules. "[The police were] isolated from the people," and
"people were afraid of their police," Lee Brown, the former
Houston and New York police commissioner credited
with introducing community policing in both cities in the
mid- and late 1980s, told the *Los Angeles Times*.

Police leaders, criminologists, and local politicians
huddled in the late 80s to try to figure out what they could
do against a frighteningly fast-rising national crime
problem, which was driving even middle-class blacks to
the suburbs and turning once-prosperous downtowns into
dead zones. They seized upon the idea that the best place
for policemen to be was not in their cruisers, hiding
behind windshields and tough-guy sunglasses, but out
talking to their people—the people they were assigned to
protect—reminding them that the police didn't have to
function as a garrison.

This new paradigm, community policing, depended in
part on technological advances, which allowed departments to map emerging crime patterns and high-crime
areas and shift officers accordingly. But a crucial component of this policy was what came to be known as the
"broken windows" theory of crime, whose most prominent proponent was the neoconservative political scientist
James Q. Wilson. In ghettos, Wilson argued, the persistent
presence of quality-of-life problems like vandalism, abandoned cars, and graffiti had profound psychological
effects: It showed residents that the police had lost control of the streets to drug dealers and criminals, shuttering

economic activity, signalling to criminals that it was open season on the neighborhood, and keeping residents from calling police when they saw crimes unfolding. Wilson said police should develop a more expansive set of goals, and not be content with simply busting murderers and drug dealers. By vigorously prosecuting small-change crimes like vandalism and graffiti, and by performing social-service functions like helping to get collapsing buildings condemned, cops could give law-abiding residents a sense of neighborhood ownership. By pursuing and jailing criminals for small crimes, the police reduced the number of thugs out on the street likely to commit more violent acts. And when cops won back the streets, residents became less scared about ratting on neighborhood bad guys, which meant the bad guys got arrested more frequently. Wilson's idea turned out, during the late 1990s, to be astoundingly correct, but it came at a cost: Such extra functions required extra enforcers.

The movement took hold in some cities in the early 1990s, with dramatic, well-publicized drops in crime in Boston, New York, and San Diego. But the idea went national in 1994, when President Clinton convinced a supportive Democratic Congress to pass the Community Oriented Policing Services (COPS) bill, which promised federal grants to help local departments put 100,000 new cops on the street. By 2000, COPS had helped departments hire about 70,000 new officers (upping local police strength by 12 percent nationally), and required that all of the new cops be out on street beats. In those six years, violent crime declined by 46 percent nationally, the most sustained, dramatic decline in the last hundred years.

But it wasn't just the sheer number of cops—by

changing the incentives for departments, the COPS program helped change police attitudes. Now, in order to compete for grants, in order to be politically viable, in order to drive down crime rates, in order to look effective and competent, police chiefs had to embrace the principles of community policing. In half a decade, this new approach became gospel for police management seminars and executive sessions. Some larger departments began to require, for the first time, college degrees of recruits—new officers no longer had to be able to simply follow orders, but were expected to deal with a broad range of community problems intelligently and sensibly. "We're talking about a subtle change in the whole culture of policing," Bueermann said.

Richmond was typical. Like many cities, it had a long history of racially charged antagonism between police and residents. By forcing cops out of their cruisers and into the street, the new model made them shake grandmothers' hands and chase down vandals and small-time thieves. It changed the public image of the cop in the city. For the first time, says Major Daniel Goodall of the Richmond police, "It let us show the people in Richmond that we were on their side." Because community policing entailed hiring new patrol cops, more crimes got solved and more criminals got put away. The crime rate began to drop dramatically, and residents, who now knew their local beat cops personally and trusted the department to put thugs in jail, were much more inclined to give tips on criminals and crimes in their neighborhoods.

Community policing also changed the way cops behaved. To win promotion, officers had to internalize the same philosophies that the department needed to display to win grants. And what was most remarkable, nearly stunning, about the Richmond police with whom I spent time last month was the thoroughness with which the department, from chief down to beat officers, had embraced the community policing model—a model almost entirely academic just 15 years ago. It has brought into being a new sort of officer. Lieutenant John Hall talks about cultivating respect from the residents: "The best way to fight crime is to have people trust you enough to report it when it happens, and tell you who did it—who did a particular crime is never a secret within the community." Sgt. Wallis, who is white, thinks his department sometimes focuses too much on the largely black housing projects, where the most visible crime occurs: "We may not be as fair in delivering justice everywhere as we'd like," he says. We're a long way from Mark Fuhrman.

But from the start, President Bush sent a very different message. In the new president's first budget, when the economy had not yet gone entirely in the tank, he zeroed out the funding for the COPS program entirely. (Congressional Democrats were able to restore some funding, but the COPS program's funds for hiring street cops are less than one-sixth the average during the Clinton administration.) For local departments, the cuts could not have come at a worse time. The lousy economy meant state and local governments had a hard time making up the federal funding cuts, and in many cases, city and state funding for cops has been slashed, too.

Caught in a crunch, local departments, understandably, came to see community policing as an add-on; it was more essential that they be able to respond to emergency calls about ongoing crimes. Departments no longer have the extra officers to staff community policing initiatives, and so even those departments most committed to broken-windows principles have had to abandon their programs. "What we're seeing now is broken windows in reverse," says nationally renowned criminologist James Alan Fox of Northeastern University.

In Richmond, with 90 fewer cops on the streets, criminals have gotten more brazen and crime has gotten more public. When the murder rate here was at its lowest, officers say, every murder stemmed from the drug trade or domestic disputes. But with fewer officers on the streets, thugs are less scared of a spot search and more willing to carry guns, and Richmond murders have gotten more senseless and surreal. This past June, a man was shot and killed after he jostled a pistol-packing tough while they were waiting in line at an ice cream truck. Detectives searched for some prior connection between the men, but it turned out there wasn't any: The murdered man really had been killed for jostling. That same week, a young mother made a wrong turn and drove into a housing project, her two children in the back seat. A group of young men hanging out in the middle of the road blocked her passage; when she honked for the crowd to move, one of them shot and killed her dead. "It makes you feel like you're losing control, when you get these murders that make no sense," Goodall said, in a softer moment. It also makes local cops feel like they're slipping back into the 1980s.

But police departments now also have new burdens that didn't exist in the 80s. The Bush administration's choice to go to war without a broader coalition has put a huge strain on U.S. military (half of the army's combat troops are now deployed in Iraq). And large numbers of reservists are cops. The Honolulu police department, which is already 291 officers short of full staffing, is sending 150 more officers overseas with the National Guard. San Antonio sent 50 cops off to war. And even one cop can sometimes be crucial to a department. The lone detective in the Crystal River, Fla., police department is back in fatigues, which has seriously hampered law enforcement in Crystal River. Worse still, departments are barred by law from replacing reservists while they're away on military duty—leaving short-handed departments with no option beyond hoping, hard, that they get their people back soon.

At home, too, the war on terror has eroded the strength and effectiveness of local enforcement. Each time the administration brightens the homeland security light from yellow to orange, police departments around the country go into a state of heightened tension—not just in New York and Washington, L.A. and San Francisco, but also in tiny towns like Richmond, Calif., where officers huddle around their port's unloading docks and their chemical plants and oil refineries, their eyes eagle-sharp for suspicious activity.

Not only are such demands eating away at local police budgets, but the security deployments are taking officers away from their primary responsibility: preventing crime. A *Hartford Courant* report found that the Connecticut state police had been forced to cut overtime for its homicide detectives while a sergeant assigned to a homeland security detail had racked up $15,000 in overtime for duties such as baby-sitting the Georgia Tech University football team during a stopover at Bradley International Airport. And a story in

Crain's Chicago Business suggests that the problem can only get worse: It concluded that most of the police departments in the Chicago area will have to lay off patrolmen because of the costs imposed by homeland security.

But what most worries criminologists is that the momentary problem of higher crime and shrinking forces may institutionalize a retrenchment in policing tactics. The Bush administration's recoil from the philosophy of community policing by choice, coupled with the local police departments' backing away from the practice by constraint, is already undermining the last decade's paradigm shift. It took a decade for the nation's cops to accept community policing, proponents say, and acceptance only came grudgingly, spurred on by a federal-funding carrot. Now that the feds have changed their tune, this revolution may collapse. "The generation I came up with had to have community policing drummed into us," Bueermann said. "I'd hoped the next generation would just sort of assume that this was how policing ought to be conducted. But if we continue to backtrack, that same assumption might not be there any longer."

HOMELAND SECURITY GUARDS

For more than a year, the FBI poured its formidable resources into a search for a terror suspect who'd been at the top of its Most Wanted list. The search for the suspect, Eric Rudolph, wanted for deadly bombings of abortion clinics, had narrowed to a rural area of western North Carolina, and the feds were determined to catch him. They sent 200 agents into the area, combing woods over and over. They posted a $1 million reward, hoping that someone in that poor area would rat Rudolph out. They came up so famously empty-handed that their failed search inspired two country-and-western songs and a best selling T-shirt: "Run, Rudolph, Run."

A 21-year-old rookie cop in Murphy, N.C., caught Rudolph after he saw him moving evasively behind a Save-a-Lot grocery store. Federal faces stayed red in the arrest's aftermath, as editorialists from local newspapers to the "Today" show pointed out that mundane police work had done what the nation's finest could not: caught one of the country's most wanted terrorists.

Policing experts say there's an important lesson here. The terrorists whom federal agents are most concerned with now may be more likely to come from Afghanistan than Murphy, but terrorism is also a local event—an attack on a local object, by men who have lived in local communities in preparation for the attack. By keeping cops out of the loop on terrorism, the feds may be wasting rare and crucial chances at nabbing terrorists.

Each of the 19 hijackers lived in the United States before the attacks and some of their names ended up in local police notebooks. By failing to link intelligence work with police work, the federal government is needlessly limiting the ways terrorists might be caught—the in-the-course-of-duty door-to-door work of local police can turn up neighborhood leads with national implications.

"Twenty-five years ago, I was a beat cop in the South Bronx, and I knocked on the door of everyone who moved into my neighborhood and introduced myself—the ones who reacted like they had something to hide, I'd keep an eye on," says Joseph Daly, now chair of Criminal Justice at Pace University in New York City. The way to catch terrorists, Daly says, may be similar.

Federal law enforcement leaders have long struggled with the knotty problem of exactly how much to tell local cops, and now this tension is further heightened by the new questions terrorism raises. The feds need to give local cops enough information to let them solve crimes and make arrests, but they have to be careful not to be too loose with crucial security information. If one local cop happens to be buddies with an al Qaeda sympathizer, the whole American intelligence apparatus could be compromised.

The solution that DHS and the FBI have arrived at makes sense, at least in theory. They've asked each department to designate a homeland security liaison (usually a command officer who's not the chief) who then goes through the FBI's most rigorous background check and, if he passes, is cleared to take part in local FBI-run terrorism task forces, which the feds use to spread intelligence and discuss tactics.

In practice, cops say, it doesn't really work—officers are not given names of terror suspects to investigate; the feds wait until they can devote enough resources to an investigation and then run it themselves. Local cops insist this frequently means that leads are tracked too slowly or by investigators sometimes shockingly devoid of local know-how. In the winter of 2001, the FBI used what later turned out to be a dubious tip to stage a sensational, headline-grabbing raid at the Chester, Pa., home of a Pakistani immigrant. The immigrant was the city's health commissioner, whom the feds eventually cleared of any wrongdoing and gave a profuse apology. Policing leaders have frequently made the point that there are 800,000 local policemen in the United States, compared to 11,000 FBI agents. If the feds let local cops take the initial steps in tracking more leads, policing experts have repeatedly argued, the FBI would have more time to follow up on the most promising investigations.

But chiefs around the country have said that the FBI still frequently discounts local police investigations. Testifying before Congress in October 2002, Baltimore Police Commissioner Edward T. Norris, since retired, talked about an investigation his officers launched against six Middle Eastern men arrested on immigration charges in a bare northwest Baltimore apartment on Sept. 10, 2002. They found literature with references to jihad, brochures from flight schools, and maps of Washington's Union Station and New York's Times Square. A federal judge released the men after the FBI did not press for their continued imprisonment. Weeks later, the bureau began to repeat the steps the Baltimore cops had already taken in their earlier investigation. Despite repeated FBI assurances that cops are equal partners in the war against terrorism, local cops say they frequently feel like second-class citizens.

The FBI has at least trusted cops to provide security for potential terrorist targets. But even in this area, liaison officers say, information is limited: They only hear that there's a "threat" and that the local force should step up patrols around essential targets. When they ask how specific the threat was, they're told that's classified. Local police chiefs also say that they're frequently not told when a threat ends, which leaves them running endless, costly patrols of all the local bridges and tunnels. "To protect ourselves adequately, we need to be given more information," said Francis Monahan, a Richmond police major who is his department's homeland security coordinator.

The situation has reached the point that many local

police chiefs say they don't trust the feds to be fully honest with them. Two years after September 11, local cops routinely say their best source for news on terrorism and terrorist threats is always "the morning paper, or CNN." Bill Hemby, a retired San Francisco detective who now runs preparedness seminars for local cops, says that federal information comes in so late and is so vague that officers he works with often "doubt that their patrols are needed at all." This spring, the Philadelphia and Seattle chiefs turned down personal pleas from Tom Ridge to increase patrols, on the grounds that the threats cited were too vague to justify the cost.

Local homeland security coordinators and cops further worry that the federal government is mismanaging the training of local officers. The current DHS training model brings single emissaries from local departments to one of four college campuses for four-day tell-em-everything seminars on terrorism. These trainees then act as trainers for the rest of their department. This is very useful for formulating policy; the trainees say they come back knowing enough to help set priorities for local homeland defense. But beat cops say that little useful information filters down to the patrol level. What departments need is not only one special officer federally versed in the ideological abstracts of the roots of Islamic fundamentalism, or how anthrax spreads. They also need each officer to know what to do if a friendly imam tells you he knows a guy who might be planning an attack, or how to respond if you come upon 10 people passed out face down in the middle of a city park.

In order to help instruct their rank and file, local departments have been relying in large part on the hundreds of private vendors who run for-profit terrorism training seminars. There's likely no way that the federal government can directly train every policeman in the nation, so at least some vendors can perform a useful service. The problem is that with nearly all of these vendors new and without reputations in the field, police departments have few means of sorting out the effective programs from the hundreds of solicitations they get. Richmond police major Francis Monahan, in charge of his department's homeland security, remembers a seminar in New York last year billed as comprehensive terrorism education. The instructors talked only about emergency centers, and when they ran out of material they sent the attendees on a tour of New York's temporary Emergency Operations Center. The seminar hadn't accounted for transportation, and so the attending chiefs had to pay for subway fare themselves. "We were command-level people attending, but it was an academy-level operation," Monahan said. Local police departments also feel unprepared when it comes to terrorism safety equipment, where they are under a similar brochure siege but have very little expert guidance. Of all the problems presented by the specter of terrorism, this one might be the easiest to solve. Should DHS put vendors through a rigorous certification process, notifying local departments which training and equipment is effective and which isn't, local police chiefs would be profoundly grateful.

CIRCLING THE PADDY WAGONS

But while Republicans have consistently and actively undermined the ability of cops to catch crooks, Democrats have played enabler, using the opposition pulpit to sound like an echo of President Bush, only a little wimpier—the

Democrats have mostly agreed with where the president is going, and are content merely to challenge him on some numerical details. Consequently, the national political debate on domestic preparedness has remained pretty resolutely banal, an outcome that is surprising, given the urgency of the topic. The whole jargoned political debate about "homeland security" and "first responders" has so far revolved around exactly how much protective gear to buy the nation's firefighters and emergency crews. The consistent Democratic line, pressed most forcefully by Sen. Joseph Lieberman (D-Conn.) has been to call for about $40 billion more than whatever the Bush administration happens to ask for. It's not a particularly useful debate. The truth is nobody really knows how many more hazmat suits is enough, and no matter what level of gear firefighters and other "first responders" have, someone will always be able to make a halfway compelling case that they could use some more.

The nine Democratic candidates have evidently been briefed on homeland security to the point of Al Gore–ishness, and each has detailed a lengthy position. Howard Dean's is representative, and telling. What we need, Dean argues, is a "circle of preparation, a circle of protection, and a circle of prevention"—words which sound consciously feminized, like they've been expertly focus-grouped with NPR listeners, but don't mean anything operationally. He's short on big ideas and long on detail, which makes his policy sound as if it was assembled from a mass email sent to favored interest groups. Dean wants to modernize Veterans Hospitals, restore $5 billion in Bush budget cuts to the Coast Guard, and more aggressively seek alternative energy sources, to reduce our dependence on bad actors like

Saudi Arabia. The other candidates aren't much better: John Kerry summoned a good bulk of the Washington press corps to a Bronx firehouse in early July for what was billed as a "major" speech on homeland security and told them that what America needed was more equipment for fire companies, which managed to make a good point sound like a play for the endorsement of the International Association of Fire Fighters. Kerry "strode to the plate like Babe Ruth," wrote *Salon*'s Nicholas Thompson, "and laid down a bunt." This full-court press of Democratic arguments is unlikely to fire even the most wonkish imagination. "The Democratic candidates start talking about where we have to spend money on cyber-terrorism and port security, and even I stop paying attention," said Jose Cerda, a policing expert at the Democratic Leadership Council.

But while the Bush administration continues to turn cops into thumb-twiddling municipal security guards, and the opposition party uses its biggest platforms to call for the government to pay for more Kevlar vests and better night-vision goggles, violent criminals are growing more brazen and police forces are getting less and less able to check them. The problems have already begun to emerge, sporadically, in some cities around the country, and experts say they will only get worse.

Both the Bush administration and its critics have become fond of forwarding their particular policy proposals by warning darkly of terrorism: We don't know where it's coming from, they say, and we're not even sure we can prevent it. The machinery of murder is far less mysterious. Good cops know where murder comes from, and they know—from long experience—how to reduce it. Over the past decade, terrorism has killed only one-fiftieth as many people as have died because of that standard menace, simple murder.

WORKING ALONE

In Richmond, I'd talked to a shift commander, Lieutenant John Hall, whose patrol had shrunk from 13 officers to 11, and asked him how he'd redeployed his officers—simple, he said. His shift was responsible for eight neighborhood beats; given 13 officers, he had five beats covered by teams of two, and three beats staffed by cops working on their own. Now, two more of the same eight beats had only a single cop to cover them. I asked him whether this made the patrol officers' jobs more difficult. "Well," he said, "one thing we worry about is safety. If you're going into a situation, it's much more dangerous if you don't have a partner there with you."

One week later, just before 5:30 p.m. on Tuesday, July 30, a routine tip came into Richmond's emergency call center—young men were dealing drugs in a crime-heavy section of South Richmond. Douglas E. Wendel, a five-year veteran of the force, responded. On this shift, he was working alone. At Midlothian Turnpike and East 33rd Street, he got out of his cruiser to walk up on the suspected dealers on the corner. But an accomplice of the dealers walked up behind Wendel, took out a gun and shot him in the back of the head. Wendel didn't have time to take his own gun out of its holster.

The crowd scampered away. Bleeding terribly, Wendel crawled back to his cruiser and radioed in. He needed some backup, he said. An hour later, he was dead. The two bullets had torn up Wendel's face so badly that emergency workers at first assumed he'd been shot from in front. He left an 11-year-old son, a 7-year-old daughter and a 4-year-old son.

Wendel was the first Richmond police officer killed on duty in five years. What was remarkable, in the news reports which followed Wendel's death, was South Richmond residents' sense that a cop's death was in some ways inevitable: They knew, better than anyone else, that criminals were winning back the streets. The *Richmond Times-Dispatch* quoted one local homeowner as saying guns were easy to buy as soda. Another, a 35-year homeowner, told the paper: "Police used to control [crime]. They can't control it now. These young boys aren't scared at all."

He Said It . . .

"And yes, we're always interested in dealing with people who have harmed American citizens."
—Washington, DC, 2/25/02

HE'S ANTI-FREEDOM

*with quotes from George W. Bush
and a cartoon by Ted Rall*

Bush and his fellow conservatives pretend to hate government—but they love it as a tool to stifle dissent. GWB cynically exploited the attacks on the World Trade Towers to launch a full-scale attack on our civil liberties. He also has presided over the most secretive administration in our nation's history, and encouraged the militarization of our society. As a result, we have lost some of the freedom we enjoyed before he took office— and we're likely to lose more.

"If this were a dictatorship, it would be a heck of a lot easier, just so long as I'm the dictator."
—Washington, DC, 12/18/00

Bush doesn't want you to know what he's doing. You can check out the full text of Pizzo's piece at MoveOn.org.

from Hiding the Truth?: President Bush's Need-to-Know Democracy

from MoveOn.org
by Stephen Pizzo

"This administration is the most secretive of our lifetime, even more secretive than the Nixon administration. They don't believe the American people or Congress have any right to information."
—*Larry Klayman, chairman of Judicial Watch*

It's been said that the first casualty of war is always truth. But with the Bush administration's war on terrorism, it's hard to know, because even before 9/11 the administration had begun hermetically sealing formerly public sources of government information.

It began when Vice President Dick Cheney refused to
provide details of his energy task force meetings with
energy companies, particularly top Enron officials. Then
came President George Bush's November 2001 executive
order allowing the administration or former presidents to
order executive branch documents withheld from the
public. At the time, the administration said the new restric-
tion on presidential papers was to protect the privacy of
former presidents and those they dealt with while in office.

> EXCERPT OF PRESIDENTIAL EXECUTIVE ORDER 13233
> (1) If under the standard set forth in Section 3
> below, the incumbent President concurs in the
> former President's decision to request withholding
> of records as privileged, the incumbent President
> shall so inform the former President. The Archivist
> shall not permit access to those records by a
> requester unless and until an incumbent Presi-
> dent advises the Archivist that the former Presi-
> dent and the incumbent President agree to
> authorize access to the records or until so ordered
> by a final court order.

But, the order also shields from public view documents
from President Bush's father's term in office that could be
awkward now. The suspicion was that the executive order
was designed to protect several current White House officials who served in the Reagan and Bush 41 administrations from embarrassment—specifically, Secretary of State
Colin Powell, Vice President Dick Cheney, White House
Chief of Staff Andrew Card, and former Budget Director
Mitch Daniels, Jr.

Each official had brushes with controversial policies in earlier administrations—not the least of which was the Iran-Contra scandal during the Reagan administration. The elder Bush, then Vice President, maintained he was "out of the loop." Documents in the Reagan archives might contradict that version of history.

Both Cheney's refusal to hand over his energy task force documents and the presidential order shielding past administrations' archived documents caused uproars among open-government advocates, historians and members of Congress.

Most of that resistance melted away in the wake of the 9/11 terrorist attacks. A scared and rattled nation was told that information was potentially dangerous. During World War II, the admonition read, "Loose lips sink ships." After 9/11, the list of perceived dangers expanded to previously unclassified information from virtually every executive branch department.

Any one of these actions would have had negligible effects. But, the cumulative effect of executive orders and new legislation restricting pubic access to public records has alarmed even many conservative groups.

"This administration is the most secretive of our lifetime, even more secretive than the Nixon administration. They don't believe the American people or Congress have any right to information," said Larry Klayman, chairman of Judicial Watch, a conservative group that is suing the administration to force it to reveal the members of the energy task force.

Gary Bass, executive director of OMB Watch, an independent public advocacy group, says that the United States, "is moving from a society based on the right to know to one based on the need to know."

The breadth and scope of the Bush administration's clamp down on information is the largest such effort to restrict public disclosure since World War II. Because much of these changes have come in little-noticed dribs and drabs since 9/11, many have largely escaped public notice or explanation. In this report we chronicle some of the most significant changes.

"Our keeping of secrets has often misled and confused our own people but has been ineffective in denying information to our enemies . . . Until recently the Soviet Union was the most secretive organization in the world; it no longer exists."
—*Dr. Edward Teller, 1992*

BIRTH OF AMERICA'S NEW "NEED TO KNOW" DEMOCRACY
Even before terrorism became the focal point of President Bush's foreign and domestic policies, slowing the flow of information openly available to the public had already become a hallmark of his administration. But the terrorist attacks of September 11, 2001, provided a context in which large swaths of formerly public information could be shielded from view on grounds that its easy availability could benefit our new enemies.

September 2001:
• Attorney General John Ashcroft moved quickly in the wake of the 9/11 attacks to put into force new rules limiting the scope of the 1966 Freedom of Information Act (FOIA). While unveiled in the context of the new war on terrorism, the changes had actually been on the administration's "to-do" list since it took office.

• Ashcroft's new rule is dubbed "Exemption 2." It empowers federal agencies to reject requests for documents from journalists and the public, whether or not they are of legitimate public interest:

> • "Whether there is any public interest in disclosure is legally irrelevant under this 'anti-circumvention' aspect of Exemption 2 . . ."

October 2001:

• Pentagon acquisition czar Pete Aldridge issues a terse memo to defense contractors warning them not to talk to the press about the kinds of contracts they are getting from the Pentagon, and to be guarded in "all public statements, press releases and communications." (Note: Aldridge retired in May 2003 and that June took a seat on the Lockheed Martin Board of Directors.)

• The Air Force's senior acquisition official, Darleen Druyun, follows up with an even sterner warning:

> • "Effective immediately, I do not want anyone within the Air Force acquisition community discussing any of our programs with the media, on or off the record."

(Note: Druyun retired from her government post at the end of 2002 and in January 2003, Ms. Druyun was appointed Deputy General Manager for Missile Defense Systems at Boeing.)

• Deputy Defense Secretary Paul Wolfowitz screws the information spigot down even tighter. In a memo to military and civilian DOD personnel Wolfowitz forbade employees as well as "persons in other organizations that support DOD" to talk about their work in public spaces or on commercial networks.

• "Even unclassified material can often be compiled to reveal sensitive conclusions . . . Much of the information we use to conduct DOD's operations must be withheld from public release because of its sensitivity. If in doubt, do not release or discuss official information except with other DOD personnel."

• The month of October ends with the passage by Congress of the Patriot Act. The law broadens law enforcement powers and, while allowing new restrictions on information available to the public about government actions, the new law allows the government to collect formerly protected information about citizens. One of the most controversial of such provisions is the right of federal authorities to learn what kinds of books individuals are borrowing from libraries.

November 2001:
• The Department of Justice closes to the public and press immigration hearings for hundreds of individuals rounded up during post 9/11 FBI and INS sweeps. Even immediate family members are

denied access or information—even though some detainees are not even accused of a crime, but rather were being held as "material witnesses."

• Administration officials begin shutting down formerly user-friendly online information sites used to keep communities and local governments apprised of health and safety issues. Among the sites shut down or gutted of data were online systems designed to warn communities about potential risks or accidents at hazardous materials and chemical facilities in or near their area. Online maps used by local first responders, citizens and environmental groups that identified the location of pipelines carrying hazardous substances were also deleted, as were Web sites containing academic studies concerning the risks associated with nuclear power plants.

• The administration's Office of Information and Privacy holds a meeting with the FOIA staffs of all executive branch agencies. The purpose of the meeting is to brief them on the new powers of Attorney General Ashcroft's FOIA Exemption 2. The meeting's minutes were classified.

December 2001:
• President Bush grants his Health and Human Services secretary power to classify his department's information secret.

2002: New Year Brings Renewed Clampdown
This would prove a busy year for those in the administration

who wielded classification stamps. The annual number of classification decisions made by classifiers in the executive branch soared. By the end of the year, more than 23 million individual "classification actions" had been taken. At the same time, declassification activity—which had surged during the Clinton administration—declined to the lowest level in seven years.

It is impossible to say how all this new secrecy affected terrorists, but law-abiding Americans whose work had become dependent on access to online public information systems quickly felt it. University of Michigan researchers lost access to an Environmental Protection Agency database they had been using to conduct a three-year study of hazardous waste facilities. Cartographers, geologists and others who relied on taxpayer-funded satellite images suddenly discovered that they were no longer available online because they had been removed by the National Imagery and Mapping Agency. Thousands of documents vanished from government Web sites.

And the pressure for yet more secrecy continued.

March 2002:

- White House Chief of Staff Andrew Card issues an "all-agency" memo ordering departments to safeguard any information, no matter how old, that "could be misused to harm the security of our Nation . . ." a standard open government advocates described as dangerously vague.

April 2002:

- A Department of Energy site that details information on the transport of hazardous materials vanishes. Asked to account for all this missing information, even the Government Accounting Office, Congress' investigative arm, said it could not figure out either how many departments had deleted information from their sites, exactly what information had been deleted or by whom.

- "I'm not sure there's any sort of inventory of what's been taken off the Web," said Tony Cicco, GAO chief information officer.

May 2002:
- President Bush grants the Environmental Protection Agency its own "Secret" stamp.

June 2002:
- The Department of Defense clamps down on the release of test data from the controversial Missile Defense System. In a June 2002 news briefing, Air Force Lt. Gen. Ronald Kadish said that "no responsible individual would make that type of information available to our adversaries." He said from now on taxpayers would simply have to trust that the decision to move forward on a missile defense system would be based on factual information. "People should have confidence in that," Kadish said.

(Note: In the previous year, a $100 million experiment failed when a U.S. missile warhead did not hit a dummy warhead in a test at the same air force base.)

- Defense Secretary Donald Rumsfeld, also citing national security and the need for flexibility, proposes exempting missile defense spending from the Pentagon's auditing and accounting rules.

September 2002:
- President Bush awards his Secretary of Agriculture her own "Secret" stamp.

November 19, 2002:
- Congress passes the administration's Homeland Security Act, which includes several provisions blocking information access. Language added to the bill by House Republicans blocks FOIA disclosures of information about technology vulnerabilities. Attempts to remove the language by Senate Democrats fail.

> - "This is the most severe weakening of the Freedom of Information Act in its 36-year history. . . . it will hurt and not help our national security, and along the way it will frustrate enforcement of the laws that protect the public's health and safety. . . . a big business wish list gussied up in security garb."
>
> (Sen. Patrick Leahy—D. Vt)

"A popular government without popular information or the means of acquiring it, is but a prologue to a farce or a tragedy or perhaps both. Knowledge will forever govern ignorance, and a people who mean to be their own governors, must arm themselves with the power knowledge gives."
—*James Madison*

2003: A YEAR OF SECRECY AND WAR

The war with Iraq created a host of additional motivations to shut the public out of the decision-making process. As war loomed early in the year, the administration struggled to rally both international and public support for attacking Iraq. When the world community refused to accept the administration's "just us" response to demands of proof that Iraq had weapons of mass destruction, the administration appeared to abandon its secrecy fetish, sending Secretary of State Colin Powell to the United Nations to describe in detail U.S. intelligence to bolster claims of Iraq's WMD programs and production.

While Powell's presentation did not succeed in swaying international opposition to the war, it went a long way toward bringing the U.S. Congress and public on board. It was only after the war was over and the U.S. in virtual possession of Iraq that the public began to learn that the information provided before the war was bogus. There were no chemical warheads or shells poised for use against U.S. troops. There were no Scud missiles ready to hit Israel. And, there was no uranium-laden yellowcake heading from Africa to Iraq, as the president claimed in his State of the Union message.

Suddenly an old and familiar question was being asked

around Washington: "What did the administration know? And when did it know it?"

It's a question that remains largely unanswered, in part because of the lid this administration has been able to maintain on disclosure of government proceedings—a process that continues.

January 2003:

• Secretary of Defense Rumsfeld complains that, even after earlier scrubbings, there is still too much sensitive information available on DOD Web sites that must be removed. Rumsfeld's warning comes in the form of a memo circulated throughout the Defense Department.

> • "One must conclude our enemies access Department of Defense Web sites on a regular basis. The fact that For Official Use Only (FOUO) and other sensitive unclassified information (e.g., CONOPS, OPLANS, SOP) continues to be found on public Web sites indicates that too often, data posted are insufficiently reviewed for sensitivity and/or inadequately protected. Over 1500 discrepancies were found during the past year. This continuing trend must be reversed."
> (Secretary Rumsfeld)

• Leading Republican senators complain that Bush administration secrecy policies are leaving them "out of the loop" on crucial defense and national security matters which they have both a right and obligation to review.

> • "I will not tolerate a continuation of what's been going on the last two years."
>
> > (Sen. John Warner, chairman of the Senate Armed Services Committee.)

March 2003:

• President Bush signs a new executive order on national security classification policy that will defer an April 2003 deadline for automatic declassification of millions of 25-year-old documents until December 31, 2006.

• President Bush's new order also stipulates that all information provided in confidence by a foreign government is automatically presumed secret. And the new order also gives the director of the CIA veto power over decisions by the Interagency Security Classification Appeals Panel, which hears appeals of government refusals to declassify information. The presidential order also allows for the reclassification of records that already have been disclosed or declassified under former President Clinton's 1995 orders to declassify records deemed overclassified.

• In a potentially momentous change in government information policy, the Federal Energy Regulatory Commission (FERC) is empowered to process public requests for access to certain kinds of sensitive energy infrastructure information on a "need to know" basis only. Under the new rules, access to "critical energy infrastructure information" would

be denied to ordinary requesters under the
Freedom of Information Act.

• Director of Central Intelligence, George J. Tenet,
signs a 28-page statement opposing declassification
of the fiscal year 2002 intelligence budget total.

April 2003:
• The Bush administration begins imposing budget
secrecy on the congressional appropriations
process where it had previously been unheard of.
For starters, President Bush asked that Congress
appropriate $2.5 billion for postwar Iraq recon-
struction, but to appropriate the money to the
White House itself where it could be spent without
further congressional interference or public
notice. A memo prepared by senior GOP staff for
the House Appropriations Committee noted that
the arrangement would erect a "wall of executive
privilege [that] would deny Congress and the Committee access to the management of the Fund."

• Routine budget justification documents are inexpli-
cably withheld from congressional appropriators,
provoking anger from even Republican lawmakers
sympathetic to the administration. Rep. Harold
Rogers (R. Ky) abruptly adjourned a hearing of a
House Appropriations Subcommittee when requisite
documents were not provided by the Department of
Homeland Security. "We need those [budget] justifi-
cations to perform our Constitutional duty," said Rep.
Rogers before terminating the hearing.

May 2003:

• The Bush administration refuses to declassify key sections of an investigation into the 9/11 attacks developed by a Bush administration working group. Intelligence officials assigned to review the document have taken a hard line against further public disclosure. Critics familiar with the findings say the administration may have wished to keep under wraps a July 2001 intelligence report warning that Al Qaeda was planning a major attack on U.S. soil "in the coming weeks." The intelligence briefing went on to say: "The attack will be spectacular and designed to inflict mass casualties against U.S. facilities or interests. Attack preparations have been made. Attack will occur with little or no warning." The warning went unheeded by the administration and President Bush spent the month of August 2001 on vacation at his Texas ranch. Nearly 30 pages of the report are also blanked out because of accusations that the Saudi government may have aided the terrorists.

June 2003:

• Attorney General John Ashcroft rejects growing congressional criticism of his Department for withholding its report on the case related to Los Alamos scientist Wen Ho Lee. The case had become a major embarrassment for the DOJ and a rallying point for Asian Americans who believed Lee was targeted solely because he was of Chinese extraction.

• "There are lots of times, especially in international intelligence security matters, when we don't release things because it's not in the national interest to do so," the Attorney General said at a House Judiciary hearing.

July 2003:

• Meanwhile, the non-partisan National Commission on Terrorist Attacks Upon the United States complains that the Bush administration is not only failing to cooperate with its investigation into what led up to the 9/11 attacks, but is actively hindering the investigation by withholding pertinent documents. The Commission named the Department of Defense, the Department of Justice, the Bureau of Immigration and the Immigration and Naturalization Service and the FBI as being slow or unresponsive in turning over requested information. "The problems that have arisen so far with the Department of Defense are becoming particularly serious," according to the group's interim report. The Commission said "records requested from DOJ are overdue." In a twist of irony, the Commission also protested the Justice Department's "insistence on having agency representatives present during interviews of serving officials. The administration pointed to a similar request by Iraq regarding interviews of its officials and scientists as proof that Iraq was trying to intimidate those officials into silence."

• White House spokesman Ari Fleischer denies that the administration has been withholding information from the public and Congress.

• "The administration has been very cooperative in providing as much information as possible to people up on Capitol Hill, and will continue to do so," he said.

• Congressional critics shot back:
"How can this administration declassify things, drop certain items into the press that are complimentary and positive from their point of view and get away with it?"

(Sen. Richard J. Durbin (D. Ill.)

• Freedom of Information Act requester Robert G. Todd asks two different agencies for a copy of the generic cover sheets they used to identify classified documents as "Confidential," "Secret" and "Top Secret." Mr. Todd was not asking for the actually classified materials, simply copies of the cover sheets. The Department of Defense refuses to provide a copy of these cover sheets, citing FOIA Exemption 2, which shields information that could enable "circumvention" of agency rules, policies or statutes.

• On a party line vote of 50–46, the Senate decides to keep the homeland security advisory process beyond the scrutiny of the general public.

August 2003:
• The Transportation Security Administration (TSA) launches an investigation to ferret out employees in the Federal Air Marshall Program, who leaked to reporters that, despite new warnings of terrorist

attacks, the TSA was going to slash the number of air marshalls to save money. The Department of Homeland Security is embarrassed by the revelations. To justify its investigation, the TSA cites the USA Patriot Act.

September 2003:
• In a letter to Senator Bob Graham, National Security Advisor Condoleezza Rice dismisses for the foreseeable future any possibility of further declassification of the report of the congressional joint inquiry into September 11.

• President Bush grants the Director of the White House Office of Science and Technology Policy (OSTP) the authority to classify information Top Secret. This ruling brought to just over 4,000 the number of executive branch employees authorized to generate classified information.

October 2003:
• Bush administration officials refuse to explain why they have classified the cost of continuing the search for weapons of mass destruction in Iraq.

• "I don't classify these things," Defense Secretary Donald Rumsfeld says evasively. "I'm sure that they have classifications for good reason."

• Over the past year, 133 secrecy orders were imposed on new patent applications. The rationale was to limit their disclosure because they could be "detrimental to the national security." More than half of the new orders affected private inventors who developed their inventions without government funding or support. Secrecy orders imposed on such private inventors are termed "John Doe" orders.

CONCLUSION

Effectively, keeping secrets means never having to say you're sorry.

It also means never having to admit you made a terrible mistake, or even lied.

He Said It . . .

"If he's—the inference is that somehow he thinks slavery is a—is a noble institution—I would—I would strongly reject that assumption. That John Ashcroft is an open-minded, inclusive person."

—interview with Tom Brokaw, *NBC News,* 1/15/01

Authoritarian regimes from Soviet Russia to Nazi Germany have relied upon the militarization of society to impose their will. American presidents, from Washington to Eisenhower have been careful to keep their distance from the military—but our current Commander-in-Chief looks to other role models.

We're in the Army Now

from *Harper's* (October 2003)

By Kevin Baker

The nationalist apotheosis of George W. Bush reached its fruition last January 3, when the commander in chief of the United States' armed forces traveled to Fort Hood, Texas. He was there, ostensibly, to sell the idea of a war in Iraq to the American people and to rally the troops to the task ahead. But, more important, he was there to reclaim for himself and his party the mantle of the true keepers of the American identity.

Fort Hood is the most populous Army base in the country and the home of its heavy armor; 340 square miles of rugged Central Texas hill country, conveniently located 50 miles from Bush's vacation ranch in Crawford and housing some 42,000 soldiers. Most of these were the men and women of the First Cavalry Division and the Fourth Infantry Division, and their presence lent an added poignancy to the commander in chief's visitation. Both units were considered all but certain to be shipped out to the Gulf.

"For God and country is what I signed the paperwork for," Brad Hastings, a twenty-year-old private from

Memphis, Tennessee, told a reporter from the *Dallas Morning News*. "If I'm called, I'm ready to go."

The *Morning News* and the *Houston Chronicle* reported that Bush spent most of the day meeting selected individuals such as Pfc. Hastings and inspecting specialized tanks with nicknames like "Burn, Baby, Burn" and "Anger Management." He then proceeded to a gymnasium off Tank Destroyer Boulevard, festooned with giant American flags and a banner proclaiming *"Fort Hood, Home of America's Hammer!!!"* where he spoke before a vast crowd of soldiers in black berets and camouflage uniforms waving small, plastic American flags. Behind him, serving as a backdrop for the TV cameras, sat the usual melting pot of men and women, blacks and whites and Hispanics and Asians, that seem to pop up like magic for Bush's every speech on a military base or airfield or warship.

"The Iraqi regime is a grave threat to the United States," he told them—and the rest of us. "Our country is in a great contest of will and purpose. We're being tested. . . . We must, and we will, protect the American people and our friends and allies from catastrophic violence wherever the source, whatever the threat."

It was very much the same sort of speech that Bush had been giving throughout his campaign to drum up support for war in Iraq. Indeed, it was much the same sort of vaguely Christian, news-bite-sized portentousness that has characterized his every address, beginning with his 2001 inaugural.

It was the response that was startling. The soldiers answered their commander in chief not with cheers or claps, or any sort of ordinary, civilian applause, but with a sudden, violent roar of "Hu-AH! Hu-AH!" Shouted simultaneously from 4,500 throats, it came across on the evening news as a primal, lusting sound; unexpected and voracious and thoroughly martial, like something one might have expected to hear from the Spartans or a Falangist street demonstration in the 1930s. It was not like anything I had ever heard at a rally convened by an American president.

The chant continued throughout the speech, turning Bush's address into a churchy call-and-response. Individual cries of "Yeah!" and "Let's go!" rose from the crowd when he explained why we would invade Iraq though not North Korea, but again and again there was that same swift chant, sweeping all before it—"Hu-AH! Hu-AH! Hu-AH!"—reverberating around the gym until Bush, who just before the rally had exchanged his dark suit coat for a green waist-length army jacket, held up his left hand, palm out, in grand, imperious acknowledgment.

The media came to dwell on a moment, four months later, when Bush took his now legendary turn across the carrier USS *Abraham Lincoln* to declare Gulf War II over. But that was only a matching shot, a triumphalist bookend, to his visit to the Home of America's Hammer. He had already become, at Fort Hood, something more than any other president has ever been, which is to say the very avatar of American power. The president of *huah*.

"*Huah* is an all-purpose expression," the journalist David Lipsky explains in his instructive new study of West Point, *Absolutely American*. "Want to describe a cadet who's very gung-ho, you call them *huah*. Understand instructions, say *huah*. Agree with what another cadet just said, murmur *huah*. Impressed by someone else's accomplishment, a soft, reflective *huah*."

And *huah* is exactly what George W. Bush's presidency
has been from the beginning—a gung-ho, in-your-face
approach to governance that has refused any hint of compromise and that has already brought about a seismic
transformation of American politics. Bush appeared at
Fort Hood only four days before the swearing-in of the
first truly Republican-controlled Congress to serve under a
Republican president in almost fifty years, a stunning triumph achieved by an off-year electoral strategy that boldly
repudiated the old notion that all politics are local and
based the entire campaign on issues of national security—
and on George Bush himself.

It was a strategy that depended in large part on deploying
the military as a campaign prop. Bush stumped at military
bases throughout the 2002 elections, blowing in dramatically on Air Force One to pump his latest tax cut or the
Homeland Security plan (indeed, he has spoken either at
a military facility or to a specifically military audience an
astounding forty-five times since March 2001). There was a
tactical advantage to these venues—no American president
over the last seventy years has been less comfortable with
unscripted appearances before the general public, and by
campaigning on military bases Bush's handlers could
assure that his crowds would always be restricted to jubi-
lant, flag-waving supporters—but above all there was the
opportunity for the commander in chief to interact personally with our men and women in uniform. He could
throw his arms around their necks, shake their hands, hug
them, dress up like them. Their physical presence and their
huah approval erased any remaining public memory of
Bush's own adroit dodge of the Vietnam War, or the fact

that he may officially be a deserter to this day after going AWOL from the Air National Guard unit he managed to join during that war, or even his rabbity scurry about the country on Air Force One in the immediate aftermath of the September 11 terrorist attacks.

Surmounting his largely pacific past, George W. Bush had made himself one with what has become the most revered institution in the country. According to a Gallup Poll published in the *New York Times* soon after the "completion" of the war in Iraq, 76 percent of all Americans expressed "a great deal" or "quite a lot" of confidence in their nation's military, as opposed to only 45 percent who had the same level of confidence in the leaders of organized religion, and only 29 percent who believed so fervently in the Congress. This sort of faith extended even to 64 percent of the baby boomers' children aged eighteen to twenty-nine. A Harvard Institute of Politics poll of 1,200 college students found that 75 percent trusted the military "to do the right thing" either "all of the time" or "most of the time," and that they characterized themselves as hawks over doves by a ratio of two to one.

Nor is this a new phenomenon. Confidence and trust in the American military have been growing steadily since its nadir, back in the mid-seventies—almost exactly the moment, not so coincidentally, that the last compulsory military draft ended and our modern all-volunteer service began.

An even more salient fact, which Bush's advisers could not have missed, is that many—perhaps most—Americans now see the military as the last remaining refuge of many *democratic* values in a society that seems ever more shallow and materialistic and ironic. David Lipsky, comparing the

West Point cadets with the other students he had become accustomed to in a career of writing about college campuses, found the America of the Army to be what his liberal father had described when he talked about "his best hopes for the country. A place where everyone tried their hardest. A place where everybody—or at least most people—looked out for each other. A place where people—intelligent, talented people—said honestly that money wasn't what drove them."

There are, of course, other sides to the military, as the rape scandal that emerged from the Air Force Academy around the time of the latest Gulf War demonstrated. But even this seemed to be handled in a direct, forthright way compared with the scandals, real and invented, sexual and financial, Democratic and Republican, that have dominated Washington over the last decade. The military remains an institution that has integrated women and minorities into its ranks more successfully than most— perhaps all—other public institutions. That gorgeous mosaic of faces behind Bush at every base may have been contrived by his handlers, but it was only possible because the military is such a mosaic.

It is no wonder that Bush—along with "the genius" Karl Rove and his other advisers—has sought to identify himself so completely with this winning cultural icon. By again defying conventional wisdom and running right at what might be thought to have been Bush's Achilles' heel—his hypocritical draft dodging—they managed to erase yet another chapter of what has to be the murkiest past in presidential history.

But there is more to Bush's identification with our armed forces than simply an effort to boost poll numbers.

It signals both a reversion to the deepest, darkest roots of the Republican Party and the new political era to come. It marks the advent of the Party of Huah, and a dangerous and unprecedented confluence of our democratic institutions and the military.

For all of their supposed conservatism, the Republicans have always been the true radical party in America. From its very inception in 1854 as a rejoinder to the "Slave Power," the G.O.P. was a repository for all sorts of crackpot notions and secret societies—the Know-Nothings and the Sons of Sam and the anti-Masons, the Sabbatarians and the Prohibitionists. Their leading, shared characteristic, what brought them together as a movement in the first place, was their willingness to try to define for the first time just what a true American was—and to enforce that definition by the sword if necessary.

From its inception, the G.O.P. has been our party of blood and iron, the (Protestant) church militant. Their first martyr was John Brown, author of the Pottawatomie massacre and armed rebellion at Harpers Ferry. During the 1860 electoral campaign, the first party activists, the "Wide Awakes," marched through city streets in torchlight parades, wearing capes and singing, "They'll find what by felling and mauling/Our railmaker statesman can do . . ."

Lincoln himself saw the incredibly bloody conflict that they would fight and win as holy war, a divine redemption that would expunge the great national sin and save not so much our individual souls but *the Union*. This would be worth any price in blood, as Lincoln made clear in his second inaugural—in what is surely the most sanguinary passage ever written by an American president—when he asserted that "if God wills that it continue until . . . every drop of blood drawn with the lash shall be paid by another drawn with the sword, as was said three thousand years ago, so still it must be said 'the judgments of the Lord are true and righteous altogether.' "

Lincoln and the Republicans were right about the Civil War, of course. They not only abolished slavery but forged the United States into what was truly one nation for the first time, upsetting the long, delicate series of compromises that the accommodationist antebellum Democrats had used to preserve the old half-slave, half-free Union.

In doing so, they set the casts of our two major parties. For better and worse, the Democrats would remain the party of moderation and compromise, trying to reconcile the customs of the past with the inevitability of change (for America has been a nation only during the modern age, and change is an intrinsic part of its character). Despite the common conception of the Democrats as the "left," all of the great liberation movements that have transformed our society over the last century and a half—populism, the labor movement, civil rights, women's liberation, gay rights—originated *outside* the Democratic Party and were gradually absorbed.

The Republicans, by contrast, would remain the party of uncompromising, self-generated, draconian solutions—and it is their agenda that has mostly driven the national political debate. As the political historian Walter Karp wrote in *The Politics of War*, the Republicans shared a belief that the party " 'was not a faction, not a group, not a wing, [but] a synonym for patriotism, another name for the nation.' " Thus they have tended to couch their arguments in terms of "conserving" essential American values while actually embracing one radical nostrum after another, from social Darwinism to progressivism, from protectionism to laissez-faire to the corporate state, from isolationism to the new imperialism.

None of these had much to do with traditional notions of conservatism. For all of the rhetoric about limited government, since the advent of Reagan and the current Republican hegemony the federal government has by almost all objective measures become larger, more intrusive, more coercive, less accountable, and more deeply indebted than ever before. It has more weapons, more soldiers, more police, more spies, more prisons. These trends have only accelerated under the present administration, whose stated agenda includes plans to privatize Social Security by forcing Americans to turn their retirement savings over to private investment firms, to turn Medicare over to HMOs, to turn most other social welfare funds over to religious organizations, and to place most American businesses under the regulation of remote, international—and unaccountable—bureaucracies.

What Republicans have really done, over the past quarter-century, is to return to their roots. They once again presume to speak for the idea of *Volk*—for the larger, mistier notion of the American people, beyond any specific, coherent ideology, or even the bonds of the Constitution.

The problem with such an ambition is that, unlike Europe, America has no mystic ties of blood. It did not have time to build a "race" before it was flooded with immigrants. The early, nativist wing of the G.O.P. was largely obliterated during the Civil War. And America as a mixed-race, multicultural, nonsectarian country came to be an accepted—then a celebrated—fact of our national character. Despite the power wielded by the G.O.P.'s white Protestant clerics, and its perfection of the coded racial appeal, the party has never been able to sustain itself simply as a movement of racial identity.

Lagging hopelessly behind the urban, Democratic machines in recruiting the new immigrant masses, Republicans were historically all the more anxious to find a national Zeitgeist that might substitute for blood. But here, too, they badly miscalculated, misreading the national will during the great, twentieth-century-long emergence of the United States as the world's foremost power. The isolationist wing of the G.O.P. opposed America's entry into both world wars, into the League of Nations, and even—under Robert Taft, the 1953 Senate majority leader—the series of alliances that would contain the Soviet Union and win the Cold War. In each instance, the Republicans were forced to scramble and later come up with Red scares that sought to judge what true "Americanism" was. These had some initial success but ultimately proved too ugly to be sustainable. Even the most frenetic examples of Republican activism, such as John Foster Dulles's stated determination to "roll back" Communism or Ronald Reagan's revived arms race, proved ultimately to be no more than variations on established, long-term Democratic strategies.

But all that changed on September 11, 2001. For the first time, Republicans found themselves more or less in charge of the federal government at a moment when a stunning new foreign threat presented itself. They immediately embraced the crisis as their own, applying the sorts of radical remedies—both at home and abroad—they have often advocated in the past but have never been able to fully put into effect. The destruction of the World Trade Center towers enabled Bush and the Republicans finally, fully, to reclaim the mantle of national identity—to become the Party of Huah.

Just what the Republicans' crowded hour portends has since become very clear, and it is disturbing for anyone who values our democratic institutions. In keeping with his party's tradition of identifying itself with a "higher" notion of the national will, Bush has not bothered to ask Congress to declare, officially, either of the two preemptive wars it has launched since 9/11, as is mandated in the Constitution. Instead, he has claimed unprecedented powers to use whatever military force he deems necessary, for as long as he wants, in this conflict of open-ended duration against terrorists and "evildoers."

At home, Bush used the issue of Homeland Security—as opposed to actual homeland security—to personify the national will and to drive the Democrats from any remaining vestiges of power. He achieved this by insisting that the new Department of Homeland Security be exempted from the usual federal government standards regarding employee compensation and job security.

Let us put aside the fact that Bush's requirements would automatically make Homeland Security the least desirable government department to work in, or that it was revealed—after the 2002 elections—that it would take several years to integrate all the parts of the new department, or that these would not include the FBI, the CIA, or any other important segment of the national-security apparatus. Or that the latest report from Warren

Rudman's Independent Task Force for the Council on Foreign Relations found that our security efforts were "underfunded" to the tune of $98 billion and that the country "remains dangerously unprepared to handle a catastrophic attack on American soil." But to understand just how much of a joke Homeland Security really is, it is necessary to live in a major urban area and see its forces in action every day.

In New York's Pennsylvania Station, for instance, pairs of uniformed National Guardsmen sit all day behind desks at what seem to have become permanent posts. When a friend of mine approached one desk, to ask if the Guardsmen would contact the police and have them remove a violent homeless man from the subway platform below, he was politely informed that the Guard's radios did not operate on the police bands.

Meanwhile, once a week or so, a helicopter comes and hovers over my Manhattan neighborhood for an afternoon, apparently expecting to see Al Qaeda operatives moving freely about in their kaffiyehs. Out on Broadway and Ninety-sixth Street, a checkpoint is sometimes set up by the curb, with police waving over vans and small trucks for inspection. Of course, the flashing police-car lights are visible for a good five blocks away, and, because they are close to a bus stop and have little space, the police wave any bigger trucks past—apparently hoping that Al Qaeda will not try to smuggle in too *large* a weapon of mass destruction.

These are a few examples of our new national-security state in action; everyone I know has his or her own stories. One can scarcely imagine the sheer scale of this non-sense; the waste of manpower and money multiplied many times over, at airports and bus stations and bridges throughout the United States.

But of course Homeland Security, the issue, is less about catching or deterring actual terrorists than about making a show of action—and of force. The men and women of our national-security agencies—just like the men and women of our armed forces—have been fetishized, made into another political prop for the Party of Huah. Homeland Security will not apprehend or deter any terrorist blessed with more than a sub-cretinous level of intelligence. But it has injected a constant military presence into our lives. Already it has become routine to see armed men in uniform roaming our streets, to hear Air Force jets and military helicopters buzzing low over our homes—one more pretense of uniformed efficiency.

Where the Bush Administration fights its real national-security battles is in the subcommittee room or in the halls of John Ashcroft's Justice Department. The administration even went so far as to try to hire Henry Kissinger in order to exculpate itself from any blame during the long-delayed investigation of the September 11 attacks. Eventually, it had to settle for temporarily classifying twenty-eight pages of the congressional investigating committee's report, in a pathetic attempt to obfuscate the leading role prominent Saudi friends of the Bush family played in funding Al Qaeda. Such political face-saving means that, incredibly, there will be no wholesale re-assessment of our intelligence capabilities even after the disaster of 9/11.

Instead, the Bush Administration has decided that it is the Bill of Rights that needs to be reassessed. As our war machine was readying for action in Iraq, Attorney General

Ashcroft—far and away the most radical individual ever to sit in a U.S. cabinet—worked up an eighty-six-page legislative draft of the "Domestic Security Enhancement Act of 2003," or "Patriot II." The bill is designed to preclude any court challenges to the original Patriot Act, the law under which Ashcroft has already claimed the power to suspend the right of habeas corpus for any American citizen he deems to be a security risk.

Section 201 of Patriot II, entitled "Prohibition of Disclosure of Terrorism Investigation Detainee Information," would provide that "the government need not disclose information about individuals detained in investigations of terrorism until . . . the initiation of criminal charges." Another crucial clause would give the government the wholly novel right to strip *any American of his or her citizenship* if he or she "becomes a member of, or provides material support to, a group that the United States has designated as a 'terrorist organization,' if that group is engaged in hostilities against the United States."

"Until now," longtime civil-liberties champion Nat Hentoff pointed out in *The Village Voice*, "an American could only lose his or her citizenship by declaring a clear intent to abandon it." Under Section 501 of Patriot II, however, "the intent to relinquish nationality need not be manifested in words, but can be inferred from conduct." It would be Mr. Ashcroft and his subordinates in Justice who would be doing all the inferring and determining just what "provides material support" to a terrorist group means.

The premature leaking of Patriot II has delayed its formal submission to Congress, but related ways of closing up Patriot I "loopholes" are already being discussed. Even the Pentagon's proposed "Total Information

Awareness" (TIA) program—a gargantuan intelligence operation under which almost every transaction Americans make would be electronically monitored—is back on the table, under the new, somewhat less Orwellian label of "Terrorist Information Awareness."

It is unclear just how any part of this purported technological fix is to stop Al Qaeda, an organization so adept at low-tech strategies that it reportedly has learned to substitute personal messengers for cell phones. But then many of our security programs seem to rely on similarly ineffectual tactics. A report issued this past June by the Clinton-appointed inspector general of the Justice Department, Glenn Fine, found that of 762 illegal immigrants caught up in Ashcroft's nets since September 11, 2001, none were terrorists. Of course, their innocence did not save them from being detained, incommunicado, for months or, in some cases, subjected to "a pattern of physical and verbal abuse," and even threatened with death, before being deported.

Fine's report did not deal with our prison at Guantanamo, which is outside his jurisdiction, being run by the U.S. military. In fact, Guantanamo's Camp X-Ray seems to operate outside the jurisdiction of every national or international body of law. Its wardens answer only to their commander in chief, George W. Bush, making it the first detention center—or, for that matter, the first institution of any kind—to be run by a U.S. president without any judicial or congressional oversight. Despite all the reports of underage captives at Camp X-Ray, despite the accounts of attempted suicides and severe psychological depression and deprivation on the part of the prisoners, the Pentagon still offers no information on when or how they will be tried—beyond a vague promise of military tribunals, "when the time is right," that would not be bound by normal rules of evidence, would offer no independent right of appeal, and would place attorneys under a permanent gag order.

And it is unclear whether, even if they knew more about it, the American people would care much about the abuse of power being perpetrated in their name. The greater question, though, is whether they could stop them anymore even if they wanted to.

The war has largely succeeded in finishing off any effective opposition. The Democratic Party is a cobweb, waiting to be swept away. In a unique disaster, it has been simultaneously de-pedded and beheaded; bereft of a dedicated, activist core and any meaningful leadership.

The Democrats' first presidential debate this spring, shown on tape delay, revealed its potential candidates to be perhaps the most singular array of non-entities, curiosities, stalking horses, and outright charlatans ever brought together on a single stage. Most of them seem to quietly agree with the Republicans' basic worldview, and those who do not agree lack the will or ability to do anything about it or to offer any alternative vision of their own. It seems all but inconceivable that the likes of either Joe Lieberman or Howard Dean will get to wear the little green jacket at the Home of the Hammer.

Unlike their counterparts in the G.O.P., political activists on the liberal left are unfocused and badly organized. Above all, they have been unable to muster a convincing worldview to counter that put forward by the Party of Huah. For all that it has dwelled on the blatant lies told by the administration about Iraqi weapons of mass destruction and terrorist connections, the American left has been unable to fashion any effective response to the inescapable conclusion that the war was the best possible (and I stress *possible*) turn of events for the people of Iraq, providing them as it did with at least a chance for freedom.

The activist left lacks any real strategy for engaging with the world as it is, preferring to retreat into the usual Chomsky-Zinn-Vidal dreamworld of outraged American innocence. There was little or no acknowledgment from the left that Afghanistan was a failed state that had become a haven for terrorists and would have to be invaded, or that destroying Al Qaeda and any related terrorist networks will involve a long-term campaign that will have to include at least some military and intelligence operations, or that there should always be, in the modern world, an ongoing effort to dislodge, by one means or another, any and all dictators, including Saddam Hussein. In failing to develop a nuanced, engaged worldview that would both reject Bush and find a way to confront Saddam and Bin Laden, the successors to the old, engaged Democratic liberalism have allowed themselves to be cast as hopelessly naive and ineffectual.

Nor can one expect any real defense of our democracy from the media any longer. The giant media conglomerates (created in good part by the Reagan-era gutting of the FCC's old anti-monopoly safeguards) have served mostly as auxiliaries to the administration since 9/11, as exemplified by Clear Channel's persecution of the Dixie Chicks.

During the latest Gulf War, the *New York Times*, for one, seemed to be recycling much of its vocabulary from the 1960s, writing of a "long-haired" opponent of the war and a "short-haired" supporter. The paper of record granted that "the antiwar movement today appears more diverse than it was during the early protests of the Vietnam War, when it often seemed hostile to 'anyone over thirty,' " but put us all on notice that "disruptive demonstrations can wear out even the most tolerant." Meanwhile, James Traub, writing in *The New York Times Magazine*, denounced as "Weimar Whiners" those acquaintances of his who claimed that such little repressions proved the United States was becoming a fascist state—as if there could be no gradations of authoritarianism.

Much more chilling than these exercises in denial has been the media's creeping acceptance of the concept, put forth for some time now by various Bush apparatchiks, that we are now an "empire." *The Atlantic Monthly*, in its July/August 2003 issue, published one in what it threatens will be a series of articles by Robert D. Kaplan intended to serve as "a kind of user's manual for managing an unruly world"—a series that, in Kaplan's own description, "will be a ground-level portrait from the remotest and most exotic regions, not a broad overview from the imperial capital."

Kaplan finds military operations of the scale employed in Iraq to be unsustainable for very long, and estimates that in any case the American worldwide empire will probably not last beyond "a few decades from now." His user's manual, though, is broken down into such indicative, and ominous, subheadings as "Rule No. 3: Emulate Second-Century Rome," "Rule No. 4: Use the Military to

Promote Democracy," and "Rule No. 10: Speak Victorian, Think Pagan," and suggests that we take our cues from "liberal empires—like those of Venice, Great Britain . . . ," which he claims were "motivated not by an appetite for conquest per se but because it was thought necessary for the security of the core homeland."

Kaplan urges us to borrow tactics from some of our bloodiest foreign adventures, including the conquest of the Philippines, our foray into Central America under Reagan, and our overthrow of the Chilean regime of Salvador Allende. He advocates that the CIA and Special Forces teams revert to running coups and carrying out assassinations. He wants a corps of Roman-style military tribunes who will make foreign policy as well as enforce it, and that we become "more pagan" in our outlook. Most chillingly of all, he complains that "the media increasingly, and dramatically, affect policy yet bear no responsibility for the outcome." Kaplan's solution for this problem is primarily that the government "find the budget and the will to hire away the best communicators," but he insists that ultimately "our intelligence officers, backed by commando detachments, should in the future be given as much leeway as they require to get the job done, so that problems won't fester to the point where we have to act in front of a battery of television cameras."

Never mind, for a moment, that the idea of Rome or the British Empire as liberal institutions of any sort would have come as a surprise to, say, the Gauls or the Carthaginians, or the Jews of Masada; or, respectively, the Zulus or the Boers or the North American Indians or the Maoris of New Zealand. Or that the dark side of these supposedly civilizing forces is, say, the Japanese Empire of the twentieth century, a venture that was also launched on the excuse of national survival and soon spiraled down into the absolute "need" to take over half the world.

Much more demoralizing, for the American prospect, is the fact that a venerable publication of the liberal arts, such as the *Atlantic*, would give its imprimatur to any screed suggesting that "intelligence officers" and "commando detachments" be empowered to get rid of journalists "as they require to get the job done." After such an immediate capitulation to secrecy and brute force, what can we look forward to in the future?

With their dominance of the national media, their vast advantages in money and organization, their tactical ruthlessness, and the disarray of the opposition, George W. Bush and his party have positioned themselves for a crushing electoral victory in 2004, and most likely for some years to come. The Republicans already control all three branches of the federal government, a majority of the governors' mansions and statehouses, even—for the third term in a row—the mayoralty of the nation's largest city. There, still another ceremony of apotheosis is in store for us, on September 11, 2004, now that the genius, Karl Rove, has scheduled the Republican convention to coincide with the third anniversary of the attack on the World Trade Center.

Rove likes to compare the Bush ascendancy to the election of William McKinley in 1896, after which the Republicans controlled the presidency and remained the majority party for all but eight of the next thirty-six years, or until they were finally ousted with the onset of the Great Depression. He may be more right than he knows.

Soon after becoming president, McKinley took the nation into its "splendid little war" with Spain, in which America took its first overseas colonies, and then waged a brutal, extended, not-so-splendid guerrilla struggle in the Philippines, one in which our armed forces—for all of Robert Kaplan's admiration—killed a larger percentage of the population than they would in Vietnam.

Currently, in Afghanistan and Iraq, we are occupying some 420,000 square miles of the most fractious territory in Asian history. Our troops there are subjected to almost daily ambushes, and the cost of occupying Iraq alone has already doubled, to some $4 billion a month. By July the Pentagon was conceding that our ground forces had been stretched nearly to their limit, with some 370,000 troops deployed in 120 countries around the world. Between our occupation forces, replacements for those troops, and troops being held in abeyance for emergency deployment in North Korea, there were only three active-duty Army brigades available for potential new missions—a situation that one official, in a beautifully evasive bit of Pentagonese, lamented as "the tyranny of fixed numbers."

It is this tyranny of fixed numbers that provides the real threat to Karl Rove's Republican millennium. They now seem to pop up everywhere. We simply cannot go on indefinitely waging war around the world while giving ourselves record tax cuts. And we cannot go on occupying vast swaths of Asia for years without resorting to a military draft.

The administration has resolutely rejected any such suggestion. A few months ago, Secretary of Defense Donald Rumsfeld even went so far as to ridicule the performance of America's old draft army before being forced to apologize. Others, such as longtime congressman Charles Rangel

(D., N.Y.), a Korean War veteran, have proposed that the draft should indeed be restored. Rangel's suggestion was mostly facetious, a small protest against what he saw as the disproportionate burden that the poor and minorities currently bear in our all-volunteer army. But it speaks very much to the hollowness of the whole politics of *huah*.

The Bush Administration rushes to repudiate even the idea of a draft because it realizes that such an eventuality would pose a mortal threat to its own popularity. It is no coincidence that public confidence in the American military, as noted above, has grown exponentially since the armed forces returned to their all-volunteer status for the first time in a generation.

For all of its merits, our military is not, and cannot be, a democratic institution. The administration, and often the Army itself, try constantly to obscure this fact, most recently under the Thoreauvian rubric "An Army of One." Surely this has to be one of the most disingenuous recruiting slogans that has ever been devised, for no army has ever been about promoting individualism but rather its exact opposite, bending the wills of many individuals into a single, blunt instrument of incredible violence.

No doubt the young men and women at Fort Hood meant every word they said about defending freedom, and some have probably already paid the last full measure of their devotion to that cause. But the world that our soldiers live in every day is one in which nearly every aspect of their lives is carefully controlled. It is—ironically, considering our victory in the Cold War—the closest thing in America to the collectivist ideal; over a million men and women working toward the same end, under the same, all-intrusive discipline. Grow your hair too long, and you will receive a threatening letter. Let the grass grow too long around the house you live in on base, and you will get another letter. Our servicemen and women shop at the same PX and BX monopolies, are subjected to a national health-care system whether they like it or not. Even the personal behavior of their spouses is carefully scrutinized, and can be cause for official reprimands and other punishments.

The old draft did not make the military a democracy either, but it did connect it organically to the democracy it was created to serve. Under the draft the armed forces were a levy of free citizens, taking up an onerous but temporary duty in order to preserve their freedom. Any military commitment that extended this duty had to be well thought out and truly important to our national security, or it was bound to founder on popular opposition.

It is well and good that this should have been so, for in a true democracy the military should never be an end unto itself, or an isolated institution, but a necessary burden that we all share in, one way or another. We should always celebrate the heroism and dedication of our troops, but we must never try to force upon them roles that they are not equipped to play.

Under the Bush Administration, the all-volunteer military has become a photo op, a fantasy; a feel-good television substitute for actual participation in our democracy. Its troops can be shuttled around like toy soldiers on an ever expanding game board, whisked to conflicts of every possible size and duration, all around the globe. The Bush attempt to substitute it for our democracy has done a terrible disservice to both institutions. It has made each one a simulacrum of its true self, rendering our democracy passive and largely unengaged while our military is over-burdened with all sorts of tasks and missions it is ulti-mately not suited for, such as nation-building and policing the streets of Baghdad.

This is the ultimate politics of *huah*—with Bush revealed as no more of a leader than, say, Al Pacino's absurd characterization of a blind retired colonel in the film *Scent of a Woman*, yelling out, "Hu-ah!" at every opportunity, in order to convince us that he had some connection with real fighting men.

And yet we go on, making an ever greater commitment to our armed forces, $329 billion in 2002 alone—or more than China, Russia, Japan, Iraq, North Korea, and all other NATO countries *combined*, according to the Center for Defense Information.

"No other military is even close to the United States," Gregg Easterbrook wrote in the *New York Times* following the fall of Baghdad. "The American military is now the strongest the world has ever known, both in absolute terms and relative to other nations; stronger than the Wehrmacht in 1940, stronger than the legions at the height of Roman power . . . The extent of American military superiority has become almost impossible to overstate."

According to Easterbrook, our Navy now has nine super-carrier battle groups, with a tenth under construction; no other navy in the world has a single supercarrier. Our Air Force has "more advanced fighters and bombers than those of all other nations combined." We possess the world's only Stealth aircraft; the world's largest aerial tanker fleet, to project our air power around the world. We have far and away the heaviest bombers, the most advanced tanks, the most deadly air-to-air and air-to-ground missiles; the most sophisticated military electronics, including armed drone airplanes and space satellites . . .

As it is written in the Bible, where your treasure is, there will your heart be also. We now substitute military solutions for almost everything, including international alliances, diplomacy, effective intelligence agencies, democratic institutions—even national security. Although a mere five months and fewer than 270 fatalities in Iraq have our ground forces dangerously extended, we continue to rattle sabers at Syria, Iran, North Korea.

The logic is inexorable. Having committed so many of our resources to the military, at the cost of so much else, there is nothing else we can do. No previous national dilemma compares with our current one. Even Vietnam was, in the end, overreaching in pursuit of the basically sound policy of containment. Our current course is no more than a blind stumbling forward, until we shall indeed run up, once and for all, against the tyranny of fixed numbers.

For the fact is that we are not an empire, no matter how fashionable it has become to say so, on both the left and the right. We have no storied class of dedicated, career civil servants; no vast surplus population, hungry for land or betterment. Nor are we some ancient race of pagan warriors. A random survey of those undecided about Gulf War II drew such comments as "I think they should finish the job fast and get out" and "I think it would be a mistake to tie down American troops for years." For all of the conditioning that the administration and the enthusiasts of empire have already subjected us to, America remains at heart an isolationist country, willing to tolerate foreign ventures only for so long as they seem vital to actual homeland security.

> Remember!
> It is the soldier, not the reporter,
> Who has given us freedom of the press.
> It is the soldier, not the poet,
> Who has given us freedom of speech.
> —Father Denis Edward O'Brien, USMC

These sentiments can be found on a poster, pasted on the side of one of four little sheds near the foot of the Lincoln Memorial. They are staffed by four different Vietnam POW/MIA groups: The Last Firebase, POW Outpost, Rolling Thunder, and Warriors. Their sheds—no bigger than an average city newsstand—have been open twenty-four hours a day since 1982, when Maya Lin's remarkable Vietnam Veterans Memorial was first dedicated, keeping a round-the-clock vigil until all of the remaining American troops missing in action in Southeast Asia "come home."

For all of the bellicosity and the schmaltz, the individuals manning the stands are soft-spoken, polite, almost shy. They are not conspiracy nuts, and as melodramatic as they often are—one shed bills itself as THE LAST FIREBASE STANDING VIGIL UNTIL THEY ALL COME HOME WORLD WAR II, KOREA, COLD WAR, VIETNAM, GULF WAR—there is a certain dignity to their vigil. Standing in the sheds for all those long nights, more than twenty years now, through the dead of winter. Alone out by the silent monuments, waiting for what they expect to be mostly a few boxes of bones. It is a grand, romantic gesture, and the sort associated only with the military among all our institutions today.

By contrast, our civilian democratic culture at home is fading away. Slowly, slowly, we are becoming conditioned to a military style of discipline. We live in a country now where anyone can be banned from flying, or detained and searched, or browbeaten and humiliated, or arrested and hauled off to prison for as long as the Supreme Commander says so—and where soon Americans may even be stripped of their citizenship at his discretion. We have become a nation of secret police raids that never make the papers, and of permanent gag orders; of military tribunals and perhaps even drumhead death sentences that cannot be appealed. In America today, federal agents can walk into a public library and confiscate any public records they choose. They can also demand lists of who has taken out which books, and they can order the librarians, under the threat of criminal prosecution, to keep quiet about it all.

We have not yet arrived at a point where we receive letters ordering us to cut our hair or our grass. But we may well be told, in the very near future, what private firms we are to trust with our retirement savings and our health care; what religious sect, or cult, the administration will turn us over to if we fall upon hard times. Fewer and fewer men tell us what we may read, or watch, or listen to, while on their television channels the *huah* heads shout down any dissent. Already, most democratic dialogue has vanished, replaced by personal insults and growing accusations of treason—even death threats.

When troubles arise in this new America, when we are no longer able to escape the tyranny of fixed numbers, it is unlikely that we will return to a befuddled, liberal opposition. Instead, we will probably look for the real thing.

When the Party of Huah can no longer keep up its various pretenses, we will seek out an even stronger, more confident hand. The one public institution we respect above all others—because most of us have never experienced it. The one that more than three quarters of us have a great deal or quite a lot of confidence in, and the one that has, after all, the longest experience running a paternalistic, authoritarian society. The one that is demographically the most like us, that does its job with startling efficiency and without complaint; the one that captures our imagination to the point that men hold twenty-one-year round-the-clock vigils to honor it.

In the end, we'll beg for the coup.

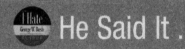 He Said It . . .

"You saw the president yesterday. I thought he was very forward-leaning, as they say in diplomatic nuanced circles."
—about meeting with Vladimir Putin, 7/23/01

HE'S
ANTI-EDUCATION

BUSH FLUNKS SCHOOLS
SUSAN OHANIAN—227

*with quotes by George W. Bush
and a cartoon by Garry Trudeau*

Ask any teacher: The policies of George W. Bush are destroying public education in this country. Public education is a crucial element of our democracy—but then Bush isn't big on democracy, is he? He's not even big on children. As a matter of fact, he seems to dislike them—much as Evil abhors Innocence.

> "*I believe the results of focusing our attention and energy on teaching children to read and having an education system that's responsive to the child and to the parents, as opposed to mired in a system that refuses to change, will make America what we want it to be—a literate country and a hopefuller country.*"
> —Washington, DC, 1/11/01

Bush Flunks Schools

from *The Nation* (11/13/03)

Susan Ohanian

At first, many people liked the sound of "No Child Left Behind," President Bush's education plan. Who could object? The press and the public responded positively to the sentiment—until the failure-to-measure-up labels started rolling in. But now, *New York Times* education columnist Michael Winerip says NCLB (pronounced "nicklebee") "may go down in history as the most unpopular piece of education legislation ever created."

Across the country, thousands of federal scarlet letters have been posted on schoolhouse doors. According to a Machiavellian federal formula, many schools well respected in their communities didn't make Adequate Yearly Progress (AYP). In Florida, only 22 percent of the schools earning A's under the state's ranking system received the NCLB imprimatur; overall, 87 percent of Florida's public schools were judged inadequate. NCLB wonks are quick to point out that nowhere in the law is the word failure used. True. But everybody reads the "in need of improvement" tag as a euphemism for failure. And schools "in need of improvement" are penalized, so the distinction is a sham.

Note that these labels apply only to public schools. Private and parochial schools are exempt from the same requirements—even when they receive vouchers paid for with public funds.

Under what is termed disaggregation, a scheme central to NCLB, kids are divided into subgroups, every one of which must show 95 percent test participation (and progress). Here are Minnesota's: All Students, American Indian/Alaskan Native, Asian/Pacific Islander, Hispanic, Black, White, Limited English Proficient, Special Education, Free/Reduced Priced Meals. It's true that in the past, schools could hide poor performance of, say, special-ed students by averaging it in with that of excellent students. Pulling out the subgroups creates what is called transparency. And that's fine, as far as it goes. But under NCLB, transparency is transmuted into school-bashing. In the words of the North Carolina State Board of Education, "A school's making AYP is an all or nothing prospect. A school will either have 'Yes' or 'No' in this field." One of Palo Alto's top high schools received a scarlet letter because some students skipped the test to study for AP exams.

And remember, this is all based on how some squirrely kids perform on a standardized test that neither the public nor the educators have a right to examine. In some states a teacher is subject to reprimand or dismissal if she even glances at it. Or tries to comfort a child sobbing over the test.

Multiply the subgroups by two, since all subgroups have to measure up in both reading and math, with science waiting in the wings. Every category must have 95 percent test-taker participation and show adequate yearly progress. In a small rural district, a couple of kids having an off day can cook a school's goose. In a large urban school, it doesn't take many more. A school can meet as many as seventeen out of eighteen target goals, and because this game is all or nothing, still be labeled failing. Ninety-four percent—and failing.

If No Child Left Behind meant what it says, it would help schools concentrate on that 6 percent, not cripple the whole school with an ugly label and crushing financial consequences. If even 6 percent of the bombast supporting NCLB was in touch with reality, they'd take heed of the American Society of Civil Engineers Report Card for America's Infrastructure, where public school buildings are ranked in worse shape than our bridges, transit systems and hazardous-waste disposal systems. Where's the Congressional breast-beating about this D-?

Of late, some Democrats have been saying they wouldn't have voted for NCLB if they'd known the Administration was going to skimp on funding. But to educators, this fiat for perfection looks like a gotcha setup; money or no, everybody will fail. As respected researcher Gerald Bracey puts it, NCLB is "a weapon of mass destruction, and the target is the public school system." Vermont Senator James Jeffords sees NCLB as "a back door to anything that will let the private sector take over public education."

If a school doesn't meet its AYP for two consecutive years, then it has to offer students the opportunity to go to a school with better scores, paying for the transportation costs. The Feds call this capacity-building; schools trying to meet already depleted budgets call it a crisis. Students with the lowest scores get first choice for moving, so consider this scenario: A receiving school's AYP is endangered by the incoming students, and the sending school's AYP improves just because they left. Then the bus can reverse direction, with the sending school becoming the recipient. Such a scheme looks at schools not as social institutions but as skill delivery systems. Already, there have been ugly incidents of cities not wanting to accept Somali refugees because they're worried about AYPs.

States must come up with a plan for achieving 100 percent proficiency by 2013–14, so they set up a grid: Oregon is typical, promising 40 percent proficiency in English/ Language Arts in 2002–03, jumping to 60 percent by 2007–08, 80 percent by 2011–12 and 100 percent by 2013–14. Note that they're putting off the utterly fantastic gains until the last years. Maybe they're counting on NCLB's self-destructing by then.

A July press release from the Business Roundtable quotes Joseph Tucci, chairman of the Roundtable's Education and the Workforce Task Force: "You can't manage what you don't measure. No executive can run a business without accurate, granular data that explains what's working and

what's not. Our school systems should be no different."
Keep those 8-year-old widgets rolling along the conveyor
belt! But man does not live by granular data alone. Neither
should children, though everywhere music, art and recess
are being cut—to make room for more test prep.

Consider this: A Steinway grand has more than 12,000
parts, and a third grader's brain has about 100 billion neu-
rons; but it's the Steinway that's acknowledged as unique,
differing not only from all other piano brands but from all
other Steinways. In an article celebrating the Steinway,
James Barron says, "Perhaps it is the wood. No matter how
carefully Steinway selects or prepares each batch, some
trees get more sunlight than others in the forest, and some
get more water. Certain piano technicians say uncontrollable factors make the difference." *Uncontrollable factors.*
These days, piano makers may talk about uncontrollable
factors, but no teacher or principal had better try it. With
test-score numbers passing for accountability, "No
Excuses" is the mantra for schools.

Ask any teacher and she will tell you how different is
each third grader in her classroom. But the corporate-
politico-media alliance long ago abandoned teacher judgments as "anecdotal," putting all their eggs in that
granular data basket. Because the governor of Florida
holds firm to a magic test score for every third grader—
disregarding the kind of work they have done all year in
class—he called on God, who has given children "the
ability to gain this power and they haven't learned it," to
justify holding back 43,000 of them. Maybe God was listening; this number was later reduced to 32,000. In the
short term, retaining kids this year will make next year's
AYP scores look better. But what about the long-term

consequences? The relationships between retention, race and dropout rates are amply documented in research on retention. Hold ten students back a grade and only three will be around on graduation day; hold those students back twice and none will complete school. None. And African-American and Latino students are retained at twice the rate of white students.

Holding back third graders a year in school is said to be in the nation's self-interest. The hysterical tone harks back to the cold war rhetoric found in 1983's *A Nation at Risk:* "If an unfriendly foreign power had attempted to impose on America the mediocre educational performance that exists today, we might well have viewed it as an act of war." Refusing to acknowledge evidence to the contrary, Business Roundtable bullies still talk this way about schools, and the national press lets them get away with it.

People are so used to thinking of issues as right wing and left wing that they often miss the business wing. Go to the Business Roundtable (BRT) website and you can download the NCLB Business Leaders Toolkit. In the name of preparing students for "the 21st century workplace," CEOs are urged to deliver the BRT-crafted messages to public officials, taking advantage of this "exceptional window of opportunity . . . [to] act strategically and with a common voice." The Roundtable cannot have missed the fact that this law, which will declare nearly all public schools failures, greases the skids for vouchers and privatization (though that danger appears to have escaped the law's Democratic supporters). NCLB also paves the way for school-to-work plans that have been sitting on the back burner ever since Clinton failed to get the national test he wanted. When school-to-work, which is a technology-based learning model training students for their place in the global economy (meaning school ends for some kids after tenth grade), is combined with NCLB-type open enrollment (in which kids revolve constantly from school to school), a marketplace model determines the relationship of people to schools. Which is exactly what business wanted in the first place.

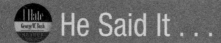

He Said It . . .

"You teach a child to read, and he or her will be able to pass a literacy test."
—Townsend, TN, 2/21/01

HE'S ANTI-
EARTH

with quotes from George W. Bush;
cartoons by Toles and Garry Trudeau;
and an anagram

Bush has done more to harm the environment than any other president—than any other person—in our country's history. He has overturned or gutted scores of regulations that protect our water and our air so that his friends in the corporate world can pollute with impunity. He'll do even more damage if we let him.

> "Arbolist . . . look up the word. I don't know, maybe I made it up. Anyway, it's an arbo-tree-ist, somebody who knows about trees."
>
> —quoted in *USA Today*, 8/21/01

ANAGRAM

George W. Bush:
Ugh! Sewer bog!

Trashing the Environment

from *The Nation* (2/3/03)

Mark Hertsgaard

George W. Bush's assault on the environment over the past two years has been so blatanly relentless that even American television now reports it as a simple fact, like gravity. Is there another issue where Bush has gotten such critical news coverage? Not Iraq, where reports have made plain the Administration's determination to go to war but declined to challenge it. Not economics, though that could change if unemployment and federal deficits keep climbing. Some stories have mentioned Bush's bias toward the rich and corporate, but the tone of most economics coverage has been relatively respectful, except during the Enron scandal, and the White House slipped that noose by changing the subject to Saddam.

The environment, however, has been one bad story after another. Every week seems to bring news of a fresh abomination, from making environmental impact assessments in the national forests optional, to excusing the country's dirtiest power plants from upgrading their pollution controls, to stripping protection from 20 million acres of wetlands, to recycling nuclear waste within consumer goods. (The latter lunacy so far remains only a proposal, but it illustrates a mindset.)

The temptation in writing a midterm evaluation like this one is to list every anti-environmental action the Bush Administration has taken over the past two years. But that would make for long and tedious reading, and besides, environmental group websites already offer the information. Suffice it to say that no Administration since the dawn of the modern environmental era forty years ago has done more to facilitate degradation of the ecosystems that make life on earth possible.

The irony is that Bush has compiled this odious record without having an environmental policy as such. Instead, his environmental achievements—an ever-lengthening list of regulations relaxed, actions delayed and foxes put in charge of henhouses—have come mainly as a consequence of policies pursued in other fields: economic, military and, above all, energy. The environment is not even an afterthought for the Bush crowd. The Administration's energy plan, for example, never once mentions the words "climate change," even though its lopsided emphasis on fossil-fuel development promises to boost US greenhouse-gas emissions between 14 and 38 percent by 2007.

It's easy enough to say that Bush's approach reflects his and his top aides' pasts in the oil, mining, timber, chemical and electric utility industries. It's likewise easy to understand Bush's actions as thanks for the $44 million in contributions those industries showered on him and the Republican National Committee in 2000. Here, the indispensable resource is Paybacks, a report prepared by the NGO's Public Campaign and Earth Justice (www.publicampaign.org/publications/reports/paybacks/Paybacks.pdf). Paybacks offers the most complete listing available of which former corporate executives now oversee their erstwhile colleagues from which federal agencies. In a crowded field, perhaps the most egregious conflict of interest belongs to Steven Griles, the Deputy Interior Secretary. During two years of government service, Griles has continued to be paid $284,000 a year by his former lobby firm, National Environmental Strategies, where he represented mining companies. Apparently not a man to take something for nothing, Griles has returned the favor by meeting with and lobbying on behalf of former clients, most notably in the Administration's attempted recasting of the Clean Water Act to allow the dumping of mining debris into streams and rivers in Appalachia.

The ecological consequences of all this are as predictable

as they are lamentable, but the questions that most urgently need answering are political. Why does the Bush Administration think it can get away with such a slash-and-burn approach to a mom-and-apple-pie issue? Surely Karl Rove, the powerful White House political director, is aware that poll after poll shows that large majorities of Americans care about clean air and water and support the goals of the environmental movement. And why have environmentalists, and specifically Democrats, had so little success in countering the Bush agenda? They turned back the last concerted effort to gut the nation's environmental laws, led by Newt Gingrich in 1995. Did that victory depend so heavily on Bill Clinton's veto threats that it can't be replicated now? Or do environmentalists need a new strategy?

George W. Bush is not the quickest calf in the pasture, but even he recognizes that it's risky for a US President to look bad on the environment. Back when Bush was running, his advisers organized dozens of tutorials to remedy his ignorance of global and presidential issues. Only one such session was devoted to the environment, and it was held in the living room of the Texas governor's mansion on an afternoon in May 1999, according to Steven Hayward, a senior fellow at the Pacific Research Institute for Public Policy, and Terry Anderson, the executive director of the Political Economy Research Center. Hayward and Anderson were two of fifteen experts who heard Bush open this meeting with the following request: "I am going to be the next President of the United States. And when I leave office, the air will be cleaner, the water will be cleaner and the environment will be better. Tell me how I'm going to make that happen."

By the end of the three-hour session, the assembled experts had assured Bush that he could accomplish this politically happy outcome without discomforting the corporate interests or right-wing groups central to his candidacy. The secret was to embrace what Gale Norton, soon to be Bush's Interior Secretary, called "a philosophy of environmental federalism." The idea, as Anderson later explained it, was that Washington should "devolve some responsibility for meeting environmental standards to local levels, where [officials] have better information about how to reduce pollution cost-effectively." A second element of the philosophy presented to Bush that afternoon was replacement of government regulation with market mechanisms such as corporate self-audits, a device Bush had implemented as governor. A third element was elevation of private-property rights over public prerogative.

These ideas had been gestating in right-wing and libertarian think tanks for years. Norton, for example, spent the first four years of her career at the Mountain States Legal Foundation, a nonprofit law firm co-founded by James Watt, Ronald Reagan's Interior Secretary, that frequently represented corporate interests. In a 1989 speech Norton's admiration for market mechanisms led her to suggest that corporations should "have a right to pollute" and then be charged accordingly. Her friend Hayward, who got Norton invited to the May 1999 meeting with Bush, conceded that she "put it poorly" but defended her underlying point: "Let's give landowners an incentive to protect species we want protected." The same basic reasoning underlies another concept that Norton championed for Bush that afternoon: "takings" theory, which asserts that government must compensate a landowner if a government policy precludes full economic exploitation of his property. Most environmentalists criticize takings theory as paying people to obey the law, but it is gaining ground under Bush. In a June 2001 decision the US Supreme Court endorsed takings theory by a 5-to-4 vote.

The intellectual rationale presented to Bush that afternoon in Austin has proven wonderfully convenient to him as President, for it enables him to tell himself he is helping the environment even as he pursues the corporate-friendly agenda that has defined his entire political career. How the philosophy translated into action became evident less than two weeks after Bush took office, when soaring electricity prices and threatened blackouts in California began making national news. Bush quickly blamed environmentalists and the overly stringent regulations they had supposedly imposed to keep the state from building enough power plants. California's energy shortages, Bush argued, were another reason to support his plan to open the Arctic National Wildlife Refuge to oil drilling (which Vice President Dick Cheney promised could be done with minimal environmental impact). Environmentalists and public officials in California scoffed that the new President was talking nonsense. Just what devious nonsense, however, only became clear a year later, with the unfolding of the Enron scandal. What had really driven up electricity prices in California, it turned out, were the artificial shortages that Enron and other companies created by manipulating a deregulated marketplace. The right-wing gospel had said leave corporations alone and the environment would prosper, but reality in California proved otherwise.

Jump ahead now to the summer of 2002. Much of the

nation has been suffering from prolonged, extreme drought. In the West, millions of acres have been ravaged by wildfires. Once again Bush is faced by a genuine public emergency. Once again he scapegoats environmentalists and federal regulators to advance a corporate agenda. During a visit to a still-smoldering forest in Oregon, the President declares that the wildfires are the result of irresponsible forest management. Excessive underbrush had accumulated, and then caught fire, because loggers had been prevented from thinning forests in a scientifically sound manner. From now on, said Bush, federal policy would promote well-managed forests and recognize that "there's nothing wrong with people being able to earn a living off of effective forest management." To set things right, Bush turned to a man who had long made a very good living from timber: Mark Rey, who was vice president of the American Forest and Paper Association before becoming Bush's Under Secretary of Agriculture. Rey's solution called for waiving fundamental stipulations of the National Environmental Protection Act, such as mandatory environmental-impact assessments, while making protection of wildlife an "optional" goal for national forest managers. With straight faces, Bush's spin doctors proclaimed it the "Healthy Forests Initiative."

In truth, the wildfires of 2002 were more likely rooted in an environmental reality that Bush refuses to confront: global climate change. Drought of the sort experienced in 2002 is exactly what scientists project will occur increasingly in the years ahead as global temperatures rise, bringing more extreme weather of all kinds. Thus killer floods punished central Europe and southern Asia in 2002, while Arctic ice is melting at record speed. The signs of impending disaster are so unmistakable and frightening that they are converting even such die-hard skeptics as Republican Senator Ted Stevens of Alaska, who has watched his state absorb billions of dollars of property damage as melting tundra buckles roads and buildings, and forests are consumed by a species of beetle suddenly able to survive in Alaska's warming climate.

Bush, meanwhile, remains loyal to his oil-industry roots: Global warming is something to study, not resist. Bush promised in a September 2000 campaign speech to regulate emissions of carbon dioxide (and three other pollutants). But it's doubtful he understood the implications of his speech, and once it became clear that honoring the promise would preclude the kind of energy plan Cheney cooked up in secret with Enron and other industry representatives, the promise obviously had to go. So did US support for the Kyoto Protocol on global warming, a move that provoked more anger overseas than perhaps any other action Bush took in his first year in office.

The White House has won the legal battle over whether it can keep secret the meetings that gave rise to the Bush energy plan, but who needs further proof of industry fingerprints when the policy speaks for itself? Its call for oil drilling in Alaska has driven discussion in Washington and therefore media coverage, but that may be a diversion. Even as environmental groups fundraise and Democratic senators threaten to filibuster over Alaska, the Administration has pursued a less-noticed but equally destructive aspect of its energy plan: encouraging drilling and mining of millions of acres of public land in the West, including national monument areas. Court rulings have blocked much of the Administration's efforts—so far.

The single most powerful action Washington could take to slow global warming would be to impose a meaningful increase in vehicle fuel-efficiency standards. The Bush philosophy instead dictates a voluntary plan to reduce emissions, one that respects corporations' freedom to make whatever products the market demands. Bush believes that, like him, America's corporate leaders care about the environment, and they will do more to protect it if government stops telling them how to do so (which explains why he has cut environmental enforcement budgets and prosecutions nearly 50 percent from Clinton-era levels). Let consumers start buying more hybrid-powered cars, and Detroit will respond.

The same faith in corporate goodness underlies the rollback of the Clean Air Act's so-called New Source Review provision, a policy that literally threatens death for thousands of Americans, especially very young and very old people who already suffer from asthma or other respiratory ailments. Approximately 75 percent of all power-plant emissions in the United States come from facilities built before 1977, which pollute four to ten times as much as plants with modern pollution controls. The Clean Air Act has long required companies to install modern pollution controls if they expand capacity at older plants. The companies complained that this requirement discouraged modernization and thereby prevented them from cutting pollution. The Administration has endorsed this logic with its new rules, which make pollution upgrades largely voluntary. The upshot, EPA Administrator Christie Whitman has promised, will be cleaner skies as corporations step up and do the right thing.

The military, however, may not even have to pretend to

do the right thing. Perhaps the single most disturbing and overlooked environmental proposal of the past two years is the Pentagon's post–September 11 suggestion that it be exempted from environmental laws. Congress rejected this request last fall, but the Pentagon is back this session with a better-prepared proposal and is confident of victory. Robert Alvarez, a senior policy adviser to the Energy Secretary during the Clinton Administration, warns that such a policy could enable the military, the nation's biggest polluter, "to write off large areas of land, bodies of water, and the people that are dependent on them, just as the Soviet Union did." Nuclear weapons sites in particular, says Alvarez, might become "national sacrifice zones."

So, will Bush end up paying a price in 2004 for his betrayal of environmental values? His supporters in corporate America and the far right are apparently so blinded by their ideological biases that they perceive little political risk. Paul Weyrich, the president of the Free Congress Foundation, told the *Washington Post* in March 2001 that things would be fine as long as the body count didn't get too high: "There's a risk with some of the swing voters, but unless something happens where lots of people turn up dead before the election, these issues are not going to resonate with lots of voters." An unnamed senior Republican agreed, asserting that "unless there's a catastrophe, these decisions aren't going to affect a mom in Fairfax."

Karl Rove, however, has a more sophisticated analysis. He knows Americans, especially the suburban swing voters so coveted by presidential campaigns, care about the environment. But he thinks they care more about other issues: the economy, security (both economic and military) and healthcare. The environment, Rove reportedly calculates, ranks eighth or ninth among the average voter's priorities. He may be right—recent polls indicate that Americans oppose Bush's environmental actions by a 2-to-1 margin, yet 60 percent of them approve of the job he is doing as President. So it may make sense for Bush to pursue an environmental agenda that rewards corporate backers and throws red meat to his right-wing base; the White House just has to make sure that it doesn't unleash its own Chernobyl in the process.

Remember the arsenic flap early in Bush's presidency? Many environmental issues are too technical or abstract to resonate with average voters, but the idea of allowing more arsenic in drinking water connects with nearly everyone, which is why the Administration quickly retreated. If opponents can make Bush's other policies equally visible in the media, and their dangers equally concrete to voters, they may force additional retreats and persuade significant numbers of voters to oppose his re-election.

Environmentalists in Washington fret that Republicans now control both houses of Congress and the White House, but this situation may be forcing the movement to recall that its true strength lies out in the country among the general public, which supports it by approximately 2 to 1. There is no reason the environmental movement has to be a marginal player in American politics. It commands significant financial resources, public credibility and intellectual capital. But too much fighting over turf and too little coordinated action has frequently left the movement in disarray. That may now be changing. According to a report in gristmagazine.com (another indispensable source of environmental news) by former *New York Times* reporter Keith Schneider, mainstream environmental groups have begun collaborating like never before in the face of the Bush threat. Their "collaborative defense campaign" mirrors part of Bush's strategy by focusing more effort on state and local resistance to environmental rollbacks, both among activist groups and such politicians as New York Attorney General Eliot Spitzer. The national groups also hope to mobilize public unease by highlighting one or two egregious, easily communicated environmental outrages (à la arsenic) and convincing politicians, both Democratic and moderate Republican, that they can win votes by opposing Bush's agenda.

In the longer run, environmentalists also need to get serious about economics if they want to make political progress. Perhaps because so much of the mainstream environmental movement is made up of affluent white people, they forget how close to the economic edge the majority of Americans live. Most Americans want to see the environment protected, but many fear the economic consequences. History shows that no issue except war has more effect on voters' views of a President than the economy. A policy to restore our damaged ecosystems and transform our technologies toward renewable energy and environmental sustainability would create more jobs and business opportunities than today's dead-end approach, but most Americans don't know that. A movement or a candidate who opened their eyes could become Bush's biggest nightmare.

6·13·02

He Said It . . .

"First, we would not accept a treaty that would not have been ratified, nor a treaty that I thought made sense for the country."
—on the Kyoto accord, quoted in the *Washington Post*, 4/24/01

HE'S
CORRUPT

with a quote from George W. Bush;
cartoons by Toles, Garry Trudeau and Joel Pett;
a quiz by Paul Slansky;
and anagrams

Think of it as affirmative action, Republican style. George W. Bush, born to wealthy and powerful parents, got rich himself through a series of shady deals and failed business ventures. These early ventures were supported by wealthy people and corporations who sought the favor of his powerful father. The same supporters have financed GWB's political career in exchange for power and influence in his administration. Conclusion: George W. Bush has made a career out of selling out the United States of America.

Quiz
Paul Slansky

Who said what?

1. "In the corporate world, sometimes things aren't exactly black and white when it comes to accounting procedures."

2. "[Osama bin Laden is] either alive and well or alive and not too well or not alive."

3. "How many Palestinians were on those airplanes on September 9th? None."

4. "First of all, let's get one thing straight: Crack is cheap. I make too much money to ever smoke crack. Let's get that straight. O.K.?"

    (a) George W. Bush
    (b) Dan Quayle
    (c) Whitney Houston
    (d) Donald Rumsfeld

Answer: 1(a), 2(d), 3(b), 4(c)

Audit This

from *The New Republic* (7/22/02)

Martin Peretz

In 1986 George W. Bush received one of the lucky breaks that would characterize his business career, when Harken Energy bought his otherwise near-worthless oil company, Spectrum 7, for more than $2 million in stock. As part of the deal, Bush was named to Harken's board of directors and was designated a member of the board's audit committee. An ordinary director of a public company has rather vague responsibilities, and many directors simply doze through their periodic meetings and collect their annual fees. But a member of the audit committee has specific obligations. Among them is the obligation to ensure that the company's books are honest. In fact, members of the audit committee are the guarantors of the company's probity.

It was during Bush's term on the audit committee in 1990 that the Securities and Exchange Commission (SEC) forced Harken to revise its books and account for millions of dollars in losses it had disguised as profit through the $12 million sale ($11 million of which was in reality financed by a note from Harken itself) of a subsidiary to a posse of insiders. If this evokes the work of Arthur Andersen, it should: Andersen was Harken's accounting firm, its legal and ethical guide. In that sense, when Bush was supposed to be exercising fiduciary oversight over the company, Harken was pioneering the very tricks that Enron and WorldCom have now made famous. The White House does not like this comparison; according to the

Associated Press, Communications Director Dan Bartlett harrumphed, "To compare a $12 million sale . . . by Harken to a deliberate attempt to hide $3.8 billion in losses is ridiculous." So, as the old joke about the whore has it, we are now just haggling over the price.

In the ordinary course of business, members of the audit committee know more about a company's financial drift than do other directors, and they know it earlier. Which is to say they really do have insider information. The vagaries of the law permit directors to buy and sell during designated windows of opportunity even though they may be in possession of information— as Bush was—that other shareholders don't have. Bush took advantage of this window when he sold his Harken stock. Unfair, maybe. But as Michael Kinsley once wrote, "[T]he scandal isn't what's illegal, the scandal is what's legal."

Nonetheless, what makes this kind of selling legally acceptable (if not exactly morally correct) is the obligation to report in a timely fashion the sale (or purchase) so outsiders know what insiders are doing. But Bush didn't do that. As the SEC has found, he failed to notify the authorities (and, through that notification, other stockholders and the public) on a timely basis that he had, in fact, sold stock. The SEC nevertheless declined to press charges, a decision that becomes more interesting when you realize, as *The Baltimore Sun* has noted, that the Commission's then–general counsel, James R. Doty— the man who supervised the legal inquiry into Bush's behavior—was also the lawyer who had facilitated the sale of the Texas Rangers baseball team to George W.'s partnership. And Bush was selling his Harken stock to pay off his debt to the bank that had financed his share of the Rangers' purchasing price.

The June 22, 1990, transaction was for 212,140 shares sold at $4 per share, for a total of $848,560. Two months after the sale (but before Bush actually reported it), Harken announced an unprecedented quarterly loss of $23 million, of which George W. could not have helped but be aware—of which, in fact, he was legally obliged to be aware. An *Associated Press* dispatch reported that "[Bush] received memos in spring 1990 that referred in stark terms to the company's cash-strapped condition. . . . One document said that the company was in the midst of a 'liquidity crisis' and another told Bush the company was 'in a state of non-compliance' with its lenders." When the loss was made public, Harken stock fell to a shade above $2 and, by year's end, was down to $1. (As we go to press twelve years later, one share of Harken Energy is worth 45 cents.)

According to Adam Entous, a *Reuters* White House correspondent, Bush was late in informing the SEC of his sales not once but four times, and one of those times he was more than eight months late. When one of these latenesses became an issue in Bush's 1994 run for governor of Texas, he simply asserted that the SEC had lost Form 4, as the relevant document is called. But that claim was sheer invention. And when asked about the filing last week—in the shadow of WorldCom and Martha Stewart—White House press secretary Ari Fleischer, on information provided by his boss, changed the story and pinned responsibility for the reporting delay on Harken's lawyers.

Given the president's well-known distaste for lawyers, it's perhaps not surprising that he blamed his blunder on members of the bar. But not every Bush lawyer involved in the Harken affair has been made a scapegoat. Bush's personal attorney at the time, the man who defended him against the SEC, was a man named Robert W. Jordan, formerly a partner at Baker Botts LLP. The Baker referred to therein is none other than James Baker, secretary of state to Bush père and the tactician behind W.'s extra-legal victory in Florida. At W.'s inaugural, Baker Botts threw a private party for, among others, Saudi Ambassador Prince Bandar. Later that year Jordan, who knows almost nothing about the Middle East, was appointed U.S. ambassador to Saudi Arabia.

James Baker now has a very influential friend and full-time interlocutor in Riyadh whenever he goes there (which he does often) on behalf of the banking consortium called the Carlyle Group. As it happens, George H.W. is also a highly remunerated senior Carlyle trustee with special responsibilities for Arab and especially Saudi Arab clients. In fact, Bush père traveled to Saudi Arabia shortly after the 2000 election. Prominent among H.W.'s clients was the family of Osama bin Laden, the money of whom was quickly disentangled from Carlyle for purposes of public decency shortly after September 11. Which raises a few questions: Why were Osama's many siblings and cousins who were in the States on September 11 apparently allowed to slip out of the country so quickly and without questioning? Did Ambassador Jordan do anything to facilitate their sudden and surprising departure? Did Jordan call his old partner Jim Baker to facilitate the mass getaway? Or did he go to the paterfamilias, who had his own interest in the bin Ladens not suffering any embarrassments? Or did Jordan simply talk directly to his boss? Maybe no one talked to anybody. Which leads back to the original question: Why were the bin Ladens not detained? These might be useful topics for a congressional committee, once it gets done with Harken Energy.

TNR 7-20A

ANAGRAMS

Compassionate Conservative:
Come, vote: save a patrician's son.

Bush Administration:
This bandit is our man!

President George W. Bush:
Greed rips the U.S. Now beg!

To the Cronies Go the Spoils
from Salon.com (10/9/03)
Farhad Manjoo

On Sept. 17, the Bush administration handed Congress a spending bill that reads like a bleeding-heart liberal's legislative fantasy, a massive, government-funded infrastructure revitalization program of the kind not seen since the days of FDR: It calls for $800 million for the police, $300 million for firefighters, and almost $3 billion for clean water systems. It sets aside tens of millions of dollars to build thousands of new public housing units, but it warns that much more money will be needed in the future. The bill allocates about $1 billion to spend on healthcare, including $150 million for a state-of-the-art children's hospital. There's even $5 million to build a women's center and a million dollars for a new museum.

Is George W. Bush finally displaying the compassion long advertised to run through his brand of conservatism? Not exactly. As you may have guessed, this particular plan isn't aimed at fixing the problems of Boston or Boise but those of Baghdad and Basra and Tikrit and Najaf. Congress is now debating—and, after many adjustments, will likely approve—the president's plan to rebuild Iraq's schools, hospitals, highways, prisons, the electricity grid, railroads, and every other institution of civilized society; of the $87 billion the administration seeks, about $20 billion is earmarked for Iraqi nation-building.

Iraq desperately needs rebuilding, and it might seem churlish to question what the administration has requested. But when the price tag is in the tens of billions, one can't help wondering: How much money will actually find its way into the hands of Iraqis? Who will profit from this reconstruction windfall?

In Congress, Democrats are asking the same questions— and many are saying that the spending request is nothing but a huge gift to Bush's moneyed friends. "Item after item [in the request] reads like a government contractor's wish list," Rep. Henry Waxman, a California Democrat, wrote in a recent letter to the White House's Office of Management and Budget.

Is Waxman right? Is the rebuilding request tailor-made to pad the accounts of U.S. corporations, and in particular, those with good connections to the White House? It's hard to get definitive answers to this question, mostly because nobody seems to know how much money

Iraq needs, and, consequently, whether the president's plan is too big, too small, or just right.

"I'm hard-pressed to criticize the particular numbers—I can see an argument for why all of these things could be good for Iraq," says Bathsheba Crocker, a post-conflict reconstruction expert at the Center for Strategic & International Studies. "But that doesn't mean that the U.S. taxpayer can or should afford all of these things, and you do have to protect against padding of the contracts."

This reconstruction fog raises all sorts of vexing problems for the average concerned citizen. You want to support the rebuilding in Iraq, but you don't want to overpay. You want to make sure the Iraqis get what they need, but you're not too thrilled about Halliburton getting a blank check. It'd be great if the work was done in a transparent manner, but since when does a government program work like that? And is there a danger of the president's pals making off with the biggest prizes—and are they trying to do that? Of course.

What you need is a guide to the main players in Iraq—a handy list of the various interests who are winning, trying to win, losing, and trying not to lose. You need to know what makes the work in Iraq so expensive, and so prone to cozy political relationships. And you need to see why rebuilding the country is going to be a long, difficult, ugly process.

Fortunately, we have created such a guide for you:

The lobbyists. Late in September, the Washington newspaper *The Hill* reported that some of the president's closest political allies had created a new firm, New Bridge Strategies, whose main goal is to help corporations "evaluate and take advantage of business opportunities in the Middle East following the conclusion of the U.S.-led war in Iraq." The company, which is headed by Joe Allbaugh, Bush's chief of staff in Texas and his campaign manager in 2000, was not exactly hard to find—it has a Web site that boasts of its intimate ties to government officials: "New Bridge Strategies principals have years of public policy experience," the site says. The company's directors "have held positions in the Reagan Administration and both Bush Administrations and are particularly well suited to working with international agencies in the executive branch, Department of Defense and the U.S. Agency for International Development, the American rebuilding apparatus and establishing early links to Congress." Other New Bridge partners include Ed Rogers, vice chairman of the lobbying firm Barbour Griffith & Rogers, and a close political aide to George H. W. Bush; and Lanny Griffith, also at Barbour Griffith, who served in several positions in Bush senior's White House, including as Southern polit-ical director in the 1988 campaign.

You might think it a bit unseemly for the president's close friends to use their proximity to power to profit from a war that the administration assured us had nothing to do with profiteering, but that's only because you're naive. According to Allbaugh and the others at New Bridge, having friends in high places is no reason not to make money; that's how things work in Washington, it's not at all unusual. "Because my friend is president of the United States, I'm supposed to check out of life?" Allbaugh asked the *New York Times* on Friday. (Nobody at New Bridge Strategies—nor at any of Washington's other lobbying firms looking for work in Iraq—returned Salon's repeated calls.) "I have nothing to hide. I'm straightforward. I deal my cards on top of the table," Allbaugh told the newspaper, and he added that there was in fact something honorable about working in Iraq. "We fought a war, we displaced a horrible, horrible regime, and as a part of that we have an obligation to help Iraqis. We can't just leave in the middle of the night."

On its Web site, New Bridge Strategies says that the business opportunities in Iraq are of an "unprecedented nature and scope," but what that means specifically is left up in the air. So far, it appears that New Bridge's only public client is MCT Corp., a cellular phone company based in Alexandria, Va., that has previously built phone systems in the former Soviet Union and Afghanistan. In August, MCT and New Bridge Strategies submitted a bid to build the mobile system in Iraq, but New Bridge's political ties do not appear to have helped it very much. On Monday, the Iraqi communications ministry announced that it had awarded mobile phone bids to three Middle Eastern firms.

But that may have just been New Bridge's bad luck. In Iraq, virtually everything that gets built is built with the approval, if not by decree, of Washington—which is, after all, funding the entire endeavor. Undignified as it may appear, New Bridge's pitch is rather logical, and after the new spending bill is signed, it's likely that many companies will decide that the best way to get to Baghdad is by way of K Street.

And perhaps that's why New Bridge Strategies is not the only lobbying firm looking to push work in Iraq. On Oct. 2, the *Washington Post* reported that the Livingston Group, the firm headed by former Rep. Robert Livingston—

the Republican whose plans to become speaker of the House in 1998 unraveled when it was revealed that he'd carried on an extramarital affair—is also quite interested in working for companies looking to take part in the Iraqi reconstruction. One firm Livingston is helping is De La Rue, a British paper company. De La Rue has already received a contract to print Iraq's new currency, and it wants to work on secure travel documents, too. A Livingston lobbyist told the *Post* that he was rather busy pitching De La Rue's case to a number of influential members of Congress. "We're trying to get the right people to ask the right questions of the right people," he said.

De La Rue, incidentally, provides a good indication of how lucrative working in Iraq can be. The company's fortunes had been flagging recently; in July, the Justice Department began an investigation of De La Rue to see if one of its subsidiaries was involved in a scheme to fix the prices of holographic security stickers used for Visa credit cards—news of the investigation sank De La Rue's stock. Thanks to Iraq, things now look fine for the firm. In September, the company said that its profits would soar, mostly due to its reconstruction work.

Halliburton. In March, Kellogg Brown & Root, a subsidiary of Halliburton, signed a contract with the Defense Department to fight fires in Iraq in the event that Saddam Hussein tried to destroy his oil fields during the war. The contract seemed fishy from the start. It was awarded on a "no-bid" basis; only Halliburton was asked to do the work. The Defense Department has subsequently been suspiciously cagey about its details, slow to answer questions about the contract's size and specific purpose. Only in April, a month after it was signed, did the Army Corps of Engineers disclose (in response to questions from Henry Waxman) that the contract was potentially worth $7 billion to Halliburton. It took another month for the Army Corps to say that Halliburton would not only fix damaged oil facilities but would also operate oil centers and even distribute the oil.

Why was Halliburton awarded this lucrative, expansive contract on a no-bid basis? To most people, the answer is obvious—in the 1990s Halliburton was run by Vice President Dick Cheney. There is no proof that Cheney's ties to the company had anything to do with Halliburton's good fortune in Iraq, but there are enough clues to make you suspect the worst. Halliburton's story—a no-bid contract, a friend in the highest place—has all the hallmarks of cronyism, and it ought to stand as the model of how not to reconstruct Iraq.

Both Cheney and Halliburton say that he played no part in the awarding of the contract. "Nobody has produced one single shred of evidence that there's anything wrong or inappropriate here, nothing but innuendo, and—basically they're political cheap shots is the way I would describe it," Cheney said on "Meet the Press" on Sept. 14. "I don't know any of the details of the contract because I deliberately stayed away from any information on that, but Halliburton is a fine company. And as I say— and I have no reason to believe that anybody's done anything wrong or inappropriate here."

In an e-mail to Salon, Wendy Hall, a spokeswoman for Halliburton, echoed Cheney's denial of impropriety. "There have been many allegations that Halliburton received the contract for the reconstruction of Iraq because of political influence," she wrote. "Certainly it's easier to assign devious motives than to take the time to learn the truth." The real reason Halliburton was awarded the contract, Hall said, is because of "our unique combination of business experience in defense contracting, engineering and construction and oilfield services." Hall added that "Our employees in the Middle East are building housing, preparing meals, delivering the mail and providing many other vital services for our troops. Our Halliburton people are sharing the hardships and the risks. Three have lost their lives while working there."

At the same time, though, Halliburton has made quite a bit of money in Iraq. So far, it has received about $1.2 billion under the oilfield contract—more money than any other firm working in Iraq. Moreover, Cheney's insistence that he has no financial stake in the company is dubious. Since he became vice president, Cheney has continued to receive checks in deferred compensation from the company—he got almost $150,000 in 2001 and $162,000 in 2002, and he will keep getting money until 2006. The White House denies that this represents a financial interest in the company; because he purchased an insurance policy on the compensation, Cheney will get the money regardless of Halliburton's fortunes. In addition, he has agreed to donate the money to charity. In late September, however, the Congressional Research Service concluded that despite these measures, the paychecks represented an actual stake in Halliburton.

The web of coincident interests here is almost comical—indeed, the most artful criticism of the Halliburton story, the one that several of its critics mention, is a joke David Letterman made on his show. The president "is asking

Congress for $80 billion to help rebuild Iraq," Letterman said. "And when you make out that check, remember—there are two L's in Halliburton." In September, the activist group American Family Voices featured Letterman's quip in an anti-Bush ad it ran in five states. Is this the image the Bush administration wants for its mission in Iraq?

There is perhaps one silver lining to Halliburton's dark deal with the government—it has so offended lawmakers that they've decided to put an end to no-bid contracts. On Oct. 2, during its deliberations over the Iraq spending bill, the Senate passed an amendment that requires all contracts in Iraq to be awarded only after a rigorous bidding process has been conducted. The House is expected to follow suit.

Bechtel. In its long history of government work, this privately owned San Francisco firm has built some of the largest public projects in the world—including the Hoover Dam, the subway systems in San Francisco and Washington, the tunnel under the English Channel, and many American nuclear power plants—and, at least according to its critics, it has also built something even more valuable: close connections to the most powerful people in the country. Former Reagan administration officials Caspar Weinberger and George Shultz have worked for the firm (Shultz is still on its board). In February, the company's CEO, Riley Bechtel, was named, along with dozens of other executives, to the president's Export Council, a White House trade advisory group.

Critics charge that it was Bechtel's ties to Republicans that helped it win one of the most lucrative Iraq rebuilding contracts—a $680 million infrastructure development grant awarded by the U.S. Agency for International Development in April. (Since then, the contract has ballooned beyond that initial sum; according to the USAID, Bechtel has so far received more than $900 million in orders through the contract.)

While Bechtel is certainly a skilled player in the Iraq game, its operations are altogether more routine, and therefore more defensible, than those of Halliburton, a company with which it is frequently lumped together for criticism. Bechtel's contract with the government was awarded in a semi-competitive bidding process (foreign firms weren't invited to apply) and there's no sign that it benefited from special favors, beyond the favors that usually accrue to giants in the military industrial complex. The firm also maintains a Web site that is frequently updated with detailed information about its work in the country; nothing about its plans in Iraq are secret.

That's not to say Bechtel doesn't have its critics. In his letter to the OMB, Henry Waxman charged Bechtel with blocking Iraqi companies from participating in the rebuilding work. Waxman said that he's uncovered evidence showing that Bechtel requires local companies to carry expensive insurance plans in order to be considered fit to subcontract from Bechtel. Waxman also said that the type of contract Bechtel has with the government—a "cost-plus" contract, in which Bechtel is paid a certain fixed fee over its costs, meaning that it's guaranteed to make money—provides little incentive for the company to reduce costs by subcontracting to Iraqis. "It is easy to understand how this arrangement is lucrative for [Bechtel]," Waxman wrote. "But what is unclear is how these arrangements protect the interests of the U.S. taxpayer or further the goal of putting Iraqis to work rebuilding their own country."

Michael Kidder, a spokesman for the company, said that Waxman's assessment of Bechtel's work is simply incorrect. "The congressman's letter inaccurately described our method of hiring Iraqi subcontractors," Kidder said. "There is no bond industry in Iraq, but this lack of construction insurance has never prevented Bechtel from awarding any subcontracts to Iraqi firms. Following USAID's direction and their priorities, a vast majority of the subcontracting work Bechtel has awarded has gone to Iraqi subcontractors." Of the 133 subcontracts the company has awarded, 98 have gone to Iraqi firms, the company says on its Web site.

Since the eve of the invasion, when Bechtel's headquarters became a prime San Francisco protesting spot, the company has generally tried hard to counter the charge that it is profiteering from the war and that it won its contracts in Iraq through its political ties. Online, Bechtel has posted a list of "media inaccuracies" that it says the press routinely reports as fact. "Through endless repetition, rather than facts, Bechtel has gained an undeserved reputation as a secretive company that succeeds through powerful friends in high places," the site says. "Over the years, we have certainly built good relationships with important people. We network like anyone in business or the professions . . . But the implication that Bechtel wins business or succeeds in a highly competitive marketplace through political connections is misguided and false."

Security guards. Iraq, as you may have heard, isn't exactly a pleasant place to do business, and when companies like

Bechtel set up shop there, they're finding that thinly stretched American forces aren't always available to protect corporate interests. Instead of relying on the military for help, many companies are hiring their own protection—elite security-service firms that provide executives with armed guards, convoys of Humvees, and all manner of amenities in order to stay alive in Baghdad. The security business is one of the few growth industries in postwar Iraq, a fact that can't be heartening to the Bush administration.

Security firms began gearing up for work in Iraq before the war, when they predicted that the chaos immediately following regime change would create temporary opportunities for their services. "We didn't know at that point how difficult it was going to be, and I think it's exceeded our expectations," says David Claridge, the managing director of Janusian, a British security firm working in Iraq. He says that few people in his business predicted "the longevity of the problem, the depth of the problem" in securing Iraq. "Probably everybody inside and outside government failed to estimate the situation."

There are at least 100 security firms working in Iraq today; most are British (Claridge says that the Brits are "regarded as the best, even by American customers") but some large American companies have won choice security contracts with the government. DynCorp, a subsidiary of CSC, an American military contractor, has been tapped to train Iraq's police force. Vinnell, a division of Northrop Grumman, is training the Iraqi army. (If you're a former Special Forces officer who can't find a job in America, you might want to consider working for Vinnell in Iraq.)

The unsafe operating conditions in Iraq have clearly

hampered the rebuilding effort, and the need for private security firms likely accounts for the larger-than-expected reconstruction costs. "One of our major clients is entitled to protection from the U.S. military in Baghdad," Claridge says, "but waiting for them left three- or four-hour delays just for their convoy of Humvees to show up. For them the only real solution was to move to private security." Claridge adds: "There's a connection between security and reconstruction. The two have to move hand in hand, and private security has the capacity to make up what is missing in the coalition effort. There isn't capacity in the military to deal with the reconstruction process."

The French. On a trip to Paris in early October, Alan Larson, the undersecretary of state for economic affairs, told a business conference that the United States is quite willing to have French firms work in Iraq. "The door is open for French companies to participate in infrastructure contracts in Iraq," he said, according to AFP. "We're open to companies from all over the world regarding the rebuilding of Iraq."

Beyond that remark, however, it appears that few French companies are participating in the country, and the French government—along with the Germans and just about everyone else in the world—has pledged relatively small sums for the reconstruction effort. Late in October in Madrid, the United Nations will hold a donor conference to raise money for Iraq; the U.N. wants about $35 billion, but only about $1 billion has been pledged so far. One wonders how much more money we'd have available if Donald Rumsfeld would learn to measure his words.

The Iraqis and the Americans. The question of whether Iraqis will ultimately benefit or suffer as a result of the U.S. occupation is the most important, and freighted, issue of the war, and it can't be answered here. But it's important to note how firmly the financial fate of the average Iraqi citizen is now dependent on the continued goodwill of the average American taxpayer. At least for the next few years, until Iraq regains its oil production capacity, the country will run on U.S. dollars. And as we all share the same pool of money, our fortunes will be mutually exclusive: When the Iraqis get money, Americans will lose money, and vice versa. This situation cannot make for a fast friendship, and it's further complicated by the political imbalance: Because it's the Americans who get to vote, the Iraqis ought to be wary.

Indeed, the Iraqis are already starting to lose. After the president presented his reconstruction plan to Congress, lawmakers immediately began trimming it. In the House, Bill Young, the Florida Republican who chairs the Appropriations Committee, has "scrubbed" the bill of about $1.7 billion of the president's reconstruction request. Young deleted the $50 million the administration wanted to buy cars for Iraq's traffic police; $153 million for "solid waste management," including the purchase of 40 trash trucks; $9 million for creating ZIP codes in the country; and the $150 million to build that advanced children's hospital in Basra.

Meanwhile, in the Senate, many Democrats and some Republicans are arguing that at least some of the money the U.S. provides to Iraq should be paid back when Iraq becomes self-sustaining. The Iraqis are obviously not pleased with this plan, and members of the governing council have cautioned senators that Iraq is already heavily burdened with Saddam Hussein's loans. But the idea of lending Iraq its reconstruction money has obvious political appeal in the U.S.—Americans faced with a ballooning deficit and the hazy notion that Iraq is sitting on billions of dollars in oil wealth might think it only fair that Iraqis pitch in. As the conservative syndicated columnist Cal Thomas wrote recently, "Why should the Iraqis complain? It's their freedom we bought. Let them help pay for it."

But the Iraqis didn't ask for the war, and they didn't volunteer to pay for it. "I'm sympathetic to the argument that it would be nice if the U.S. could get paid back some of this money," says Bathsheba Crocker, the reconstruction expert at CSIS. "But I don't think the loan is the way to do it. I'm worried about how it looks to make Iraq fairly heavily indebted to the United States. It's not something that looks all that great given the heavy degree of suspicion about what our motives are here."

In other words, we wouldn't want to be in the position of reminding the Iraqis that, when they make their checks out for the reconstruction, there are two L's in Halliburton.

ANAGRAMS

Compassionate Conservative:
Conspire to save a vast income

George Bush with Dick Cheney:
Heck, be cheesy, right wing duo!

 He Said It . . .

"I've got a preference for friends."
—Washington, DC, 2/5/01

HE'S A
BULLY

with quotes from George W. Bush;
cartoons by Ward Sutton, Garry Trudeau and Pat Oliphant;
quizzes by Paul Slansky;
and anagrams

George W. Bush is emotionally and spiritually weak. His weakness helps explain his lust for empire and his endless search for enemies who (he thinks) will be easy to destroy—both at home (single mothers, migrant workers, the unemployed) and abroad.

IN THE AFTERMATH OF THE VIETNAM WAR CAME *RAMBO*. NOW COMES A NEW TALE WE'VE ALL BEEN WATCHING SLOWLY UNFOLD ...

★ **DUMBO** ★
by WARD SUTTON

DO WE GET TO WIN THIS TIME, SIR?

YES, WE GET TO WIN.

"WE" MEANING HALIBURTON.

THE TUMULTUOUS LATE 1960s FIND OUR HERO SO "WRAPPED UP" IN HIS STUDIES THAT HE IS LEFT "AMBIVALENT" ABOUT THE WAR IN VIETNAM ...

...MORE SOLDIERS CONTINUE TO DIE...

HEY! ISN'T *BONANZA* ON??

BEER

DKE

BEER

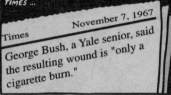

IN 1967, WHEN HUGE NUMBERS OF COLLEGE STUDENTS WERE MARCHING ON WASHINGTON, GEORGE HAD HIS OWN CAUSE: DEFENDING THE BRANDING OF FRAT PLEDGES IN THE *NEW YORK TIMES* ...

Times   November 7, 1967

George Bush, a Yale senior, said the resulting wound is "only a cigarette burn."

IN 1968, ARMED WITH THE LOWEST ALLOWABLE SCORE ON THE PILOT APTITUDE TEST, OUR HERO ENTERS THE NATIONAL GUARD ON THE FAST TRACK.

ENTER

ONE SIDE! CONGRESSMAN'S SON COMING THROUGH.

DKE

APPLICATION
Name *George W. Bush*
Date *1968*

Do you wish to volunteer for overseas duty?

☐ Yes
☑ No

HEH, HEH!

Texas National Guard
PRESS RELEASE
March 24, 1970

"I've always wanted to be a Fighter Pilot"

- G. W. Bush

THEN, JUST 22 MONTHS AFTER HIS TRAINING, HE QUITS FLYING. HE MUST HAVE KNOWN HE WAS DESTINED FOR BIGGER THINGS. LIKE GOING AWOL FROM MAY 1972 - MAY 1973.

≈SNIFF!≈ I'M GON' BE PRESSYDENT SOMEDAY!

SHORE YOU WILL, GEORGE!

HAW-HAW!

XX

FAST FORWARD TO 1991: GEORGE'S DAD LEADS A VALIANT MILITARY VICTORY.

KUWAIT'S OIL FIELDS HAVE BEEN LIBERATED!

YAY! YAY!

YAY! YAY!

George W. Bush seizes every opportunity to unleash America's military power on our so-called "enemies." Why? One answer: he is a willing tool of political fanatics bent on world domination.

American Dominance
from *The Bergen Record* (2/23/03)
Chris Floyd

SUNDAY, FEBRUARY 23, 2003

An attack on Iraq. Vast increases in military spending. Planting new American bases all over the world, from the jungles of South America to the steppes of Central Asia. Embracing the concept of preemptive war and unilateral action as cornerstones of national strategy.

These policies may seem like reactions to the changed world confronting America after the Sept. 11 terrorist attacks. But in fact, each one of them—and many other policies now being advanced by the Bush administration—was planned years before the first plane ever struck the doomed Twin Towers.

They are the handiwork of an obscure but influential conservative group called Project for the New American Century, whose members—including Vice President Dick Cheney and Defense Secretary Donald Rumsfeld—now sit at the highest reaches of power. The papers they produced during the 1990s are like a roadmap of the course that America is following—a course that PNAC hopes will lead to an utterly dominant America in world affairs.

PNAC was formed in 1997, with a roster of conservative heavy-hitters, many of whom are now major players in the Bush administration. In addition to Cheney and Rumsfeld, the lineup included Paul Wolfowitz (now deputy defense secretary), Lewis Libby (Cheney's chief of staff), Zalmay Khalilzad (special emissary to Afghanistan), John Bolton (undersecretary of state for arms control), and Elliot Abrams, who was convicted of lying to Congress in the Iran-Contra scandal but was pardoned by George H. W. Bush (now White House director of Middle East policy).

Other influential participants included publisher Steve Forbes, conservative Christian activist Gary Bauer, former Secretary of Education William Bennett, former Vice President Dan Quayle, and Jeb Bush, brother of the president-to-be and now governor of Florida.

PNAC fired its first shot across the bow in 1998, with letters to President Clinton and congressional leaders calling for regime change in Iraq, by force if necessary, and the establishment of a strong U.S. military presence in the region. Then in September 2000, just months before the disputed election that brought George W. Bush to power, the group published a highly detailed, 90-page blueprint for transforming America's military—and the nation's role on the world stage.

The document, "Rebuilding America's Defenses," advocated a series of "revolutions" in national defense and foreign affairs—all of which have come to pass, in a very short time, since the Sept. 11 terrorist attacks.

The measures proposed in PNAC's 2000 report included:

Projecting American dominance with a "worldwide network of forward operating bases"—some permanent, others "temporary access arrangements" as needed for various military interventions—in the Middle East, Asia, and Latin America. These additions to America's already-extensive overseas deployments would act as "the cavalry on the new American frontier"—a frontier that PNAC declared now extended throughout the world.

Withdrawing from arms control treaties to allow for the development of a global missile shield, the deployment of space-based weapons, and the production of a new generation of battlefield nuclear weapons, especially so-called "bunker-busters" for penetrating underground fortifications.

Raising the U.S. military budget to at least 3.8 percent of gross domestic product, with annual increases of tens of billions of dollars each year.

Developing sophisticated new technologies to "control the global commons of cyberspace" by closely monitoring communications and transactions on the Internet.

Pursuing the development of "new methods of attack— electronic, non-lethal, biological . . . in new dimensions, in space, cyberspace, and perhaps the world of microbes."

Developing the ability to "fight and decisively win multiple, simultaneous major theater wars." This means moving beyond the two-war standard of preparedness that has guided U.S. strategy since World War II in order to account for "new realities and potential new conflicts." It lists countries such as Iraq, Iran, Syria, North Korea, and Libya as targets for those potential new conflicts, and urges Pentagon war planners to consider not merely containing them or defeating them in battle, but "changing their regimes."

Oddly enough, although regime change in Iraq was still clearly a priority for PNAC, it had little to do with Saddam Hussein and his brutal policies or his aggressive tendencies. Instead, removing Hussein was tied to the larger goal of establishing a permanent U.S. military presence in the Persian Gulf in order to secure energy supplies and preclude any other power from dominating the vital oil regions of the Middle East and Central Asia.

The PNAC report puts it quite plainly: "The United States has for decades sought to play a more permanent role in Gulf regional security. While the unresolved conflict with Iraq provides the immediate justification, the need for a substantial American force presence in the Gulf transcends the issue of the regime of Saddam Hussein."

Many critics say this is why the Bush administration has offered a constantly shifting menu of rationales for the impending attack on Iraq: because the decision to remove Hussein was taken long ago as part of a larger strategic plan, and has little to do with any imminent threat from the crippled Iraqi regime, which is constantly bombed, partially occupied (with U.S. forces already working in the autonomous Kurdish territories), and now swarming with United Nations inspectors. If the strategic need for the attack "transcends the issue of the regime of Saddam Hussein," then almost any rationale will do.

Perhaps due to the presence of Washington insiders like Cheney and Rumsfeld, the PNAC report recognized that thorny political difficulties could stand in the way of implementing the group's far-reaching designs. Indeed, in one of the most striking and prescient passages in the entire 90-page document, PNAC acknowledged that the revolutionary changes it envisaged could take decades to bring about— unless, that is, the United States was struck by "some catastrophic and catalyzing event—like a new Pearl Harbor."

That new Pearl Harbor did come, of course, in the thunderclap of Sept. 11, 2001. And the PNAC alumni now in government were quick to capitalize on this catalyzing event.

All of the PNAC recommendations listed above were

put into place, with almost no debate from a shellshocked Congress and a populace reeling from the unprecedented assault on American security.

In the very first days following the attack, Rumsfeld urged the Bush Cabinet to make "Iraq a principal target of the first round in the war against terrorism," despite the lack of any proof connecting Baghdad to the terrorist atrocity, according to Bob Woodward's insider account, *Bush at War*.

But Rumsfeld was overruled by Colin Powell, who counseled that "public opinion has to be prepared before a move against Iraq is possible."

The "war on terrorism" was launched initially against Afghanistan, where the Taliban regime was harboring the Saudi terrorist Osama bin Laden and his band of international extremists. The attack on Afghanistan was accompanied by the construction of new American bases and "temporary access arrangements" throughout Central Asia, giving America a military "footprint" in the strategically vital region for the first time.

At the same time, new U.S. forces were dispatched to East Asia, to the Philippines, for example, where just last week American troops were ordered into direct combat against Muslim insurgents, and to South America, to help Colombia fight "narco-terrorists" and to protect that nation's vital oil pipelines.

Meanwhile, at home, military budgets skyrocketed to deal with the "new realities and potential new conflicts." As it had earlier indicated it would, the Bush administration withdrew from the landmark ABM arms control treaty and began construction of missile defense facilities. It provided new funds for the militarization of outer space (dubbed "Full Spectrum Dominance") and the development of "non-lethal" biochemical weapons. Pentagon technicians, led by another convicted Iran-Contra figure, John Poindexter, began the development of Internet data-mining and monitoring technology (which, despite some recent congressional restrictions, continues today).

And the U.S. announced a new nuclear strategy, including the willingness to use tactical nuclear weapons—a move supported by the Republican-led House of Representatives, which approved Pentagon plans to develop the bunker-buster nukes specifically recommended by PNAC. And just this month, Rumsfeld told Congress that he has asked the president for a special waiver that will allow American forces to use non-lethal chemical arms in subduing enemy armies—and enemy populations. The long-standing international treaties banning combat use of chemical weapons have "tangled us up so badly," Rumsfeld testified.

Finally, much of the PNAC philosophy was enshrined as official U.S. policy last September when Bush proclaimed a new National Security Strategy. Bush even adopted some of the same language found in the PNAC reports. He stated that no global rival would be allowed even the "hope of surpassing or equaling the power of the United States" and pledged that America would maintain its "global leadership" through "the unparalleled strength of the United States armed forces and their forward presence" around the world.

Bush pledged the United States to PNAC's cherished principle of preemptive war, saying the nation will act not only against imminent threats but also "against emerging threats before they are fully formed." Bush called this "the path of action—the only path to peace and security." He declared that America would use its power of global leadership to promote the "single sustainable model of national success"—a free enterprise system that Bush describes in some detail, including low taxes, little government regulation of business, and open markets for international investors.

The existence of PNAC and its influence on the Bush administration is not some sinister conspiracy theory. It follows a pattern frequently seen in American history: A group of like-minded people band together in think tanks, foundations, universities, and other institutions, where they lay out their vision for America's future. And when they at last have access to the levers of power, they try to make that vision a reality. In that sense, the PNAC group is not so different from the academics and activists behind Lyndon Johnson's Great Society programs, for example.

What is different now is that the Sept. 11 attacks have given this particular group an unprecedented amount of political capital—not to mention cold, hard federal cash—to put their long-held dreams into practice, virtually without opposition. What is also different is the essential goal of that vision: the establishment of what might almost amount to an American empire.

This empire would be different from the old Roman or British models, of course. It would not entail direct occupation of foreign lands, but instead offer paternal protection and guidance—albeit backed up with strategically placed military bases and "temporary access arrangements" for the inevitable "constabulatory duties" required to enforce PNAC's longed-for "Pax Americana."

However, the intent is not conquest or plunder, but the chance to bring "the single sustainable model of national success" to all the world, to set people, and their markets, free—as long as no "regional or global challenges to America's leadership" arise, of course.

But there will be costs to taking up what Thomas

Donnelly, the principal author of the PNAC blueprint, calls "the free man's burden." Donnelly, a former journalist and legislative aide, wrote in the journal *Foreign Affairs* last year that America should look to its "imperial past" as a guide to its future.

Reviewing *The Savage Wars of Peace*, a pro–American dominance book by journalist Max Boot, Donnelly cites approvingly the "pacification" of the Philippines by American forces in 1898–1900, in which at least 100,000 Filipinos were killed in a bid for independence. He also points to the U.S. Army's success in subduing the Native American tribes in a series of small wars, and, closer to our time, the efficient "constabulatory operation" in Panama, which was invaded by the first President Bush in 1989.

Similar "savage wars of peace"—pacifications, counterinsurgencies, police actions, invasions—will be required to maintain American dominance, says Donnelly.

And here, too, George W. Bush has clearly echoed the thinking of the PNAC members who now surround him in the White House. Speaking at a Republican fund-raiser last August, the president seemed keenly aware of the heavy price in blood and treasure the nation will have to pay to maintain its imperium in the New American Century:

"There's no telling how many wars it will take to secure freedom in the homeland."

He Said It . . .

"Redefining the role of the United States from enablers to keep the peace to enablers to keep the peace from peace-keepers is going to be an assignment."
—quoted in *New York Times*, 1/14/01

"Bring 'em on."
—encouraging Iraqi militants to attack U.S. forces in Iraq, 7/3/03.

ANAGRAMS

George Walker Bush, President of the USA:
The bugger seeks of oil. He's a warped runt.

George W. Bush and Tony Blair:
Beware! Blood-hungry giants!

President George Bush:
Oh! Desert purge begins!

Quiz

Paul Slansky

What did George W. Bush do immediately before announcing the commencement of the war against Iraq?

(a) He winked at Laura and blew her a kiss.
(b) He shook his fist and declared, "I feel good."
(c) He called the Prime Minister of Turkey and said, "I loathe you."
(d) He said, "Let's go kick some Iraqi butt."

Answer: (b)

ANAGRAM

President George Bush:
He gestured! Big person!

Quiz
Paul Slansky

Who explained that the Bush Administration waited until September to push publicly for war with Iraq because, "from a marketing point of view, you don't introduce new products in August"?

(a) Attorney General John Ashcroft
(b) Chief of Staff Andrew Card
(c) Press Secretary Ari Fleischer
(d) National-security adviser Condoleezza Rice.

Answer: (b)

An entry from George W. Bush's journal.

Crazy Eights
from My First Presidentiary
John Warner and Kevin Guilfoile

		George	Jeb
1955	Crazy Eights	25	1
1959	rock/paper/scissors	8	65
1960	"Who-loves-Mom-more" hugging contest	1	0
1962-2000	RISK	0	356
1965	Tic Tac Toe	465 ties	
1974	Beeropoly	48	6
1977	Pong	934	0
1972, 76, 80	Beer Bong Olympics	4	0
1990's	Governor of major state	1 I was first	1
1996	Crash Bandicoot	50	0
1997	Crash Bandicoot 2	345	0
2000	President	I kicked his ass!	

John Pilger wishes to register his objection to the title of this collection. He believes that "it personalises a corrupt system, thereby letting it off the hook. George W Bush is no more hateful than Bill Clinton or indeed Woodrow Wilson, whose Christian fanaticism set in train the American imperialism of which Bush is merely the latest administrator, if an especially dangerous one."

Crime Against Humanity

from *The New Statesman* (4/14/03)

John Pilger

A BBC television producer, moments before he was wounded by an American fighter aircraft that killed 18 people with "friendly fire", spoke to his mother on a satellite phone. Holding the phone over his head so that she could hear the sound of the American planes overhead, he said: "Listen, that's the sound of freedom."

Did I read this scene in *Catch-22*? Surely, the BBC man was being ferociously ironic. I doubt it, just as I doubt that whoever designed the *Observer's* page three last Sunday had Joseph Heller in mind when he wrote the weasel headline: "The moment young Omar discovered the price of war".

These cowardly words accompanied a photograph of an American marine reaching out to comfort 15-year-old Omar, having just participated in the mass murder of his father, mother, two sisters and brother during the unprovoked invasion of their homeland, in breach of the most basic law of civilised peoples.

No true epitaph for them in Britain's famous liberal newspaper; no honest headline, such as: "This American marine murdered this boy's family". No photograph of Omar's father, mother, sisters and brother dismembered and blood-soaked by automatic fire. Versions of the *Observer*'s propaganda picture have been appearing in the Anglo-American press since the invasion began: tender cameos of American troops reaching out, kneeling, ministering to their "liberated" victims.

And where were the pictures from the village of Furat, where 80 men, women and children were rocketed to death? Apart from the *Mirror*, where were the pictures, and footage, of small children holding up their hands in terror while Bush's thugs forced their families to kneel in the street? Imagine that in a British high street. It is a glimpse of fascism, and we have a right to see it.

"To initiate a war of aggression," said the judges in the Nuremberg trial of the Nazi leadership, "is not only an international crime; it is the supreme international crime differing only from other war crimes in that it contains within itself the accumulated evil of the whole." In stating this guiding principle of international law, the judges specifically rejected German arguments of the "necessity" for pre-emptive attacks against other countries.

Nothing Bush and Blair, their cluster-bombing boys and their media court do now will change the truth of their great crime in Iraq. It is a matter of record, understood by the majority of humanity, if not by those who claim to speak for "us". As Denis Halliday said of the Anglo-American embargo against Iraq, it will "slaughter them in the history books". It was Halliday who, as assistant secretary general of the United Nations, set up the "oil for food" programme in

Iraq in 1996 and quickly realised that the UN had become an instrument of "a genocidal attack on a whole society". He resigned in protest, as did his successor, Hans von Sponeck, who described "the wanton and shaming punishment of a nation".

I have mentioned these two men often in these pages, partly because their names and their witness have been airbrushed from most of the media. I well remember Jeremy Paxman bellowing at Halliday on *Newsnight* shortly after his resignation: "So are you an apologist for Saddam Hussein?" That helped set the tone for the travesty of journalism that now daily, almost gleefully, treats criminal war as sport. In a leaked e-mail Roger Mosey, the head of BBC Television News, described the BBC's war coverage as "extraordinary—it almost feels like World Cup football when you go from Um Qasr to another theatre of war somewhere else and you're switching between battles".

He is talking about murder. That is what the Americans do, and no one will say so, even when they are murdering journalists. They bring to this one-sided attack on a weak and mostly defenceless people the same racist, homicidal intent I witnessed in Vietnam, where they had a whole programme of murder called Operation Phoenix. This runs through all their foreign wars, as it does through their own divided society. Take your pick of the current onslaught. Last weekend, a column of their tanks swept heroically into Baghdad and out again. They murdered people along the way. They blew off the limbs of women and the scalps of children. Hear their voices on the unedited and unbroadcast videotape: "We shot the shit out of it." Their victims overwhelm the morgues and hospitals—hospitals already denuded of drugs and painkillers by America's deliberate withholding of $5.4bn in humanitarian goods, approved by the Security Council and paid for by Iraq. The screams of children undergoing amputation with minimal anaesthetic qualify as the BBC man's "sound of freedom".

Heller would appreciate the sideshows. Take the British helicopter pilot who came to blows with an American who had almost shot him down. "Don't you know the Iraqis don't have a fucking air force?" he shouted. Did this pilot reflect on the truth he had uttered, on the whole craven enterprise against a stricken third world country and his own part in this crime? I doubt it. The British have been the most skilled at delusion and lying. By any standard, the Iraqi resistance to the high-tech Anglo-American machine was heroic. With ancient tanks and mortars, small arms and desperate ambushes, they panicked the Americans and reduced the British military class to one of its specialities—mendacious condescension.

The Iraqis who fight are "terrorists", "hoodlums", "pockets of Ba'ath Party loyalists", "kamikaze" and "feds" (fedayeen). They are not real people: cultured and cultivated people. They are Arabs. This vocabulary of dishonour has been faithfully parroted by those enjoying it all from the broadcasting box. "What do you make of Basra?" asked the *Today* programme's presenter of a former general embedded in the studio. "It's hugely encouraging, isn't it?" he replied. Their mutual excitement, like their plummy voices, are their bond.

On the same day, in a *Guardian* letter, Tim Llewellyn, a former BBC Middle East correspondent, pointed us to evidence of this "hugely encouraging" truth—fleeting pictures on Sky News of British soldiers smashing their way into a family home in Basra, pointing their guns at a woman and manhandling, hooding and manacling young men, one of whom was shown quivering with terror. "Is Britain 'liberating' Basra by taking political prisoners and, if so, based on what sort of intelligence, given Britain's long unfamiliarity with this territory and its inhabitants . . . The least this ugly display will do is remind Arabs and Muslims everywhere of our Anglo-Saxon double standards—we can show your prisoners in . . . degrading positions, but don't you dare show ours." Roger Mosey says the suffering of Um Qasr is "like World Cup football". There are 40,000 people in Um Qasr; desperate refugees are streaming in and the hospitals are overflowing. All this misery is due entirely to the "coalition" invasion and the British siege, which forced the United Nations to withdraw its humanitarian aid staff. Cafod, the Catholic relief agency, which has sent a team to Um Qasr, says the standard humanitarian quota for water in emergency situations is 20 litres per person per day. Cafod reports hospitals entirely without water and people drinking from contaminated wells. According to the World Health Organisation, 1.5 million people across southern Iraq are without water, and epidemics are inevitable. And what are "our boys" doing to alleviate this, apart from staging childish, theatrical occupations of presidential palaces, having fired shoulder-held missiles into a civilian city and dropped cluster bombs?

A British colonel laments to his "embedded" flock that "it is difficult to deliver aid in an area that is still an active battle zone". The logic of his own words mocks him. If Iraq was not a battle zone, if the British and the Americans were not defying international law, there would be no difficulty in delivering aid.

There is something especially disgusting about the

lurid propaganda coming from these PR-trained British officers, who have not a clue about Iraq and its people. They describe the liberation they are bringing from "the world's worst tyranny", as if anything, including death by cluster bomb or dysentery, is better than "life under Saddam". The inconvenient truth is that, according to Unicef, the Ba'athists built the most modern health service in the Middle East. No one disputes the grim, totalitarian nature of the regime; but Saddam Hussein was careful to use the oil wealth to create a modern secular society and a large and prosperous middle class. Iraq was the only Arab country with a 90 per cent clean water supply and with free education. All this was smashed by the Anglo-American embargo. When the embargo was imposed in 1990, the Iraqi civil service organised a food distribution system that the UN's Food and Agriculture Organisation described as "a model of efficiency . . . undoubtedly saving Iraq from famine". That, too, was smashed when the invasion was launched.

Why are the British yet to explain why their troops have to put on protective suits to recover dead and wounded in vehicles hit by American "friendly fire"? The reason is that the Americans are using solid uranium coated on missiles and tank shells. When I was in southern Iraq, doctors estimated a sevenfold increase in cancers in areas where depleted uranium was used by the Americans and British in the 1991 war. Under the subsequent embargo, Iraq, unlike Kuwait, has been denied equipment with which to clean up its contaminated battlefields. The hospitals in Basra have wards overflowing with children with cancers of a variety not seen before 1991. They have no painkillers; they are fortunate if they have aspirin.

With honourable exceptions (Robert Fisk; al-Jazeera), little of this has been reported. Instead, the media have performed their preordained role as imperial America's "soft power": rarely identifying "our" crime, or misrepresenting it as a struggle between good intentions and evil incarnate. This abject professional and moral failure now beckons the unseen dangers of such an epic, false victory, inviting its repetition in Iran, Korea, Syria, Cuba, China.

George Bush has said: "It will be no defence to say: 'I was just following orders.'" He is correct. The Nuremberg judges left in no doubt the right of ordinary soldiers to follow their conscience in an illegal war of aggression. Two British soldiers have had the courage to seek status as conscientious objectors. They face court martial and imprisonment; yet virtually no questions have been asked about them in the media. George Galloway has been pilloried for asking the same question as Bush, and he and Tam Dalyell, Father of the House of Commons, are being threatened with withdrawal of the Labour whip.

Dalyell, 41 years a member of the Commons, has said the Prime Minister is a war criminal who should be sent to The Hague. This is not gratuitous; on the prima facie evidence, Blair is a war criminal, and all those who have been, in one form or another, accessories should be reported to the International Criminal Court.

Not only did they promote a charade of pretexts few now take seriously, they brought terrorism and death to Iraq. A growing body of legal opinion around the world agrees that the new court has a duty, as Eric Herring of Bristol University wrote, to investigate "not only the regime, but also the UN bombing and sanctions which violated the human rights of Iraqis on a vast scale". Add the present piratical war, whose spectre is the uniting of Arab nationalism with militant Islam. The whirlwind sown by Blair and Bush is just beginning. Such is the magnitude of their crime.

Sore Winner

from *The New Republic* (5/12/2003)

Peter Beinart

Americans sometimes wonder why so many non-Americans view the United States as a bully. Are they jealous, resentful, irrationally afraid? Perhaps. But there's a simpler explanation for the widespread perception that the United States is vindictive, arrogant, and petty. Under this administration, it's true.

Consider the Bush team's behavior over the past few weeks toward countries that opposed the war in Iraq. Almost as soon as the fighting stopped, the French government started trying to mend fences. Paris abandoned its long-standing opposition to NATO control over the peacekeeping force in Afghanistan. In a surprise concession, and a break with Russia, it agreed to suspend (though not remove) U.N. sanctions on post–Saddam Hussein Iraq. Jacques Chirac warned Syria not to harbor Iraqi officials and telephoned George W. Bush, breaking a months-long silence between the two men. Jean-David Levitte, France's ambassador to the United States, said his government wanted to "turn this bitter page and think positively about what we have to do together."

The Bush administration responded with a high-level meeting to decide how to punish Paris for opposing the war. According to reports in *The New York Times* and *The Washington Post*, the Bushies are considering downgrading France's status at international meetings and bypassing the North Atlantic Council, NATO's governing body, because France is a member. Bush officials noted that when the president attends the G-8 summit in Evian, France, this June, he will stay across the border in Switzerland. No pettiness here.

And it's not only France. President Bush, who famously refused to place a congratulatory phone call to Gerhard Schroeder after he was reelected on an antiwar platform, has not spoken to the German leader yet this year. The White House recently canceled a Bush trip to Ottawa, leading one Canadian academic to tell the *Times* that relations between the two countries were at "the lowest moment since the early 1960s." The United States has pointedly refused to set a date for signing a long-planned free-trade deal with Chile, which refused to use its rotating Security Council seat to back a second resolution authorizing war. (There are also reports, denied by Bush officials, that the United States has slowed talks on a trade deal with Thailand as punishment for its lukewarm stance on the war.) White House Envoy to the Americas Otto Reich recently warned Caribbean countries that their antiwar stance might bring U.S. "consequences." And, in a slap at Mexican President Vicente Fox, the former Bush pal who refused to back the Iraq war, the White House has scrapped this year's Cinco de Mayo celebrations. Pettiness? Perish the thought.

This retaliation isn't just vindictive; it's deeply stupid. First of all, it will hurt Iraq. Andrew Natsios, administrator of the United States Agency for International Development (USAID), recently told "Nightline"'s Ted Koppel that USAID would spend $1.7 billion this year—and not a penny more—to reconstruct Iraq. That's quite an admission, considering that the Council on Foreign Relations has put the cost of rebuilding Iraq at roughly $15 billion per year for the rest of the decade, and the Center for Strategic and Budgetary Assessments has put the cost far higher. (When experts hear Bush officials claim that exports from Iraq's decrepit oil industry will fund the reconstruction, they generally laugh.)

After the first Gulf war, America's allies wrote most of the checks that rebuilt Kuwait. In fact, over and over in recent years—in Bosnia, Kosovo, Afghanistan—the United States has bled to win the war, and its democratic allies have paid to win the peace. It's a formula that needs to be vastly expanded if Iraq is to become a stable, liberal country. But, by doling out postwar snubs and restricting postwar contracts to U.S. firms, the Bush administration is doing its best to ensure that countries such as France, Germany, and Canada don't fork over the money Iraq desperately needs. Tony Blair sees the folly in this. Which is why Britain supports a large U.N. role in post-Saddam Iraq, a role that will give countries that opposed the war the political cover they need to fund Iraqi reconstruction. The White House, however, isn't listening to Blair—after all, even British companies weren't invited to bid for USAID contracts in postwar Iraq.

But the bigger problem isn't the impact of White House score-settling on Iraq; it's the impact on the United States. Key Bush officials—particularly Dick Cheney and Donald Rumsfeld—clearly believe Al Qaeda and Saddam were emboldened in the 1990s by U.S. weakness. Their solution: Show terrorists and dictators that the United States hasn't gone soft; restore some good old-fashioned fear of Uncle Sam.

As an analysis of Saddam, Osama bin Laden, and Kim Jong Il, this makes sense. What has become appallingly clear in recent weeks, however, is that many in the Bush team apply the same logic to independent-minded Western democracies such as France, Germany, Canada, and Chile. The problem with America's relationships with its allies, they seem to feel, is that we don't throw our weight around enough. If we make countries that opposed the war suffer, they'll be more pliant next time around.

But there's a key difference between the way Bashar Al Assad makes decisions and the way Gerhard Schroeder does. It's called democracy. Supporters of the administration train their anger on antiwar leaders. Ask many American conservatives why France opposed the war, and, without missing a beat, they'll say it was because Chirac has a corrupt history with Iraq and feared what the United States might find in the Baghdad archives once Saddam was gone. What they generally overlook is that public opinion in France—and virtually everywhere else in Europe—massively opposed the war. I think those large antiwar majorities were wrong, but they were a response to perceived American arrogance and aggression. As Charles Grant, director of London's Center for European Reform, recently noted to *BusinessWeek*, "In every West European country, polls show that George W. Bush is seen as a greater threat to world peace than Saddam." Europeans ignored Saddam's horrors and identified with Iraq as a small country being pushed around by the United States. That public sentiment led leaders in Europe and in democracies such as Chile, Canada, Mexico, and Turkey to oppose the war. (In the case of Schroeder, a pro-war stance would probably have cost him reelection.)

In other words, governments across the world opposed the Iraq war to appease citizenries angered by perceived U.S. bullying. So now that the war is over—and our military victory gives us a chance to improve America's image—the Bush administration has responded with a fresh round of bullying. Sounds like a winning strategy to me.

Quiz
Paul Slansky

What happened during George W. Bush's first post-election meeting with California's governor-elect, Arnold Schwarzenegger?

(a) Schwarzenegger wondered if the Constitution said anything about whether the Vice-President had to be a natural-born citizen, and joked that it might be time to say, "Hasta la vista, Cheney."

(b) Schwarzenegger explained to Bush that "Bring 'em on!" didn't really work as a catchphrase, because it was inappropriate for a leader to invite an attack on his own troops.

(c) Schwarzenegger said to Bush, "You were governor of a big state," and then asked for some general advice.

(d) They agreed that terrorism was great for both of them, because it made so many Americans feel that their safety depended on giving power to bullies.

Answer: (c)

He Said It . . .

"I understand that the unrest in the Middle East creates unrest throughout the region."
—Washington, DC, 3/13/02

HE GETS
AWAY WITH IT

with quotes from George W. Bush;
quizzes by Paul Slansky;

a cartoon by Toles;

and anagrams

George W. Bush believes he can fool us by saying one thing while he does quite another—and he often succeeds. Some Americans who suffer from his destructive and corrupt policies still believe that he's a decent and compassionate man who cares about them. They're wrong.

> **"I'm the master of low expectations."**
> —Aboard Air Force One, 6/4/03

The media's shameful, kid-gloves treatment of George W. Bush began during the 2000 campaign and continued into his presidency, providing cover for many of his worst policies and clumsiest pratfalls.

W's World
from *What Liberal Media?* (2003)
Eric Alterman

Journalists and presidents, especially Republican presidents, both prefer to portray the media under a mutually self-serving myth as an allegedly cynical, heartless, anti-authoritarian left-wing animal. The president and his people play along because the myth brings them as much sympathy from the largely inattentive public as it does from their fiercely ideological supporters. The idea of an indefatigable press, rumbling for trouble, also connects to the right's apparently universal wellsprings of self-pity and imagined persecution. The media enjoys the stereotype because it ennobles their self-image and disputes their own fears of being stenographers in the unstoppable spin machine. Of course, the stereotypes against which the myth is written are not always true of every reporter or every member of every administration. But those reporters who make careers of breaking through barriers of incessant spin and media to establish themselves as independent voices are few and far between. Journalists, like most people, go along to get along.

The result of this mutually reinforcing myth is that presidents are popular with the media and the public until proven otherwise. The campaign over, they are given a "clean slate" regardless of what happened on the campaign trail. As David Carr, former correspondent for Inside.com, now a *New York Times* media reporter, observed shortly after the Florida debacle, "In order to tee themselves up for the coming four years, reporters have to find a way to turn the nincompoop they bashed throughout the election into something resembling the leader of the free world. That's a bit of a lift with George W., who doesn't exactly send out statesman-like vibes." Carr went on to observe, however, that Bush had done himself a favor by choosing to vacation in Florida with his father and brother Gov. Jeb Bush immediately after the Supreme Court decision, thereby offering the media the opportunity to indulge in a plethora of Henry V allusions. "The rules of the press pool dictate that you are never close enough to engage in genuine dialogue with the target," Carr wryly noted, "so reporters can't ask impertinent questions like, 'Shouldn't you be back in Texas with your hospitalized daughter?' Or, 'Doesn't this seem like a good time to be catching up on Cliff Notes for World Peace?' "

The Osric-like coverage goes beyond the widely acknowledged "honeymoon period" and can last indefinitely—as it did under John Kennedy—or at least until it is in the interest of one side or the other to upset this cozy arrangement. (The Clinton presidency was the exception that proved the rule in this regard. His honeymoon occurred during the campaign.) Presidents and the media enjoy an informal agreement entitling every occupant of the Oval Office a certain amount of hero worship merely for being there.

The White House and the media need one another in order to be successful in their jobs. The White House depends on the media to make its case to the public; the media need the White House to fill their airtime and news columns. It is in neither side's interest to push the other too far. But the administration maintains a major advantage in the power calculus, particularly if it can maintain a united front, because it is singular and the media are plural. This is where the Bush people truly excelled. As David Brooks complained of the Bush crew: "They don't leak. They don't gossip. They don't stab each other in the back. ... It's a nightmare." Unity allows administration spinners to divide and conquer. The top members of the Clinton administration, for instance, treated leaks as a form of personal therapy, detailing every single screw-up and then some to almost any reporter who would listen. Josh Micah Marshall noted in the neoliberal *Washington Monthly,* "Even successful legislative battles like the 1993 budget reconciliation bill—the measure that set the stage for declining deficits and the groundwork for sustained growth—were drawn out with an almost masochistic relish and always left within a hair's breadth of failure. The Bush guys do none of this. As a result, they exude a kind of cocky confidence, and competence regardless of whether it's authentic." There's just no story there, beyond the boring policy stuff, which most reporters prefer to leave to wonks at the Brookings Institution.

Unlike Republicans, reporters just about never play as a team. The authors of ABC's *The Note* write, with considerable justice, "If we could change one thing about Washington journalism, we would ask White House reporters to not help out the press secretary, in contradiction to the public interest, by interrupting a colleague who is trying to elicit important information or establish a non-answer for the public record." Moreover, the Bush team plays a kind of hardball that the Clintonians were never able to master. When *Houston Chronicle* reporter Bennett Roth asked press spokesman Ari Fleischer about underage drinking by the president's daughters, Fleischer informed him, Don Corleone–style, that his question had been "noted in the building." The implication was clear to all: More such unfriendly questions and Roth would be cut off, unable to do his job, and useless to his employers. The outcries of solidarity from Roth's colleagues in the press corps in the face of this public threat would not have disturbed the sleep of a napping newborn.

Clinton proved the exception to the rule, but in truth, much of what the media reports about the White House, any White House, is little more than spoonfed public relations pabulum. When NBC contracts to broadcast, more than a year into George W. Bush's first term, a special hour about an alleged day in the life of the "real" *West Wing*, Tom Brokaw must claim the broadcast will not be "an infomercial for the White House" to defend his own reputation and that of his network's news division. But of course it is. Otherwise, the profoundly image-conscious and message-disciplined Bush White House communications operation would not allow it to take place. Certainly no one at NBC News is sufficiently naïve to labor under the illusion that

Karen Hughes and Karl Rove were about to leave their president's public image at the mercy of a bunch of journalists and network executives. Rather, the deal works as follows: NBC agrees to provide twelve camera crews along with an invaluable hour of prime-time air; the White House provides the "actors" playing idealized versions of themselves, going about their business in exactly the manner we all wish they would. Maybe the conditions of this deal are spelled out on paper somewhere; maybe not. It really doesn't matter. Like the actors playing wrestlers in a WWF grudge match, all the players understand the ground rules before anyone enters the "ring."

NBC has offered this same deal to all recent presidents, but few managed the opportunity as well as Rove and Hughes for Bush. For the January 2002 production, the White House came up with what the *New York Times* noted was "an unusually full schedule of public activities for Mr. Bush's day on camera." Instead of the usual single public event per day, NBC's "typical day" included: a meeting with labor leaders at Teamster headquarters; a bill-signing ceremony in the East Room; a photo-op with the president of Lithuania in the Oval Office; a 4-H award presentation in the Roosevelt Room, and finally, a cocktail party for Republican members of Congress in the White House residence. In addition, viewers saw the famously relaxed-about-work George W. Bush working out in the gym, stopping in on a meeting of his Council on Bioethics, and walking into the famed Situation Room for a top-secret national security briefing. White House spokesman Ari Fleischer insisted that the perspective offered to NBC viewers was "as real as it gets." This was clearly nonsense, as even Hughes admitted, since NBC's "typical" day contained "an education component" that was added at the last minute to round out the administration's domestic pitch. One cocktail party guest, New York Representative Peter King, later described the experience as similar to attending the Academy Awards.

Like most lucky people, George W. Bush helped make his own luck, particularly with regard to charming the media. Consider the coverage of the brief China "crisis" of spring 2001: A U.S. spy plane collided with a Chinese fighter, killing its pilot. I dwell a bit on this now-forgotten incident to demonstrate that Bush, the unelected conservative Republican, received extremely indulgent coverage from the so-called "liberal media" long before September 11. In fact, Bush's behavior was often examined with little more critical distance than I employ when critiquing the art projects of my four-year-old daughter.

Recall that the Chinese held twenty-four U.S. soldiers and demanded an apology. Even the hint of such an admission would have likely crippled the Clinton administration among punditocracy hawks, who dominate all discourse in times of perceived military threat. But the Bush administration managed to say "sorry" to the Commies and paid almost no political price whatever. Moreover it succeeded in manipulating the media to the point where its incompetence was portrayed as heroism, despite the amazingly thin gruel it offered up in support of this case. The *Washington Post,* for instance, presented readers with a twenty-six-paragraph, front-page analysis of Bush's talks, replete with inside anecdotes designed to make the president appear somehow simultaneously in charge and comfortable with delegation of details.

Never mind that no *Post* reporters were present during the events they so breathlessly reported as fact. To question the official version of events handed out by the president's propaganda machine is apparently no longer part of the job description. As Josh Marshall pointed out of this incident, "Sadly enough, such articles are too often the result of an unspoken, almost Faustian arrangement. Official sources provide the essential inside details and reporters then regurgitate the official line, giving up their independence and skepticism for a quotation from the boss that he might or might not actually have said."

Bush actually screwed up quite a few times during this crisis, but you'd be hard-pressed to learn this from the press coverage. For no apparent reason, and perhaps without even knowing what he was doing, the president appeared on ABC's *Good Morning America* to announce that the United States would do "whatever it took" to defend Taiwan if China attacked. This pledge, long desired by the Taiwanese, had been specifically avoided by every U.S. president since the beginning of the nation's "two-China" policy in 1979, owing to the concern that it might embolden Taiwan's rulers to start a war. Various administration spokespeople tried to pretend that that U.S. policy remained unchanged, but nobody really knew for certain whether Bush was trying to change it or even if he understood it in the first place. But the Chinese surely noted it in *their* buildings. "This shows that the United States is drifting further down a dangerous road," averred Foreign Ministry spokeswoman Zhang Qiyue. "It will . . . harm peace and stability across the Taiwan Strait, and further damage U.S.-China relations." Even so, Bush enjoyed oceans of SCLM slack. As an April 13 *Los Angeles Times* news analysis put it, "Bush Gets High Marks for Low-Key Approach." Just about the only vocal criticism to be found in the media during this period came from the right. Writing in the *Weekly Standard,* for instance, Robert Kagan and William Kristol thundered about "the profound national humiliation that President Bush has brought upon the United States." With his hemming and hawing, they complained, "President Bush has revealed weakness. And he has revealed fear. . . . The American capitulation will also embolden others around the world who have watched this crisis carefully to see the new administration's mettle tested." (To read these words in hindsight would be to see an implication that perhaps Mr. bin Laden was among those "emboldened" by the administration's "capitulation." And we can imagine that exactly such an accusation might have been leveled by these very authors—if it had been President Clinton "capitulating.")

In addition to papering over Bush's still-unexplained decision to shoot off his mouth, what was almost as odd in the incident with China was the White House spinmeisters' strategy for portraying George W. Bush as "deeply involved" in the solution of the crisis. The word was that while Bush let the diplomatic team do its own work, he stayed abreast of things by peppering his staff with questions. These were dutifully relayed by the media, and consisted of the following: "Do the members of the crew have Bibles? Why don't they have Bibles? Can we get them Bibles? Would they like Bibles?" He also inquired, "Are they getting any exercise?" The *Guardian*'s Jonathan Freedland wondered why in the world Bush's aides wished to "confirm the satirists' caricature of Bush as a 'know-nothing fundamentalist fitness freak.' " But it worked.

That the elite media—much less the SCLM—chose to celebrate the performance of an unelected president who apparently lacked the intellectual curiosity to learn the finer points of his job may inspire a bit of cognitive dissonance on the part of those seeking to make sense of American politics, but there it is. And it would prove the rule, rather than the exception, of Bush's pre–September 11 presidency. Frank Bruni, whose issueless *New York Times* coverage of Bush's campaign had proven so indulgent that it inspired Bush to frequently tell Bruni that he "loved" him, continued the kind of reporting on Bush's presidency that would earn any politician's affection. On a trip to Mexico where Bush met with that nation's new president, Vincente Fox, Bruni professed to spy Bush's boots "peek[ing] out mischievously" from beneath his trousers. He did not elaborate as to what variety of mischief said boots might have in mind. On a later trip to Europe, Bruni seemed to find absolutely everything Bush said or did to be unspeakably fabulous. The reporter noted that upon meeting Tony Blair, Bush "broke into a smile, indulged a mischievous impulse and offered him a greeting less formal than the ones the British leader usually hears. 'Hello, Landslide!' Mr. Bush shouted out. It was a reference—an irreverent, towel-snapping one at that—to Mr. Blair's recent re-election, and it recalled the playful dynamic . . . when he cracked during a news conference that he and Mr. Blair liked the same brand of toothpaste." It was odd to say the least. Past *New York Times* coverage of presidential missions abroad have not, by and large, celebrated "irreverent towel-snapping" comments to leaders of other nations. The "playful dynamic" of the toothpaste "crack" might just as easily have been termed a "doltish" or "obnoxious frat-boy" crack. And, since Tony Blair actually did win his job in a landslide, it's hard to see just what is so "irreverent" about pointing it out. (Now if the Prime Minister had greeted the unelected/court-appointed Bush as "Landslide," I might have laughed.)

Ari Fleischer could not have scripted the *Times* presidential coverage more generously. "Still pumped up," according to Bruni, Bush professed to detect "a willingness for countries to think differently and to listen to different points of view," though he offered no evidence. Finally, speaking of Bush's strange meeting with Vladimir Putin, Bruni still felt compelled to celebrate the apparently amazing fact that Bush refrained from drooling all over himself at a state dinner. "Rarely," Bruni wrote of Bush and Putin, "have the two nations' leaders so surpassed the limited expectations of their meeting." Nowhere, however, does the reporter bother to explain how rarely; whose expectations; how limited; limited by whom to what? (Beware, dear reader, of the passive voice.) Bush did indeed, after a fashion, surpass people's expectations on this trip when he claimed to be able to see into the soul of Russian President Vladimir Putin and find a friend, though one suspects that Bruni did not have the viewers of the Psychic Friends Network in mind when parceling out his praise. Perhaps it's a bit unfair to focus so closely on Bruni, as clearly this is the kind of coverage his editors deemed appropriate and the *Times* wanted. Indeed, why else assign to cover the presidency a man whose book-length pre-election examination of the man and his work informs readers of the exact number of seconds that George and Laura Bush danced at each of their nine Inaugural Balls but contains nary a word about what the president intended to do the next day when he finally sat down at his desk to get to work?

The kid-gloves approach to Bush puzzled many, as the SCLM myth had grown into a monolith by the time of the Bush presidency. Early in the administration, *Washington Post* White House correspondent John Harris felt compelled to explain the apparent contradiction in the form of a kind of public mea culpa. "The truth is," he wrote, "this new president has done things with relative impunity that would have been huge uproars if they had occurred under Clinton. Take it from someone who made a living writing about those uproars." He made the following comparison:

> Take the recent emergency landing of a U.S. surveillance plane in China. Imagine how conservatives would have reacted had Clinton insisted that detained military personnel were not actually hostages, and then cut a deal to get the people (but not the plane) home by offering two "very sorrys" to the Chinese, while also saying that he had not apologized. What is being hailed as Bush's shrewd diplomacy would have been savaged as "Slick Willie" contortions.
>
> Try to recall this major news story during Clinton's first 100 days: Under pressure from Western senators, the president capitulated on a minor part of his 1993 budget deal, grazing fees on ranchers using federal lands. A barrage of coverage had an unmistakable subtext: Clinton was weak and excessively political and caved to special interests. Bush has made numerous similar concessions on items far more central to the agenda he

campaigned on, such as deemphasizing vouchers in his education plan and conceding that his tax cut will be some $350 billion smaller than he proposed. For the most part these repositionings are being cast as shrewd rather than servile. Do you suppose there would have been an uproar under Clinton if Democrats had been rewarding donors with special closed-door briefings by Cabinet secretaries? The *New York Times* reported the other day that GOP donors received just such a briefing with Health and Human Services Secretary Tommy Thompson as thanks for their efforts. Far from an uproar, the story has had only a faint echo. Clinton's "donor maintenance" coffees led to a year of congressional inquiries.

Harris could not note, because it had not yet happened, that while the Clinton fund-raisers were front-page/lead-the-news-every-night affairs for years, they were chicken feed compared to Bush's uncovered fund-raising efforts. Federal Election Commission records demonstrated that between January 2001 and mid-August 2002, for instance, despite a four-month moratorium he set following September 11, George W. Bush raised $100.03 million. Clinton, for all the outrage he generated, raised just $38.7 million during the same period of his first term. That's more than two-and-a-half times as much money with a tiny fraction of the number of unflattering stories written. (Howard Kurtz termed Clinton officials' defenses of these efforts as attempts "to defend the indefensible.")

The media, as we have seen, turned parsing Bill

Clinton's words into an obsession, hoping to catch the president in a lie about whether or not he had sex with Monica Lewinsky. "We have our own set of village rules," complained David Gergen, editor at large at *U.S. News and World Report*, who had worked for both Ronald Reagan and Richard Nixon, as well as Clinton, and therefore could not claim to be a stranger to official mendacity. "The deep and searing violation took place when he not only lied to the country, but co-opted his friends and lied to them." Chris Matthews explained that, "Clinton lies knowing that you know he's lying. It's brutal and it subjugates the person who's being lied to. I resent deeply being constantly lied to." Pundit George Will, a frequent apologist for Reagan, went so far as to insist that the president's "calculated, sustained lying has involved an extraordinarily corrupting assault on language, which is the uniquely human capacity that makes persuasion, and hence popular government, possible. Hence the obtuseness of those who say Clinton's behavior is compatible with constitutional principles, presidential duties and republican ethics."

As president, however, George W. Bush regularly lied about far more significant matters relating to both war and peace, and the media could barely bring themselves to make note of them. In fact, in a front-page story devoted to this very topic in the *Washington Post*, the writer, Dana Milbank, could not bring himself (or was not allowed by his editors) to pen the words, "The president lied." Instead, readers were treated to complicated linguistic circumlocutions like: Bush's statements represented an "embroidering of key assertions." Presidential assertions were clearly "dubious, if not wrong." The president's "rhetoric has taken some flights of fancy . . . taken some liberties . . . omitted qualifiers," and "simply outpace[d] the facts." But "Bush lied"? Never.

ANAGRAMS

George Walker Bush, President of the United State of America:
Damn! Result is garbage, takes pretender to White House office.

George Walker Bush, President of the USA:
Pretender grabs White House:
—flag use ok?

Quiz
Paul Slansky

How did Canadian Prime Minister Jean Chrétien respond when his spokeswoman called George W. Bush a "moron"?

(a) He pulled out a photograph of Bush reading an upside-down book and said, "She may have a point."
(b) He said, "She calls me Cretin. Do you see me getting all upset?"
(c) He accepted her resignation and said that Bush is "not a moron at all."
(d) He held up a photograph of Bush looking through binoculars with the lens caps still on and said, "You tell me, does he look like a moron?"

Answer: (c)

ANAGRAM

Bush Administration:
Duh . . . I ain't bin so smart.

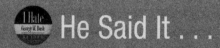

He Said It . . .

"And there's no doubt in my mind, not one doubt in my mind, that we will fail."
—Washington, DC, 10/4/01

This account of GWB's early days in the White House is a parody.

West Winging It:
George Bush's First Hundred Days
from The Modern Humorist (11/8/00)

January 20: Take oath to uphold the honor and dignity of the office of President of the United States. Nudge Rehnquist, ask what he's wearing under that dress.

January 23: Award Presidential Medal of Freedom to Ralph Nader.

January 24: Help Alec Baldwin pack.

January 30: Memo to Jeb: in your face, Poindexter!

January 31: Get people working on stuff.

February 3: Bring Democrats and Republicans together.

February 4: Bring peanut butter and chocolate together.

February 5: Unite North, South Dakota; North, South Carolina; New, Old Mexico.

February 7: Get loaded, fail to name designated driver, don't tell anyone for 25 years, usher in an era of personal responsibility.

February 9: Change pitch and tone of Washington to something that will only annoy dogs.

February 12: Replace Affirmative Action with Affirmative Access. Replace Medicare with Medicool. Replace Department of Transportation with Department of Fantabulation.

February 18: Offer Jeb important cabinet position—possibly Secretary of My Asshole.

February 20: Invite NRA executives into Oval Office to write legislation, play Madden NFL 2001.

March 1–March 31: Halftime!

April 1: Plant flowers in Rose Garden: daisies?

April 7: Give younger workers the opportunity to responsibly invest a portion of their payroll taxes in eBay bids.

April 9: Open up Yellowstone National Park, the Appalachian Trail and Chappaqua, NY, for oil exploration.

April 12: State dinner for Emperor Akihito of Japan. Do "Samurai Dry Cleaner" sketch.

April 15: Replace soft bigotry of low expectations with hard nougat of candy.

April 18: Try Oval Office fellatio (once or twice; what's the harm?).

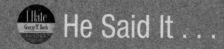

He Said It . . .

"You're free. And freedom is beautiful. And, you know, it'll take time to restore chaos and order—order out of chaos. But we will."
—Washington, DC, April 13, 2003

Security Concerns
from *Harper's Weekly Review* (10/21/03)
Roger D. Hodge

President George W. Bush traveled to Asia and gave a speech in Manila comparing Iraq to the Philippines, a former U.S. colony that was "liberated" from Spain in 1898 and occupied for 48 years. Bush said that the Philippines, which he called "the oldest democracy in Asia" should be seen as the model for a new democratic Iraq, and then quickly left the country because of security concerns.

Quiz
Paul Slansky

Who is John Brady Kiesling?

(a) The Christian conservative who withdrew his nomination to Bush's Advisory Council on H.I.V. and AIDS after it became known that he referred to AIDS as "the gay plague."

(b) The commentator who said, referring to Bush's plan to eliminate taxes on stock dividends, "This isn't even trickle-down economics. It's mist-down economics."

(c) The State Department diplomat whose resignation letter said, "Until this Administration it had been possible to believe that by upholding the policies of my president I was also upholding the interests of the American people and the world. I believe it no longer."

(d) The White House aide, known for his calm disposition, about whom Karl Rove said, "I'd use the word 'sweet' if it didn't make me look odd."

Answer: (c)

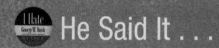

He Said It . . .

"My administration has been calling upon all the leaders in the—in the Middle East to do everything they can to stop the violence, to tell the different parties involved that peace will never happen."
—Crawford, TX, 8/13/01

"This foreign policy stuff is a little frustrating."
—NY Daily News, 4/23/02

Homeland Insecurity
from *The Nation* (9/22/03)
David Corn

In early August, as George W. Bush was beginning a monthlong working vacation at his Texas ranch, he told reporters, "We learned a lesson on September the 11th, and that is, our nation is vulnerable to attack. And we're doing everything we can to protect the homeland."

Everything we can. That was a bold statement. But it was not accurate. Indeed, it was one of the more galling misrepresentations of his presidency, for crucial areas of homeland security—ports, chemical plants, emergency response, biodefense—are not getting adequate attention or funding. Two years after the nation's vulnerability was exposed, at the price of 3,000 lives, everything is *not* being done. Why? Because, in part, of the Administration's strategic and ideological assumptions.

Here are a few recent and troubling indicators:

- In June a Council on Foreign Relations task force—headed by former Republican Senator Warren Rudman—issued a report noting that "the United States remains dangerously ill-prepared to handle a catastrophic attack on American soil." According to this study, most fire departments are short on radios and breathing apparatuses and only 10 percent are able to handle a building collapse. Police departments across the country lack the protective gear necessary to secure a site struck by a weapon of mass destruction. Most public health labs do not have the personnel or equipment to respond to a chemical or biological attack. The task force estimated the country will fall $98.4 billion short in funding needs for emergency responders over the next five years. And a study released by RAND in August essentially seconded the CFR task force report.

- According to a June report by the Century Foundation's Homeland Security Project, "State and local governments have complained that they cannot improve their preparedness without more money. The federal government promised $3.5 billion in aid, but only $2.2 billion has been made available so far."

• In June Homeland Security Secretary Tom Ridge announced about $300 million in funding for improving security at ports. The Coast Guard, though, has estimated that $1 billion is needed. Ports throughout the United States have asked for nearly that much to finance 1,380 security projects. "Any and all funding is helpful, but [the money provided] really doesn't even come close to what is needed," Maureen Ellis, a spokeswoman for the American Association of Port Authorities, told the *Baltimore Sun*. Stephen Flynn, a retired Coast Guard commander and a senior fellow at the Council on Foreign Relations, worked on a CFR terrorism study that preceded the report on emergency responders. He complains that the government has spent only about $10 million on security for maritime containers. "We've invested so little to date," he warns.

• A review conducted by the Partnership for Public Service, a nonpartisan good-government outfit, found that the government is drastically short on medical and scientific employees for its biodefense programs.

• In late July the Transportation Security Administration asked Congress for permission to reduce its air marshal program by 20 percent, at a time when the Bush Administration was issuing warnings about hijackings. To counter the ensuing bad PR, Ridge declared there would be no reduction in the program. (He later announced its reassignment to another agency.) Since the TSA has received nearly $1 billion less than it had requested, it has been forced to implement other program cuts.

• The Bush Administration and Congress have yet to take action to enhance security at chemical plants. More than 100 facilities nationwide handle chemicals that, if released, could threaten a million or so people, and there are 15,000 other chemical sites to worry about. Yet no security standards have been established for these sites. The White House is supporting Senate legislation that would require chemical firms to conduct their own security assessments and has opposed a more stringent bill by Democratic Senator Jon Corzine that would grant Homeland Security the power to order specific security measures. Almost a year ago, Ridge himself said that voluntary industry efforts would not be sufficient to protect the public. Yet that's the Administration's approach. In March the General Accounting Office declared that "the federal government has not comprehensively assessed the chemical industry's vulnerabilities to terrorist attacks." Six months later, no such assessment has been made.

So Bush is wrong. Not all steps are being taken. His White House has even opposed certain security measures. For example, the Administration has blocked legislation being pushed by Representative Edward Markey, a Massachusetts Democrat, that would require automated or manual screening of cargo shipped on passenger planes. Currently, most of this cargo—unlike travelers' checked baggage—is not screened. The House approved Markey's amendment by a 278-to-146 vote. But the Senate—pressed by the aviation industry and the White House—has ignored the issue. On the larger front, in July, Senator Robert Byrd and other Senate Democrats proposed adding $1.75 billion to the Department of Homeland Security budget—including about $730 million for first-responders, $602 million for port and transportation security, $100 million for examining air cargo and $80 million for handling chemical weapons attacks. The package was defeated on a mostly party-line vote, 50 to 43.

The question is not whether the government under Bush is adopting all obvious precautions, but why it is *not*. Rudman says the answer is "very complicated" and that it is difficult to push "a government this size to move with alacrity." He notes that the government has yet to conduct a comprehensive examination of the nation's domestic vulnerabilities and needs. "With national defense," he explains, "if there's a crisis and a need for two more air wings, the Pentagon does a requirement study and presents a case. We haven't had a requirement study on homeland security. Until that's done, you tend to throw money at it helter-skelter." Shouldn't reviewing the risks and creating a plan be a fundamental post-9/11 responsibility of the Administration? "I'm not being critical of anyone," Rudman adds. Not explicitly, that is.

No doubt, bureaucratic sclerosis is partly to blame. The Department of Homeland Security has been so busy merging various entities into one superagency that it's a wonder it can find the time to put out color-coded terrorism alerts. And one good example of bureaucratic lack of imagination was provided (unintentionally) by Al Martinez-Fonts, a top Ridge aide, in an interview for PBS's *NOW With Bill Moyers* this past March. Asked why the government had not moved to regulate security at chemical plants, he replied that on September 11 "it was not chemical plants that were blown up."

But the continuing gaps in domestic security are also a result of the biases of Bush and his lieutenants. "We're responding dysfunctionally to the new threat environment," Flynn comments. As an example, he notes, "There is no means of saying, Will one dollar on missile defense be better spent on preparing the local public-health-system response to a bioattack? If there is a smallpox attack, it could be equivalent to a nuclear-missile attack." What inhibits rational planning and management, he asserts, is that the Bush Administration has an ideological objection to a strong federal role in domestic security. Much of the crucial infrastructure—perhaps more than 90 percent of it—is in the hands of commercial interests. If the Administration were serious about making Americans more secure, it would have to intervene forcefully in the private sector, which would likely raise industry costs. "The Administration has made it very clear it is not interested in regulation," Flynn says. "So much of homeland security then ends up being just a talkfest." Flynn characterizes the White House attitude this way: "Homeland security costs too much money and involves too much government, so we have to go straight to the source"— that is, the terrorists. "It's a seductive argument," he adds. "We can deal with the problem over there and don't have to conduct assessments and make investments here. . . . But we'll never succeed at eliminating these problems at the source and go around the planet and identify every possible angry young man who has the means to do what happened on 9/11. It's a fool's game."

Ivo Daalder, a Brookings Institution scholar, agrees, noting that a conceptual obsession hinders the Bush Administration's domestic security actions: "These guys think that if you get rid of the tyrants, you solve the problem." The Bush crowd, he suggests, really does—to an extent—consider the true source of evildoing to be not Al Qaeda and other on-the-ground terrorists but regimes that supposedly back them, even if the evidence does not support this position. "We analysts and commentators have not understood the centrality of rogue states in their worldview," Daalder maintains. "The mindset is, We cannot defend every target, so it's better to go after those who would do us harm." And that means zeroing in on Saddam Hussein and other rogue leaders. Both Flynn and Daalder point to the basic numbers to make their case. The Pentagon is receiving close to $400 billion; Homeland Security is in the mid-twenties range. "It's pretty clear," Daalder says. "One is fifteen times more important than the other."

Is Bush, with his less-than-everything approach, assuming any political risk? "People cannot believe," Flynn remarks, "that no one in the federal government has inspected security plans for chemical plants or that the US Coast Guard has conducted only ten port-vulnerability studies in the past year." If there is another terrorist assault on the country, he adds, "there will be an accounting, and people will be shocked by how little has been done. The American people will be enraged." Maybe not, says Daalder. "The American people cannot fathom that Bush isn't doing everything. Another attack could either reinforce the notion that he's trying to protect the country or that he's incapable. I used to think this was a golden issue for Democrats: tax cuts for 1 percent of Americans or security for 100 percent. But the American people cannot comprehend that a US President is not doing all that is necessary and not spending all the money that needs to be spent."

Bush might get away with misrepresenting his Administration's efforts. But more important than whether he ends up paying for his hollow promises is the possibility that thousands of Americans, if not more, might bear the cost of his negligence and false assurances.

Quiz
Paul Slansky

What was Tom Ridge, the Secretary of Homeland Security, talking about when he referred to an "unusual series of events"?

(a) George W. Bush giving a speech that was designed to raise his poll numbers, followed by a plunge in those numbers to their lowest point yet.
(b) Warnings about increased hijacking threats, accompanied by stories about budget cuts that would mean fewer air marshals on commercial flights.
(c) General John P. Abazaid referring to the ongoing fighting in Iraq as a "classical guerrilla-type campaign" after Donald Rumsfeld had spent two weeks insisting that the attacks on U.S. troops were anything but guerrilla-like.
(d) George W. Bush acknowledging that no link had ever been found connecting Saddam Hussein and the 9/11 attacks, even as Vice-President Dick Cheney continued to insinuate that such a link existed.

Answer: (b)

He Said It . . .

"I've coined new words, like 'misunder-standing' and 'Hispanically.'"
—Radio/Television Correspondents Association dinner, 3/29/01

"These terrorist acts and, you know, the responses have got to end in order for us to get the framework—the groundwork—not framework, the groundwork to discuss a framework for peace, to lay the—all right."
—on George Mitchell's report on Middle East peace, Crawford, TX, 8/13/01

He Said It . . .

"She was neat."
—on meeting Queen Elizabeth II, in *Times of London*, 7/18/01

"The thing that's important for me is to remember what's the most important thing."
—St. Louis, MO, 2/20/01

Quiz
Paul Slansky

True or False:

Barring an economic miracle, George W. Bush will end his first term as the first President since Jimmy Carter to oversee a net loss in employment.

Answer: False. He'll be the first President since Herbert Hoover.

Quiz
Paul Slansky

Match the observation about Bush with the columnist who made it.

1. "There is some kind of anger in the man, a hostility that sometimes seems barely under control—as if he were, in street parlance, being 'dissed.'"
2. "He has the unreflective person's immunity from irony, that great killer of intellectual passion. Ask him to reconcile his line on Iraq with his line on North Korea and he just gets irritated."
3. "Mr. Bush's greatest weakness is that too many people, at home and abroad, smell that he's not really interested in repairing the world."
4. "A steady hand on the helm in high seas, a knowledge of where we must go and why, a resolve to achieve safe harbor. More and more this presidency is feeling like a gift."
5. "This is the worst president ever. He is the worst president in all of American history."

    (a) Peggy Noonan
    (b) Helen Thomas
    (c) Richard Reeves
    (d) Thomas L. Friedman
    (e) Michael Kinsley

Answers: 1(c), 2(e), 3(d), 4(a), 5(b)

This piece offended conservatives. The truth hurts.

Mad About You

from *The New Republic* (9/29/03)

Jonathan Chait

I hate President George W. Bush. There, I said it. I think his policies rank him among the worst presidents in U.S. history. And, while I'm tempted to leave it at that, the truth is that I hate him for less substantive reasons, too. I hate the inequitable way he has come to his economic and political achievements and his utter lack of humility (disguised behind transparently false modesty) at having done so. His favorite answer to the question of nepotism—"I inherited half my father's friends and all his enemies"—conveys the laughable implication that his birth bestowed more disadvantage than advantage. He reminds me of a certain type I knew in high school—the kid who was given a fancy sports car for his sixteenth birthday and believed that he had somehow earned it. I hate the way he walks—shoulders flexed, elbows splayed out from his sides like a teenage boy feigning machismo. I hate the way he talks—blustery self-assurance masked by a pseudo-populist twang. I even hate the things that everybody seems to like about him. I hate his lame nickname-bestowing—a way to establish one's social superiority beneath a veneer of chumminess (does anybody give their boss a nickname without his consent?). And, while most people who meet Bush claim to like him, I suspect that, if I got to know him personally, I would hate him even more.

There seem to be quite a few of us Bush haters. I have

friends who have a viscerally hostile reaction to the sound of his voice or describe his existence as a constant oppressive force in their daily psyche. Nor is this phenomenon limited to my personal experience: Pollster Geoff Garin, speaking to *The New York Times*, called Bush hatred "as strong as anything I've experienced in 25 years now of polling." Columnist Robert Novak described it as a "hatred . . . that I have never seen in 44 years of campaign watching."

Yet, for all its pervasiveness, Bush hatred is described almost exclusively as a sort of incomprehensible mental affliction. James Traub, writing last June in *The New York Times Magazine*, dismissed the "hysteria" of Bush haters. Conservatives have taken a special interest in the subject. "Democrats are seized with a loathing for President Bush— a contempt and disdain giving way to a hatred that is near pathological—unlike any since they had Richard Nixon to kick around," writes Charles Krauthammer in *Time* magazine. "The puzzle is where this depth of feeling comes from." Even writers like David Brooks and Christopher Caldwell of *The Weekly Standard*—the sorts of conservatives who have plenty of liberal friends—seem to regard it from the standpoint of total incomprehension. "Democrats have been driven into a frenzy of illogic by their dislike of George W. Bush," explains Caldwell. "It's mystifying," writes Brooks, noting that Democrats have grown "so caught up in their own victimization that they behave in ways that are patently not in their self-interest, and that are almost guaranteed to perpetuate their suffering."

Have Bush haters lost their minds? Certainly some have. Antipathy to Bush has, for example, led many liberals not only to believe the costs of the Iraq war outweigh the benefits but to refuse to acknowledge any benefits at all, even freeing the Iraqis from Saddam Hussein's reign of terror. And it has caused them to look for the presidential nominee who can best stoke their own anger, not the one who can win over a majority of voters—who, they forget, still like Bush. But, although Bush hatred can result in irrationality, it's not the *product* of irrationality. Indeed, for those not ideologically or personally committed to Bush's success, hatred for Bush is a logical response to the events of the last few years. It is not the slightest bit mystifying that liberals despise Bush. It would be mystifying if we did not.

One reason Bush hatred is seen as inherently irrational is that its immediate precursor, hatred of Bill Clinton, really did have a paranoid tinge. Conservatives, in retrospect, now concede that some of the Clinton haters were a little bit nutty. But they usually do so only in the context of declaring that Bush hatred is as bad or worse. "Back then, [there were] disapproving articles—not to mention armchair psychoanalysis—about Clinton-hating," complains Byron York in a *National Review* story this month. "Today, there appears to be less concern." Adds Brooks, "Now it is true that you can find conservatives and Republicans who went berserk during the Clinton years, accusing the Clintons of multiple murders and obsessing how Vince Foster's body may or may not have been moved. . . . But the Democratic mood is more pervasive, and potentially more self-destructive."

It's certainly true that there is a left-wing fringe of Bush haters whose lurid conspiracy-mongering neatly parallels that of the Clinton haters. York cites various left-wing websites that compare Bush to Hitler and accuse him of murder. The trouble with this parallel is, first, that this sort of Bush-hating is entirely confined to the political fringe. The most mainstream anti-Bush conspiracy theorist cited in York's piece is Alexander Cockburn, the ultra-left, rabidly anti-Clinton newsletter editor. Mainstream Democrats have avoided delving into Bush's economic ties with the bin Laden family or suggesting that Bush invaded Iraq primarily to benefit Halliburton. The Clinton haters, on the other hand, drew from the highest ranks of the Republican Party and the conservative intelligentsia. Bush's solicitor general, Theodore Olson, was involved with *The American Spectator*'s "Arkansas Project," which used every conceivable method—including paying sources—to dig up dirt from Clinton's past. Mainstream conservative pundits, such as William Safire and Rush Limbaugh, asserted that Vince Foster had been murdered, and GOP Government Reform Committee Chairman Dan Burton attempted to demonstrate this theory forensically by firing a shot into a dummy head in his backyard.

A second, more crucial difference is that Bush is a far more radical president than Clinton was. From a purely ideological standpoint, then, liberal hatred of Bush makes more sense than conservatives' Clinton fixation. Clinton offended liberals time and again, embracing welfare reform, tax cuts, and free trade, and nominating judicial moderates. When budget surpluses first appeared, he stunned the left by reducing the national debt rather than pushing for more spending. Bush, on the other hand, has developed into a truly radical president. Like Ronald Reagan, Bush crusaded for an enormous supply-side tax cut that was anathema to liberals. But, where Reagan followed his cuts with subsequent measures to reduce revenue loss and restore some progressivity to the tax code, Bush proceeded to execute two *additional* regressive tax cuts. Combined with his stated desire to eliminate virtually all taxes on capital income and to privatize Medicare and Social Security, it's not much of an exaggeration to say that Bush would like to roll back the federal government to something resembling its pre–New Deal state.

And, while there has been no shortage of liberal hysteria over Bush's foreign policy, it's not hard to see why it scares so many people. I was (and remain) a supporter of the war in Iraq. But the way Bush sold it—by playing upon the public's erroneous belief that Saddam had some role in the September 11 attacks—harkened back to the deceit that preceded the Spanish-American War. Bush's doctrine of preemption, which reserved the right to invade just about any nation we desired, was far broader than anything he needed to validate invading a country that had flouted its truce agreements for more than a decade. While liberals may be overreacting to Bush's foreign policy decisions—remember their fear of an imminent invasion of Syria?—the president's shifting and dishonest rationales and tendency to paint anyone who disagrees with him as unpatriotic offer plenty of grounds for suspicion.

It was not always this way. During the 2000 election, liberals evinced far less disdain for Bush than conservatives did for Al Gore. As *The New York Times* reported on the eve of the election, "The gap in intensity between Democrats and Republicans has been apparent all year." This "passion gap" manifested itself in the willingness of many liberals and leftists to vote for Ralph Nader, even in swing states. It became even more obvious during the Florida recount, when a December 2000 ABC News/*Washington Post* poll showed Gore voters more willing to accept a Bush victory than vice-versa, by a 47 to 28 percent margin. "There is no great ideological chasm dividing the candidates," retiring Democratic Senator Pat Moynihan told the *Times.* "Each one has his prescription-drugs plan, each one has his tax-cut program, and the country obviously thinks one would do about as well as the other."

Most Democrats took Bush's victory with a measure of equanimity because he had spent his campaign presenting himself as a "compassionate conservative"—a phrase intended to contrast him with the GOP ideologues in Congress—who would reduce partisan strife in Washington. His loss of the popular vote, and the disputed Florida recount, followed by his soothing promises to be "president of all Americans," all fed the widespread assumption that Bush would hew a centrist course. "Given the circumstances, there is only one possible governing strategy: a quiet, patient, and persistent bipartisanship," intoned a *New Yorker* editorial written by Joe Klein.

Instead, Bush has governed as the most partisan president in modern U.S. history. The pillars of his compassionate-conservative agenda—the faith-based initiative, charitable tax credits, additional spending on education—have been abandoned or absurdly underfunded. Instead, Bush's legislative strategy has revolved around wringing out narrow, party-line votes for conservative priorities by applying relentless pressure to GOP moderates—in one case, to the point of driving Vermont's

James Jeffords out of the party. Indeed, when bipartisanship shows even the slightest sign of life, Bush usually responds by ruthlessly tamping it down. In 2001, he convinced GOP Representative Charlie Norwood to abandon his long-cherished patients' bill of rights, which enjoyed widespread Democratic support. According to a *Washington Post* account, Bush and other White House officials "met with Norwood for hours and issued endless appeals to party loyalty." Such behavior is now so routine that it barely rates notice. Earlier this year, a column by Novak noted almost in passing that "senior lawmakers are admonished by junior White House aides to refrain from being too chummy with Democrats."

When the September 11 attacks gave Bush an opportunity to unite the country, he simply took it as another chance for partisan gain. He opposed a plan to bolster airport security for fear that it would lead to a few more union jobs. When Democrats proposed creating a Department of Homeland Security, he resisted it as well. But later, facing controversy over disclosures of pre–September 11 intelligence failures, he adopted the idea as his own and immediately began using it as a cudgel with which to bludgeon Democrats. The episode was telling: Having spent the better part of a year denying the need for any Homeland Security Department at all, Bush aides secretly wrote up a plan with civil service provisions they knew Democrats would oppose and then used it to impugn the patriotism of any Democrats who did—most notably Georgia Senator Max Cleland, a triple-amputee veteran running for reelection who, despite his support for the war with Iraq and general hawkishness, lost his Senate race thanks to an ugly GOP ad linking him to Osama bin Laden.

All this helps answer the oft-posed question of why liberals detest Bush more than Reagan. It's not just that Bush has been more ideologically radical; it's that Bush's success represents a breakdown of the political process. Reagan didn't pretend to be anything other than what he was; his election came at the crest of a twelve-year-long popular rebellion against liberalism. Bush, on the other hand, assumed office at a time when most Americans approved of Clinton's policies. He triumphed largely because a number of democratic safeguards failed. The media overwhelmingly bought into Bush's compassionate-conservative facade and downplayed his radical economic conservatism. On top of that, it took the monomania of a third-party spoiler candidate, plus an electoral college that gives disproportionate weight to GOP voters—the voting population of Gore's blue-state voters exceeded that of Bush's red-state voters—even to bring Bush close enough that faulty ballots in Florida could put him in office.

But Bush is never called to task for the radical disconnect between how he got into office and what he has done since arriving. Reporters don't ask if he has succeeded in "changing the tone." Even the fact that Bush lost the popular vote is hardly ever mentioned. Liberals hate Bush not because he has succeeded but because his success is deeply unfair and could even be described as cheating.

It doesn't help that this also happens to be a pretty compelling explanation of how Bush achieved his station in life. He got into college as a legacy; his parents' friends and political cronies propped him up through a series of failed business ventures (the founder of Harken Energy summed up his economic appeal thusly: "His name was George Bush"); he obtained the primary source of his wealth by selling all his Harken stock before it plunged on bad news, triggering an inconclusive Securities Exchange Commission insider-trading investigation; the GOP establishment cleared a path for him through the primaries by showering him with a political war chest of previously unthinkable size; and conservative justices (one appointed by his father) flouted their own legal principles—adopting an absurdly expansive federal role to enforce voting rights they had never even conceived of before—to halt a recount that threatened to put his more popular opponent in the White House.

Conservatives believe liberals resent Bush in part because he is a rough-hewn Texan. In fact, they hate him because they believe he is *not* a rough-hewn Texan but rather a pampered frat boy masquerading as one, with his pickup truck and blue jeans serving as the perfect props to disguise his plutocratic nature. The liberal view of Bush was captured by *Washington Post* (and former *TNR*) cartoonist Tom Toles, who once depicted Bush being informed by an adviser that he "didn't hit a triple. You were born on third base." A puzzled Bush replies, "I thought I was born at my beloved hardscrabble Crawford ranch," at which point his subordinate reminds him, "You bought that place a couple years ago for your presidential campaign."

During the 1990s, it was occasionally noted that conservatives despised Clinton because he flouted their basic values. From the beginning, they saw him as a product of the 1960s, a moral relativist who gave his wife too much power. But what really set them off was that he cheated on his wife, lied, and got away with it. "We must teach our children that crime does not pay," insisted former California Representative and uber-Clinton hater Bob Dornan. "What kind of example does this set to teach kids that lying like this is OK?" complained Andrea Sheldon Lafferty, executive director of the Traditional Values Coalition.

In a way, Bush's personal life is just as deep an affront to the values of the liberal meritocracy. How can they teach their children that they must get straight A's if the president slid through with C's—and brags about it!—and then, rather than truly earning his living, amasses a fortune through crony capitalism? The beliefs of the striving, educated elite were expressed, fittingly enough, by Clinton at a meeting of the Aspen Institute last month. Clinton, according to *New York* magazine reporter Michael Wolff, said of the Harken deal that Bush had "sold the stock to buy the baseball team which got him the governorship which got him the presidency." Every aspect of Bush's personal history points to the ways in which American life continues to fall short of the meritocratic ideal.

But perhaps most infuriating of all is the fact that liberals do not see their view of Bush given public expression. It's not that Bush has been spared from any criticism—far from it. It's that certain kinds of criticism have been largely banished from mainstream discourse. After Bush assumed office, the political media pretty much decided that the health of U.S. democracy, having edged uncomfortably close to chaos in December 2000, required a cooling of overheated passions. Criticism of Bush's policies—after a requisite honeymoon—was fine. But the media defined any attempt to question Bush's legitimacy as out-of-bounds. When, in early February, Democratic National Committee Chairman Terry McAuliffe invoked the Florida debacle, *The Washington Post* reported it thusly: "Although some Democratic leaders have concluded that the public wants to move past the ill will over the post-election maneuvering that settled the close Florida contest, McAuliffe plainly believes that with some audiences—namely, the Democratic base of activists he was addressing yesterday—a backward-looking appeal to resentment is for now the best way to motivate and unite an often-fractious party." (This was in a *news* story!) "It sounds like you're still fighting the election," growled NBC's Tim Russert on "Meet the Press." "So much for bipartisanship!" huffed ABC's Sam Donaldson on "This Week."

Just as mainstream Democrats and liberals ceased to question Bush's right to hold office, so too did they cease to question his intelligence. If you search a journalistic database for articles discussing Bush's brainpower, you will find something curious. The idea of Bush as a dullard comes up frequently—but nearly always in the context of knocking it down. While it's described as a widely held view, one can find very few people who will admit to holding it. Conservatives use the theme as a taunt—if Bush is so dumb, how come he keeps winning? Liberals, spooked, have concluded that calling Bush dumb is a strategic mistake. "You're not going to get votes by assuming that, as a party, you're a lot smarter than the voters," argued Democratic Leadership Council President

Bruce Reed last November. "Casting Bush as a dummy also plays into his strategy of casting himself as a Texas common man," wrote *Washington Post* columnist E. J. Dionne in March 2001.

Maybe Bush's limited brainpower hasn't hampered his political success. And maybe pointing out that he's not the brightest bulb is politically counterproductive. Nonetheless, however immaterial or inconvenient the fact may be, it remains true that Bush is just not a terribly bright man. (Or, more precisely, his intellectual incuriosity is such that the effect is the same.) On the rare occasions Bush takes an extemporaneous question for which he hasn't prepared, he usually stumbles embarrassingly. When asked in July whether, given that Israel was releasing Palestinian prisoners, he would consider releasing famed Israeli spy Jonathan Pollard, Bush's answer showed he didn't even know who Pollard is. "Well, I said very clearly at the press conference with Prime Minister [Mahmoud] Abbas, I don't expect anybody to release somebody from prison who'll go kill somebody," he rambled. Bush's unscripted replies have caused him to accidentally change U.S. policy on Taiwan. And, while Bush's inner circle remains committed to the pretense of a president in total command of his staff, his advisers occasionally blurt out the truth. In the July issue of *Vanity Fair*, Richard Perle admitted that, when he first met Bush, "he didn't know very much."

While liberals have pretty much quit questioning Bush's competence, conservatives have given free rein to their most sycophantic impulses. Some of this is Bush's own doing—most notably, his staged aircraft-carrier landing, a naked attempt to transfer the public's admiration for the military onto himself (a man, it must be noted, who took a coveted slot in the National Guard during Vietnam and who then apparently declined to show up for a year of duty). Bush's supporters have spawned an entire industry of hagiographic kitsch. You can buy a twelve-inch doll of Bush clad in his "Mission Accomplished" flight suit or, if you have a couple thousand dollars to spend, a bronze bust depicting a steely-eyed "Commander-in-Chief" Bush. *National Review* is enticing its readers to fork over $24.95 for a book-length collection of Bush's post–September 11, 2001, speeches—any and all of which could be downloaded from the White House website for free. The collection recasts Bush as Winston Churchill, with even his most mundane pronouncements ("Excerpted Remarks by the President from Speech at the Lighting of the National Christmas Tree," "Excerpted Remarks by the President from Speech to the Missouri Farmers Association") deemed worthy of cherishing in bound form. Meanwhile, the recent Showtime pseudo-documentary "DC 9/11" renders the president as a Clint Eastwood figure, lording over a cringing Dick Cheney and barking out such implausible lines as "If some tinhorn terrorist wants me, tell him to come on over and get me. I'll be here!"

Certainly Clinton had his defenders and admirers, but no similar cult of personality. Liberal Hollywood fantasies—"The West Wing," *The American President*—all depict imaginary presidents who pointedly lack Clinton's personal flaws or penchant for compromise. The political point was more to highlight Clinton's deficiencies than to defend them.

The persistence of an absurdly heroic view of Bush is what makes his dullness so maddening. To be a liberal today is to feel as though you've been transported into some alternative universe in which a transparently mediocre man is revered as a moral and strategic giant. You ask yourself why Bush is considered a great, or even a likeable, man. You wonder what it is you have been missing. Being a liberal, you probably subject yourself to frequent periods of self-doubt. But then you conclude that you're actually not missing anything at all. You decide Bush is a dullard lacking any moral constraints in his pursuit of partisan gain, loyal to no principle save the comfort of the very rich, unburdened by any thoughtful consideration of the national interest, and a man who, on those occasions when he actually does make a correct decision, does so almost by accident.

There. That feels better.

An I Hate George W. Bush *Timeline:*
1946–2004

Nate Hardcastle

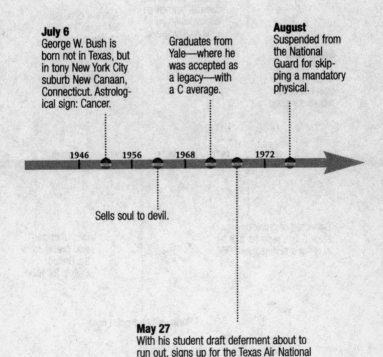

July 6
George W. Bush is
born not in Texas, but
in tony New York City
suburb New Canaan,
Connecticut. Astrolog-
ical sign: Cancer.

Graduates from
Yale—where he
was accepted as
a legacy—with
a C average.

August
Suspended from
the National
Guard for skip-
ping a mandatory
physical.

1946   1956   1968   1972

Sells soul to devil.

May 27
With his student draft deferment about to
run out, signs up for the Texas Air National
Guard and is accepted despite a long
waiting list of applicants with higher test
scores.

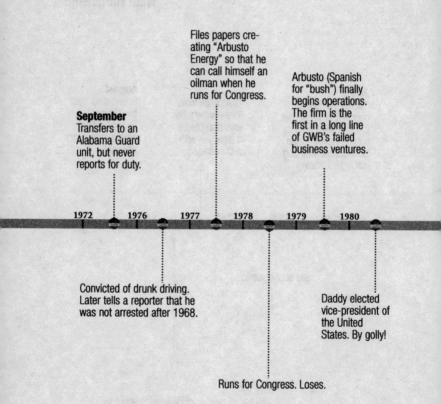

September
Transfers to an Alabama Guard unit, but never reports for duty.

Files papers creating "Arbusto Energy" so that he can call himself an oilman when he runs for Congress.

Arbusto (Spanish for "bush") finally begins operations. The firm is the first in a long line of GWB's failed business ventures.

1972   1976   1977   1978   1979   1980

Convicted of drunk driving. Later tells a reporter that he was not arrested after 1968.

Daddy elected vice-president of the United States. By golly!

Runs for Congress. Loses.

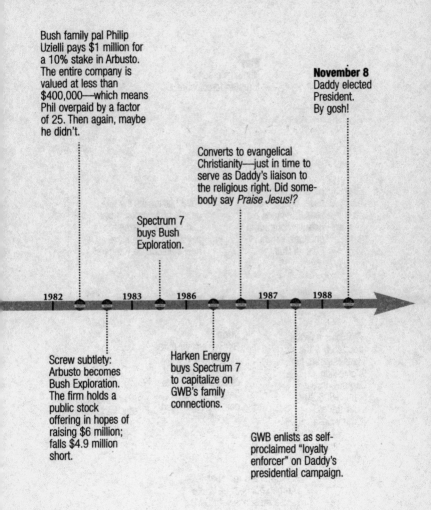

Bush family pal Philip Uzielli pays $1 million for a 10% stake in Arbusto. The entire company is valued at less than $400,000—which means Phil overpaid by a factor of 25. Then again, maybe he didn't.

November 8
Daddy elected President. By gosh!

Converts to evangelical Christianity—just in time to serve as Daddy's liaison to the religious right. Did somebody say *Praise Jesus!?*

Spectrum 7 buys Bush Exploration.

1982   1983   1986   1987   1988

Screw subtlety: Arbusto becomes Bush Exploration. The firm holds a public stock offering in hopes of raising $6 million; falls $4.9 million short.

Harken Energy buys Spectrum 7 to capitalize on GWB's family connections.

GWB enlists as self-proclaimed "loyalty enforcer" on Daddy's presidential campaign.

AN *I HATE GEORGE W. BUSH* TIMELINE

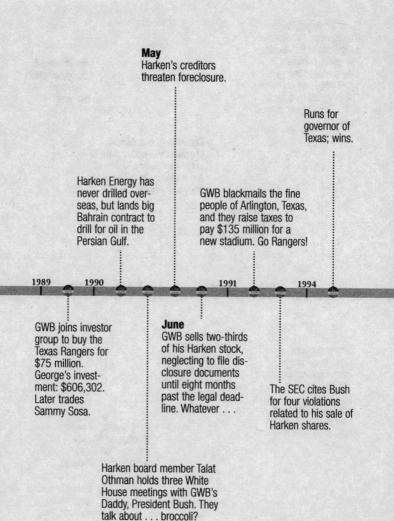

May
Harken's creditors
threaten foreclosure.

Runs for
governor of
Texas; wins.

Harken Energy has
never drilled over-
seas, but lands big
Bahrain contract to
drill for oil in the
Persian Gulf.

GWB blackmails the fine
people of Arlington, Texas,
and they raise taxes to
pay $135 million for a
new stadium. Go Rangers!

1989   1990   1991   1994

GWB joins investor
group to buy the
Texas Rangers for
$75 million.
George's invest-
ment: $606,302.
Later trades
Sammy Sosa.

June
GWB sells two-thirds
of his Harken stock,
neglecting to file dis-
closure documents
until eight months
past the legal dead-
line. Whatever . . .

The SEC cites Bush
for four violations
related to his sale of
Harken shares.

Harken board member Talat
Othman holds three White
House meetings with GWB's
Daddy, President Bush. They
talk about . . . broccoli?

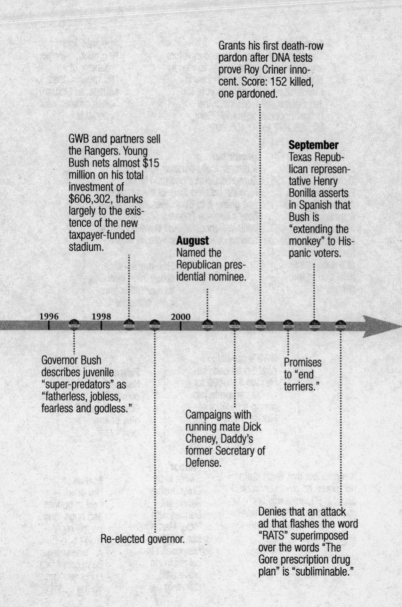

Grants his first death-row pardon after DNA tests prove Roy Criner innocent. Score: 152 killed, one pardoned.

GWB and partners sell the Rangers. Young Bush nets almost $15 million on his total investment of $606,302, thanks largely to the existence of the new taxpayer-funded stadium.

September
Texas Republican representative Henry Bonilla asserts in Spanish that Bush is "extending the monkey" to Hispanic voters.

August
Named the Republican presidential nominee.

1996   1998   2000

Governor Bush describes juvenile "super-predators" as "fatherless, jobless, fearless and godless."

Promises to "end terriers."

Campaigns with running mate Dick Cheney, Daddy's former Secretary of Defense.

Re-elected governor.

Denies that an attack ad that flashes the word "RATS" superimposed over the words "The Gore prescription drug plan" is "subliminable."

AN *I HATE GEORGE W. BUSH* TIMELINE

November
Thousands of African-American voters are illegally denied the right to vote in Florida; thousands of Palm Beach County Jewish Democrats vote for . . . *Pat Buchanan*? GWB loses the national popular vote to Al Gore, 50,999,897 to 50,456,002.

Appoints John Negroponte, former organizer of Nicaraguan death squads, as United States ambassador to the U.N.

December
A disgracefully partisan vote by the Supreme Court stops the Florida recount, robbing Gore of the presidency and giving it to Bush. Historians please note: Clarence Thomas, Antonin Scalia, William Rehnquist, Anthony Kennedy and Sandra Day O'Connor vote for Bush.

October
First debate with Al Gore; Bucknell linguistics professor Robert Beard points out that Bush speaks at a sixth-grade level during the debate.

First day in office: orders nine new worker protection rules postponed.

2000

2001

GWB's campaign pays Enron and Halliburton $15,400 for use of corporate jets during a recount of Florida votes.

February
Names fellow oilman Dick Cheney head of new energy task force.

It comes out that Bush during his tenure as governor worked about six hours a day and spent approximately 15 minutes reviewing each death-penalty case.

January
Sworn in by Chief Justice Rehnquist. Dances with Ricky Martin in front of Lincoln Memorial. Lincoln spins in grave (still spinning).

March
Unveils draconian budget and huge (and hugely regressive) tax cuts. An aide reveals Bush spent five hours working on the budget.

Announces that he will break his campaign promise to seek regulation of carbon dioxide. Adds that he isn't convinced global warming is real.

Proposes dropping random salmonella tests for ground beef in school lunches; the idea is withdrawn after public protest.

Says his tax cut is the best way to deal with high energy costs.

August
Gives speech to National Urban League: "An equal society begins with an equally excellent schools."

Opposes international plan to encourage non-polluting energy.

Announces human stem-cell research policy that seems to allow the research but effectively bans it.

July
Admits the budget surplus might disappear.

May
Displays ignorance of basic U.S. strategic policy and a reckless disregard of diplomacy, asserting that the U.S. would do "whatever it took" to defend Taiwan if China attacked the island. *Bring 'em on!*

April
U.S. withdraws from the Kyoto Protocol on global climate change. Bush: "We will not do anything that harms our economy, because first things first are the people who live in America."

Takes month-long vacation on environmentally correct pseudo-ranch in Crawford, Texas.

42% of his 189 appointments to federal office served in Daddy's administration.

Gives the military its biggest budget increase since Reagan.

AN *I HATE GEORGE W. BUSH* TIMELINE

Announces plan to withdraw from the 1972 Antiballistic Missile Treaty.

415,000 people lose their jobs. Fortunately, most of them are not Republicans and did not contribute to GWB's presidential campaign.

September
Planes hijacked by bin Laden's followers crash into the World Trade Center and the Pentagon. Bush disappears for most of the day.

The Miami Herald finds that Al Gore probably received more votes in Florida than George Bush.

October
Congress passes the Orwellian USA Patriot Act. Bush notes that the law will prevent "more atrocities in the hands of the evil ones."

2001

Receives warnings that Osama bin Laden plans to hijack airplanes in the U.S.

The Bush administration announces that it won't veto destructive mining projects on public land.

Signs executive order allowing the government to try terrorism suspects by military tribunal.

Days after the terrorist attacks, Bush's administration begins formulating plans to use them as a pretext to invade Iraq.

November
Signs a legally dubious executive order blocking the public from seeing 68,000 pages of Ronald Reagan's presidential papers. This action reduces the risk of revelations that could hurt Daddy and his friends, including current Administration officials.

Notes that the disappearance of the $1.2 trillion budget surplus is "incredibly positive news" because it will force the government to resist overspending.

February
GWB's first State of the Union address: labels Iran, Iraq and North Korea an "axis of evil."

April
Senate kills Bush's plan to open the Arctic National Wildlife Refuge to oil exploration.

January
Faints after choking on a pretzel while watching football.

Announces "doctrine" stating that the U.S. reserves the right to attack any country for more or less any reason.

December
Helps kill an international agreement to limit tobacco advertising.

Professed free-marketer GWB places illegal tariffs on imported steel to score political points.

2002

Enron—poster company for corporate corruption, which has contributed more to Bush's campaigns than any other entity—files for bankruptcy. Thousands of employees lose their retirement savings.

Signals Stevie Wonder by smiling and waving.

July
Asks Congress to raise federal debt ceiling before the government runs out of money.

March
A Texas organization reveals that 43 Bush "Pioneers" (donors of $100,000 or more) have received ambassadorships and other government appointments.

May
Makes conversation with Brazil's President: "Do you have blacks too?"

Despite mounting budget deficits, pursues another massive tax cut for the wealthy and goes after $48 billion more for the military.

AN *I HATE GEORGE W. BUSH* TIMELINE

September
Asserts that Saddam Hussein could be six months away from developing nuclear weapons. Cites two reports as evidence. The reports are based on information from 1998 or earlier.

December
U.N. weapons inspectors begin the process of finding no Iraqi weapons of mass destruction.

August
Takes another month-long vacation at his environmentally correct but incredibly barren and hot—in short, hell-like—ranch in Crawford, Texas.

Refers to Saddam as "a guy that tried to kill my dad at one time."

Chooses convicted Iran-Contra conspirator Eliot Abrams to direct Middle Eastern affairs at the White House.

2002

Announces "Healthy Forests" initiative—to allow more logging in national forests.

Cancels federal reporting of mass layoffs—on Christmas Eve.

October
The International Atomic Energy Agency disputes Bush's statement that Iraq could develop a nuclear bomb within six months.

GWB names celebrated statesman and alleged war criminal Henry Kissinger to lead a commission to investigate the September 11 attacks.

Asserts that Saddam could attack the U.S. "on any given day." Makes the following assertion without blushing: "Neither the United States of America nor the world community of nations can tolerate deliberate deception and offensive threats on the part of any nation, large or small."

March
The House of Representatives strips the word "French" from its cafeteria menus.

Lands on an aircraft carrier wearing a military jumpsuit with "Commander in Chief" written on the back, and stands under a banner reading "Mission Accomplished" to declare that major combat operations in Iraq are over.

January
Claims in the State of the Union address that Iraq recently has sought to buy uranium in Africa.

April
Signs an executive order to keep more government documents secret.

June
Lies to Polish journalists: "We found the weapons of mass destruction."

2003

February
UN weapons inspectors complain that intelligence tips from the U.S. are "garbage after garbage after garbage."

July
"Bring 'em on": Invites Iraqi dissidents to attack U.S. soldiers.

Orders invasion of Iraq. Gives up sweets.

Signs a bill allowing the government to borrow unprecedented sums, then signs a new tax cut that could save Dick Cheney $100,000.

May
Signs a proclamation making May 1 "Loyalty Day."

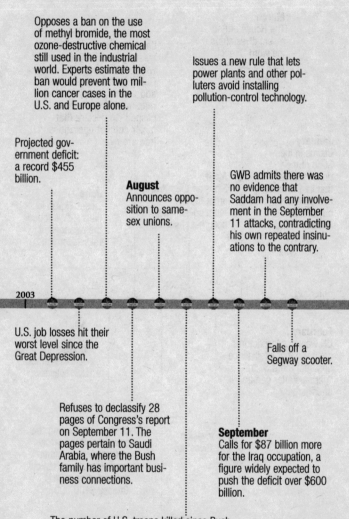

Opposes a ban on the use of methyl bromide, the most ozone-destructive chemical still used in the industrial world. Experts estimate the ban would prevent two million cancer cases in the U.S. and Europe alone.

Issues a new rule that lets power plants and other polluters avoid installing pollution-control technology.

Projected government deficit: a record $455 billion.

August
Announces opposition to same-sex unions.

GWB admits there was no evidence that Saddam had any involvement in the September 11 attacks, contradicting his own repeated insinuations to the contrary.

2003

U.S. job losses hit their worst level since the Great Depression.

Falls off a Segway scooter.

Refuses to declassify 28 pages of Congress's report on September 11. The pages pertain to Saudi Arabia, where the Bush family has important business connections.

September
Calls for $87 billion more for the Iraq occupation, a figure widely expected to push the deficit over $600 billion.

The number of U.S. troops killed since Bush declared victory on the U.S.S. *Abraham Lincoln* exceeds the number killed during the war. Bush avoids soldiers' funerals, in order not to be associated politically with the deaths he has caused.

The Justice Department begins investigating whether the Bush White House leaked the name of undercover CIA agent Valerie Plame to punish her husband—administration critic and former ambassador Joseph Wilson.

Despite Bush's statements to the contrary, Press Secretary Scott McClellan admits that the White House produced the "Mission Accomplished" banner that hung on the U.S.S. *Abraham Lincoln*.

Visits troops in Iraq; poses for photographs holding a picture-perfect roast turkey. Pretends to serve American soldiers, who actually eat turkey from nearby steam trays.

Nobel Prize–winning economist George Akerlof describes the Bush budget as "a form of looting."

Travels to Great Britain with an entourage of 650 people, including five personal chefs.

The independent commission investigating the September 11 attacks threatens to subpoena White House documents after Bush and company refuse to turn them over.

December
Repeals illegal tariffs on imported steel.

Brother Neal Bush admits that while in Thailand he accepted the sexual favors of strange women who knocked on his door; says he doesn't know whether they were prostitutes.

October
Head CIA weapons inspector David Kay issues a report saying the inspectors have found no unconventional weapons. Bush claims that the report justifies the invasion.

November
Signs a bill outlawing a rare abortion procedure called "intact dilation and extraction"—a step toward outlawing abortion altogether.

AN *I HATE GEORGE W. BUSH* TIMELINE

Claims there's no difference between weapons of mass destruction and weapons programs.

Announces plans to build a space station on the moon and send astronauts to Mars—a plan that could mean big profits for the likes of Halliburton, Lockheed Martin and Boeing. Promises to invest $750 million during each of the next five years—but experts say the amount is ridiculously small given the task. NASA decides to stop maintenance on the Hubble Space Telescope—its most scientifically valuable asset—in order to make room for the new initiatives.

Signs Medicare prescription-drug bill to boost drug-company profits over protests from senior citizens.

January
God tells Pat Robertson that Bush will be reelected.

Worried that trouble in Iraq could hurt Bush's reelection campaign, his Administration asks the U.N. for help with Iraq's elections.

2003   2004

Announces plans to let companies buy and sell rights to release mercury into the environment. Ignores the EPA decision that doing so would violate the Clean Air Act.

The Mars idea doesn't poll well; Bush ignores it in his State of the Union address. He claims inspectors have found "weapons of mass destruction–related program activities," whatever that means.

A federal judge says Bush's overturning of Clinton's ban on snowmobiles in Yellowstone was "politically driven."

February
Interviewed by Tim Russet: Asserts "good momentum" on jobs, offers more fuzzy deficit math, and waffles on his shaky National Guard record.

Former Bush Treasury Secretary Paul O'Neill releases a book, called *The Price of Loyalty*. He describes Bush during Cabinet meetings as "a blind man in a room full of deaf people," and reports that Bush during the first weeks of his presidency begin looking for reasons to invade Iraq.

Acknowledgments

Many people made this anthology.

At Thunder's Mouth Press and Avalon Publishing Group:
Thanks to Will Balliett, Maria Fernandez, Linda Kosarin, Dan O'Connor, Neil Ortenberg, Paul Paddock, Susan Reich, David Riedy, Michelle Rosenfield, Simon Sullivan, Mike Walters, and Don Weise for their support, dedication and hard work.

I am especially grateful to Nate Hardcastle, who did most of the research for this book, participated fully in all editorial decisions, created the George W. Bush timeline that appears on page 361, chased down rights and sorted out other assorted problems. This is his book, too. Any errors or omissions are his fault.

At the Portland Public Library in Portland, Maine:
The librarians helped collect books from around the country.

Finally, I am grateful to the writers and artists whose work appears in this book.

Permissions

Bibliography

Alterman, Eric. "Bush Lies, Media Swallows." Originally published in *The Nation*, November 5, 2002.

Alterman, Eric. *What Liberal Media? The Truth about Bias and the News.* New York: Basic Books, 2003.

Baker, Kevin. "We're in the Army Now." Originally published by *Harper's*, November 2003.

Beinart, Peter. "Sore Winner." Originally published by *The New Republic*, May 12, 2003.

Brooks, Renana. "A Nation of Victims." Originally published by *The Nation*, June 30, 2003.

Chait, Jonathan. "Mad About You." Originally published by *The New Republic*, September 29, 2003.

Conason, Joe. "Where's the Compassion?" Originally published by *The Nation*, August 28, 2003.

Corn, David. "Homeland Insecurity." Originally published by *The Nation*, September 22, 2003.

Floyd, Chris. "American Dominance." Originally published by *The Bergen Record*, February 23, 2003.

Frank, Thomas. "Get Rich or Get Out." Originally published by *Harper's*, June 2003.

Greider, William. "Rolling Back the 20th Century." Originally published by *The Nation*, May 12, 2003.

Hertsgaard, Mark. "Trashing the Environment." Originally published by *The Nation*, February 3, 2003.

Ivins, Molly. *Bushwhacked! Life in George W. Bush's America.* New York: Random House, 2003.

Manjoo, Farhad. "To the Cronies Go the Spoils." Originally published by Salon.com, www.salon.com, October 9, 2003.

The Modern Humorist. "West Winging It: George W. Bush's First Hundred Days." Originally published by *The Modern Humorist*, www.modernhumorist.com.

Ohanian, Susan. "Bush Flunks Schools." Originally published by *The Nation*, November 13, 2003.

Peretz, Martin. "Audit This." Originally published by *The New Republic*, July 22, 2002.

Pilger, John. "Crime Against Humanity." Originally published by *The New Statesman*, April 14, 2003.

Pizzo, Stephen. "Hiding the Truth: President Bush's Need-to-Know Democracy." Originally published by MoveOn. www.moveon.org.

Scheer, Christopher. "Ten Appalling Lies We Were Told About Iraq." Originally published by AlterNet, www.alternet.org, June 27, 2003.

Schrag, Peter. "Getting the Blues." Originally published by *The Nation*, August 24, 2003.

Smith, Sam. "The Revision Thing." Originally published by *Harper's online*, www.harpers.org, September 2003.

Stauber, John and Sheldon Rampton. "Taking Responsibility." Originally published by AlterNet, www.alternet.org, August 14, 2003.

Thompson, Nicholas. "Science Friction." Originally published by *The Washington Monthly*, July/August 2003.

Trillin, Calvin. "A Silver Lining View of George Bush's Not Attending Military Funerals, Lest He Become Associated With Bad News." Originally published by *The Nation*, December 31, 2003.

Wallace-Wells, Benjamin. "Bush's War on Cops." Originally published by *The Washington Monthly*, September 2003.

Warner, John. "Encyclopedia Brown and the Case of Death Row Dubya." Originally published by *The Modern Humorist*, www.modernhumorist.com, May 15, 2000.

Warner, John and Kevin Guilfoile. *My First Presidentiary*. New York: Three Rivers Press, 2001.

CLINT WILLIS has edited more than 30 anthologies, on subjects ranging from meditation *(Why Meditate)* to mountaineering *(Epics on Everest)*. He edited (with Nathaniel May) *We Are the People: Voices from the Other Side of American History*. Clint studied political Science at Williams College and Yale University. He lives with his family in Maine.